100 Road Movies

100 ROAD MOVIES

BFI Screen Guides

Jason Wood

First published in 2007 by the
British Film Institute
21 Stephen Street, London W1T 1LN

The British Film Institute's purpose is to champion moving image culture in all its
richness and diversity across the UK, for the benefit of as wide an audience as
possible, and to create and encourage debate.

Series cover design: Paul Wright
Cover image: *Two-Lane Blacktop* (Monte Hellman, 1971,
    © Universal Pictures/Michael S. Laughlin Enterprises)
Series design: Ketchup/couch
Set by Fakenham Photosetting Limited, Fakenham, Norfolk
Printed in the UK by The Cromwell Press, Trowbridge, Wiltshire

British Library Cataloguing-in-Publication Data
A catalogue record for this book is available from the British Library

ISBN 978–1–84457–160–4 (pbk)
ISBN 978–1–84457–159–8 (hbk)

Contents

Acknowledgments

I would first and foremost like to thank Rebecca Barden for commissioning *100 Road Movies* and for not losing patience with me as various deadlines invariably came and went. My gratitude is also extended to Tom Cabot, Sophia Contento, Claire Milburn and Sarah Watt at BFI Publishing.

Sincere thanks also to: Geoff Andrew, Nicky Beaumont, City Screen (Deborah Allison, Clare Binns, Jo Blair, Daniel Graham, Tony Jones, Damian Spandley), Gareth Evans, Steve Jenkins, Michael Leake, Andy Leyshon, Verena von Stackelberg, Gavin Whitfield, Mark Williams, Felix Wood and Rudy Wood.

Chris Petit deserves my deepest appreciation for agreeing to write the preface.

Finally, I dedicate this book to Richard Beaumont, who is very fond of cars and of driving them.

Preface

Back in the 1970s, I drove a lot and liked driving. I thought the portable radio cassette one of the great twentieth-century inventions and whoever thought to put a radio in a car was a genius. Music and speed, combined with the ratio of the windscreen, made for an experience that was often more cinematic than the films I had to review for *Time Out*. Driving with the radio on transcended the dreary reality of Britain, hinted at possibilities of a mythic landscape denied by the realism of the English cinema. I saw nothing on the English screen that corresponded to a modern life that for me combined drift and boredom, jukeboxes, *Alphaville*, J. G. Ballard and Kraftwerk. I saw no reason why contemporary England could not be a cinematic landscape or why you could not show it through the road.

England made me restless, which is why I liked US cinema with its recurring themes of migration, pioneering and journey. I was never bored by an American road movie as long as it kept moving. Driving, like viewing film, is a suspended state and any drive – well, perhaps not those to the supermarket – has its own narrative: what is being driven away from (the past) and driven towards; a simultaneous journey of flight and progression. I summed up my feelings about the road in a film, *Negative Space*, a profile essay on the great American movie critic Manny Farber:

> America. Sheer physical space. No irony, no metaphor. Distance no object. Itinerary instead of narrative. Movement, space and light rather than words on a page. Eight dollars of gas to cross three states, driving insane distances for the hell of it. After the cramped spaces of Europe, emotional and physical, America feels wide open and literal. The road

becomes a movie – becomes the memory of other movies, the physical space of the country reflected in its movie stars, who always knew how to move.

But there was little that could be applied to trying to make films in England from watching *Bring Me the Head of Alfredo Garcia*. Another part of me appreciated the austere aesthetic of European directors Bresson, Straub and Huillet, who taught me to prefer watching people by themselves to dialogue scenes, and how aloneness, as much as loneliness, lies at the heart of cinema (and the road). Godard used the road to doodle (*Pierrot le fou*) but it wasn't until seeing Rossellini and Wenders that I began to appreciate how making films might be possible. If directing is about correct shot selection and knowing where to put the camera, then I wouldn't change a frame of *Voyage to Italy*.

Lured into Wenders' early film *The Goalkeeper's Fear of the Penalty Kick* by its title and not knowing what to expect, I was intrigued by the way it squandered its plot – goalkeeper loses game, hangs around, strangles cinema cashier and takes to the road – in favour of heightened lesser moments: a bright yellow cigarette machine at a bus station or listening to a familiar song on a crappy transistor with variable reception. Wenders did none of the expected things, preferring the extended journey, which he followed up in subsequent German films, *Alice in the Cities*, *Kings of the Road* and *Wrong Movement*, voyages of discovery through landscapes suffering cultural amnesia and a country refusing to face up to its past. Where his contemporary Werner Herzog dealt with the same issues by making arduous treks through remote and hostile terrain, Wenders revealed the strangeness of the everyday – the forlorn beauty of lay-bys, fast-food stands and the sort of downbeat poetry that usually passes us by.

It was Wenders who gave me my break. *Radio On* was partly produced by his company Road Movies (what else?). I wasn't given any audition beyond being asked how I would shoot it. 35mm black and white, I said. Looking back, I'm amazed. I hadn't a clue really.

Main reasons for a film-maker (or anyone) to go on the road: fresh horizons; to save a failing relationship; to look back. Road movies are cinematic because they are not a substitute for something else. They are not filmed theatre, like a lot of movies. Despite the limited angles of filming in a car, I am thrilled by a camera inside any vehicle the way I am not when it is in a room. I was never much interested in the filmed story anyway: the-what-happens-when. Film was about space or moments or visual geometry. Godard summed it up best:

> The important thing is to be aware that one exists. For three-quarters of the time during the day one forgets this truth, which surges up again as you look at houses or a red light, and you have the sensation of existing in that moment.

The road movie is a subgenre rather than one in its own right (often an afterthought of the US Western) but, returning to that idea of the subjective windscreen, among the most memorable shots in cinema are those POV driving shots in *Vertigo* (not a road movie as such but the most driven of films). Also there is the romantic aspect of a man and a woman in a car (as opposed to the world's most depressing sight: four men in a car), or a man alone in a car looking for a woman (*Vertigo* again). For practical reasons, a road movie's ideal unit is two. Two in a car is easier to shoot than three or four. Couples then went along for the ride, with the men giving directions: Rossellini and Bergman; Eastwood and Sondra Locke; Godard and Karina; Fellini and Masina. Going on the road failed to revive Rossellini and Godard's marriages; Locke did not last long either.

The road flatters bad directors and brings out the best in good ones. Peckinpah, by association, is a recurring name. Rudy Wurlitzer wrote *Pat Garrett and Billy the Kid* for him, a kind of pre-road movie. Wurlitzer co-directed *Candy Mountain* with Robert Frank, the great photographer chronicler of the American road and a major influence on Wenders and Jim Jarmusch. Wurlitzer wrote *Two-Lane Blacktop*, the last word on the

American road: strung out, existential, narcotic. Three out of a main cast of four died prematurely, Warren Oates while washing his car. Its director Monte Hellman barely worked subsequently. The fate of *Two-Lane Blacktop*, masterpiece or not, as a *film maudit* epitomises the doomed romanticism of the road movie and its relationship to cinema, corresponding to Ballard's key image of the modern age as that of 'a man sitting in a car driving down a superhighway'.

Chris Petit, October 2006.

Chris Petit is a film-maker and writer who started his career as film editor at *Time Out* magazine. His first film, *Radio On* (1979), was re-released in 2004 at Tate Modern. Recent film work includes feature collaborations with the writer Iain Sinclair, including *The Falconer* and *London Orbital*. He is the author of *Robinson* (1993, 2000), *The Hard Shoulder* (2000) and *The Psalm Killer* (1996). The film rights to his most recent novel, *The Passenger* have been optioned by Andrew MacDonald.

Introduction

In archetypal terms, road movies commonly entail the undertaking of a journey by one or more protagonists as they seek out adventure, redemption or escape from the constricting norms of society and its laws. A manifestation of America's fascination with the road, and by extension the mythology of freedom, the road movie arguably ranks among the American cinema's most enduring gifts to contemporary film culture.

However, closer inspection reveals the dream of the road to be tarnished, a dead end in which love and dreams are dashed and hopes vanquished by harsh reality. The road movie frequently begins with the expression of a search for self by an individual or individuals disenfranchised from society on social, economic, racial or sexual grounds – criminals feature heavily too – but the journey's end rarely brings peace or contentment, but most likely further suffering or even death at the hands of everyday life. As a disenchanted character with one flat tyre eloquently puts it in Hal Hartley's road movie *Simple Men* (1992), 'There is no such thing as adventure. There's no such thing as romance. There's only trouble and desire.'

The evolution of the road movie in American cinema is closely aligned with the development of the motorcar itself and the way directors, including D. W. Griffith, utilised them to provide effective travelling shots. These travelling shots, later framed so as to include front and rear windscreens, would later become one of the key visual road-movie motifs in terms of composition and style.

Providing a window onto the world and the earliest signs of automotive fetishism (later advanced to include low-angle travelling shots of wheels and wing mirrors), these exterior and interior shots served multiple functions, primarily perhaps placing the spectator in the position of the character undertaking the journey. This could include breathtaking local scenery, or it could merely illustrate the monotony of forward motion, as evidenced in Vincent Gallo's *The Brown Bunny* (2003), featuring an extended sequence of bugs hitting Gallo's front windscreen. Shot from the outside looking into the vehicle, the technique also gave a sense of claustrophobia, telegraphing an enclosed environment with the possibility of introspection and rancour. This is particularly effective when you have two people in a confined space who are not getting along: the bickering couple in Godard's *Weekend* (1967); the distant father and son in Ismaël Ferroukhi's *Le Grand Voyage* (2004); or the mismatched travelling duo thrown together by fate's cruel hand in John Hughes' *Planes, Trains and Automobiles* (1987).

Cars were also from their earliest invention incorporated into film narrative as a means by which couples eloped, gangsters escaped and even whole families went in search of a better life. This is applicable to John Ford's *The Grapes of Wrath* (1940), a film dealing with enforced social migration and the search for employment in Depression-era America. In one of the key texts on the road movie, *Driving Visions*, author David Laderman (2002, p. 24) cites Depression-era social-conscience films and screwball comedies as essential in the development of the road movie in terms of their use of 'mobility to express a rebellious response to the social crisis', describing *The Grapes of Wrath* as one of the classical Hollywood predecessors of the genre. Ford's Steinbeck adaptation is also important in that it reveals the indelible links between the road movie and literature, with roots stretching back to Homer and Voltaire, and even forward to Walter Salles' upcoming adaptation of Jack Kerouac's Beat classic, *On the Road*.

Built to traverse the country after the US entered World War II, the expansive freeways would come to play a fundamental thematic role in road movies, and in terms of a distinctive iconography, with recurring shots of a speeding vehicle heading towards distant vistas. The glory of construction was tempered by social fragmentation as families were split asunder by the need to travel greater distances to work in artillery factories. Once the war ended, returning GIs found themselves unable to regain their place in a shifting society, and alienation and disenchantment crept into the American psyche. As this cultural psychosis took hold, films such as Edgar G. Ulmer's *Detour* (1945) and Nicholas Ray's *They Live by Night* (1948, a key work also in regards to its location shooting, informed by Italian neo-realism, one of the earliest examples of the European influence on the genre) mined this terrain, with the pursuit of dreams becoming the stuff of nightmares. As idealism soured, so the protagonists of road movies became not merely outsiders, but criminals, outlaws and fugitives on the run (see also later works such as Arthur Penn's *Bonnie and Clyde*, 1967, and Terrence Malick's *Badlands*, 1973) and, with a pinch of film noir in its fateful encounters and dead-end fatalism, the road snaked its way to death and destruction.

Advancing the politically rebellious spirit of *Bonnie and Clyde*, *Easy Rider* (1969) is another key work in American counter-culture cinema, its pioneering spirit made partly possible by advances in technology such as more mobile cameras. For Laderman, the film marked the moment when the road movie became a distinct genre in its own right. Developing the road-movie characteristics of Penn's revisionist history of Clyde Barrow and Bonnie Parker, Hopper's film also significantly contributed to the genre by pairing two men together, its use of non-diegetic soundtrack, the equation of 'transient mobility with rebellious liberation' (Laderman 2002, p. 71), montage travelling sequences, flash-forward scene transitions and the crystallisation of a sense of postmodern anxiety and restlessness.

Distinct genre or not, it is essential to note that the conferring of full genre status on the road movie has proved problematic because it so clearly infracts with films in more recognisable and more established genre categories or film types. Some examples include: the buddy movie – *Thunderbolt and Lightfoot* (Michael Cimino, 1974); the comedy – *Midnight Run* (Martin Brest, 1988); the Western – *The Searchers* (John Ford, 1956); the documentary – *Sherman's March* (Ross McElwee, 1985) and the horror film – *Near Dark* (Kathryn Bigelow, 1987). As my hopefully diverse selection of road movies shows, road movies even occur in experimental and non-narrative cinema – James Benning's *North on Evers* (1992) being the example included in this volume. In fact, with its combination of exterior long shots, intense interior close-ups, troubled relationships and attention to American mythology, the road movie has often been cited, most recently by Leslie Dick (1997) in his superlative *Sight and Sound* entry on the road movie, as the intersection of film noir and the Western. From the road movie, other substrata have arguably evolved, including the cycle of 1970s American chase movies such as *The Gumball Rally* (Chuck Bail, 1976) and *Smokey and the Bandit* (Hal Needham, 1977), 'walking movies' (Wim Wenders, *Paris, Texas*, 1984, one of the films I most regret not affording a personal entry here), and films in which a collection of people make a trip by coach or bus with enlightening or horrific results. Examples include *Get on the Bus* (Spike Lee, 1996) and *Jeepers Creepers II* (Victor Salva, 2002). The former in fact points to another mini-division that plays on a combination of teenagers in danger and the perils of the road theme. A brief sample from a long list of films of this nature includes *The Texas Chainsaw Massacre* (Tobe Hooper, 1974), *The Hitcher* (Robert Harmon, 1986) and the more recent *Turistas* (John Stockwell, 2006). The latter extends the fear of the road to a fear of foreign countries.

To return briefly to Hopper's film, in which a trio of anti-authoritarian bikers go in search of the real America but are unable to 'find it anywhere', it cast an estimable shadow over the road movies that proliferated in the 1970s and 80s. Monte Hellman's *Two-Lane Blacktop* and Richard Sarafian's *Vanishing Point* (both 1971) are two of the key films that trailed in the wake of *Easy Rider*'s exhaust fumes. Similarly, Hellman and Sarafian, with their off-kilter, out-of-synch heroes, were instrumental in refuelling the road-movie renaissance of the 1990s. Tapping into the genre's propensity for nihilistic cool and the iconography of cultural isolation, directors such as Jim Jarmusch and Gus Van Sant conceived of a new breed of existentialist traveller for whom the journey itself frequently outweighed the destination.

Other film-makers during this period saw the road movie as serving a more political purpose in regards to confronting the conflicting social forces bearing down upon their band of outsiders. Ushering in a new decade, Ridley Scott's *Thelma & Louise* (1991), a rare example of a road movie with female protagonists in what is a traditionally male terrain, examined sexual politics alongside its automotive fetishism. Compromised by its debated denouement in which the titular heroines take their own lives, Scott's film, scripted by Callie Khouri, is nonetheless an arguably feminist Hollywood work. The following year saw Gregg Araki's remarkable *The Living End* (1992), a key picture in the New Queer Cinema of the 1990s, in which two gay, HIV-positive outlaws go on the run after shooting a cop. Araki's film, to be considered in conjunction with the serial-killer-spree series of road movies that also unfortunately gave us *Kalifornia* (Dominic Sena, 1993) and *Natural Born Killers* (Oliver Stone, 1994), is perhaps more informed by Godard's *Pierrot le fou* (1965).

It is essential to note that the road movie is by no means an exclusively American domain and has been historically embraced by film-makers from across the globe as a means of exploring national identity and confronting social and political issues springing from disenchantment with the dominant ideology. Some key examples from Europe include Cocteau's *Orphée* (1950), Bergman's *Wild Strawberries* (1957), Fellini's *La strada* (1954), Alain Tanner's *Messidor* (1978) and Andrew Kötting's *Gallivant* (1996). On a broader international scale, George Miller's *Mad Max* series (1979–85), Fernando Solanas' *El viaje* (1991) and Yeo Kyundong's *Out to the World* (*Sae sang bakuro*, 1994) have performed similar functions. Recent years have seen a particular engagement with road-movie topography from Latin American film-makers, with Alfonso Cuarón's *Y tu mamá también* (2001), Walter Salles' *The Motorcycle Diaries* (2004) and Carlos Sorin's *Bombón el perro* (2004) arriving in quick succession.

Directors working outside the US have also frequently reformulated the American road movie as a means of sustaining a dialogue with the notion of American imperialism and the global exportation of American culture. Wim Wenders, a director so beholden to road movies that he named his production company after them, considered this fully in his seminal *Kings of the Road* (1976), wherein a character remarks, 'The Yanks have even colonised our unconscious.'

Wenders is one of the directors with more than one entry to his name in this volume, and frankly he could have had several, as most, if not all, of his films are road movies in one sense or another. The director is also of interest as an émigré figure, leaving Germany to explore America's expansive highways and horizons in works such as *Alice in the Cities* (1974), *Paris, Texas* and the recent reuniting with Sam Shepard, 2005's *Don't Come Knocking*. Wenders apart, who are the other filmmakers whose work make up my selection and by what criteria and for what purpose did I arrive at the films I have included?

Echoing the words to be found in the introductions to many of the books in the BFI's ongoing *Screen Guides* series, including my own previous *100 American Independent Films* (2004), I must first start by stating that my list is not intended as authorative and I do not suggest that it is anywhere near definitive. It is simply my personal selection of 100 films that may be considered in historical, aesthetic or thematic terms representative of what may be broadly termed a road movie. In making my selection, I tried to include as many films as possible that have come to be regarded as staples of the genre (the aforementioned *The Grapes of Wrath*, *Easy Rider* etc.) and that in some way were formative in shaping its future direction. I also tried to look at those films that developed from these key examples, and which were then in turn influenced by other genres and national and international film movements and technological developments.

I also endeavoured to ensure that as well as being expansive in a historical sense, the selections were diverse in terms of geography and nationality, selecting titles wherever possible from numerous continents. While it was impossible to select a film from each and every country, it was certainly my intention to attempt to provide a broad perspective. In doing so, I hoped to illustrate how the road-movie template was adapted within other countries and, through the trajectory of a quest, journey or personal odyssey of some kind, to examine issues relating to culture, politics, economics and social conditions. In turn, I wished also to examine how these road movies made in Europe, South America and further afield then bled back into the American film-making landscape.

I could quite easily have selected an alternative 100 films for this volume and, reading the selections, you may get the clear impression that I am not necessarily personally particularly fond of a number of the films included here. In these instances, the inclusion was based upon a combination of historical or stylistic significance, or simply because the film in question was the best and most readily acknowledged example of a particular type of road movie, such as the aforementioned star-cameo and stunt-driven 'race' films of the 1970s. I have endeavoured in these examples not to let my subjectivity get the better of me. And, after all, these films may be ones that other readers are justifiably very fond of.

In this introduction, I have already cited *Paris, Texas* as a title I was unable to find room for, asides from passing but admirable acknowledgment. I already have two other films by the same director, and though I chose not to impose any kind of limit in regards to the number of films by the same film-maker – Bertrand Blier, Carlos Sorin, Steven Spielberg, Gus Van Sant, John Ford and Michael Winterbottom all have more than one entry to their name – I felt that an entry was equally deserving elsewhere. This may well be seen as a glaring omission and no doubt there will be others. Some obviously important films were omitted quite simply because, despite the assistance of numerous research facilities, broadcasting companies and the increasing availability of a disparate range of titles on DVD, I was unable to gain access to them for viewing purposes. One such example is Peng Xiaolian's *A Story of Women* (1998), by all accounts a vital and fascinating work from China that offers a feminist perspective on the plight of Chinese women in transit.

I would argue that one of the objectives of any kind of 'list' or guide style of book is to stimulate debate, conjecture and hopefully, if only very occasionally, agreement. This book, and the selections therein, certainly aims to provoke discourse, but most importantly perhaps it seeks to inspire viewing, both of films that may be very well known, and also those that may be sought out for the very first time. However, and for personal satisfaction if nothing else, listed below are ten other titles whose absence from this book in single-entry form I particularly mourn. No doubt readers will note their absence too:

Calendar, Atom Egoyan (1993)
Delusion, Carl Colpaert (1991)
Electra Glide in Blue, James William Guerico (1973)
Pierrot le fou, Jean-Luc Godard (1965)
Road Movie, Joseph Strick (1974)
Since Otar Left, Julie Bertucelli (2003)
Smoke Signals, Chris Eyre (1998)
They Live by Night, Nicholas Ray (1948)
Wild at Heart, David Lynch (1990)
The Wild One, László Benedek (1953)

Finally then, what is the current state of the road movie? It would certainly seem to be in rude health, with a continuing spate of global titles proving that there is plenty of petrol in the tank in regards to the road/travelogue format. There have been continued aesthetic advancements, evolving most notably from inroads into digital film-making technology, as exemplified by Iranian auteur Abbas Kiarostami's remarkable and remarkably intimate *Ten* (2002) and Nick Broomfield's *Ghosts* (2006); while other pictures, such as Tommy Lee Jones' Guillermo Arriaga-scripted *The Three Burials of Melquiades Estrada* (2005), have continued to successfully mine the subject of American cultural domination and a post-9/11 international superpower with extensive borders to patrol.

One of the biggest critical and commercial successes of 2006 was Jonathan Dayton and Valerie Faris' *Little Miss Sunshine*. The story of a dysfunctional family learning to hate and then love themselves all over again during an eventful cross-country trip to a California beauty pageant, the film follows on the heels of Pablo Trapero's *Familia rodante* (2004) in its examination of a mobile family unit. Also released in the same year was *London to Brighton* by confident first-time film-maker Paul Andrew Williams, a gritty and grimly realistic tale of flight (by train) by a young prostitute and the barely teenage girl she is shielding from a paedophile. And so we have road movies that are also Westerns, *The Grapes of Wrath*-style migrations and a tale involving two fugitives on the run – who in the course of the film also become buddies. The road movie has certainly travelled a fair distance, but never strayed too far from its origins.

The Adventures of Priscilla, Queen of the Desert
Australia, 1994 – 102 mins
Stephan Elliott

A bitchy, liberating and ultimately poignant road movie, Stephan Elliot's *The Adventures of Priscilla, Queen of the Desert* is also a camp and thrillingly enjoyable ode to alternative lifestyles, camaraderie and the music of Abba.

1960s British icon Terence Stamp raises a few eyebrows playing heavily against type as Bernadette Bassenger, an ageing postoperative transsexual who tours the backwaters of Australia with his stage partners, Mitzi Del Bra (Weaving) and Adam Whitely, aka Felicia Jollygoodfellow (Pearce). Their act, well known in Sydney, involves wearing lots of makeup and extravagant gowns and lip-synching to records, but Bernadette is getting a bit tired of it all and remains haunted by the recent death of an old lover. Nevertheless, when an offer to perform at a large nightclub and casino complex in the remote town of Alice Springs arises, the threesome venture into the outback with 'Priscilla, Queen of the desert', a lavender-coloured school bus that doubles as dressing room and home on the road. In the road-movie tradition, the trio struggle to get along, encountering a number of eccentric Australian anachronisms, homophobia and off-road incidents involving Aborigines. All the while, Bernadette becomes increasingly concerned about the path his life has taken.

Though frequently very funny, Elliot respects the dignity of his subjects too much to play the film purely for laughs, instead offering a rich and at times complex mediation on how public exuberance sometimes masks very private pain. Elliot also avoids presenting his trio as freakish caricatures, showing them as complicated individuals for whom drag acts as a natural expression of who they are. There is also some neat subversion of stereotypes, the central protagonists out-brawling and out-boozing the small-minded backwater locals before finally winning them over with their kitsch routines. The three-dimensional nature of the

Mitzi Del Bra (Hugo Weaving) experiences the thrill of the open road in *The Adventures of Priscilla, Queen of the Desert*

characters, one of the many strengths of Elliot's writing, is further enhanced by the exceptional central performances. Free from the constricting normality of *Neighbours*, Pearce proves what a talented actor he is, providing a glimpse of the complexity he would bring to his future roles. Stamp is a pure delight as the weathered, world-weary Bernadette, a strutting peacock who senses that this may be a last hurrah. Weaving perhaps provides the film's emotional anchor, struggling to hold the troupe together while undertaking his own personal journey of self-discovery.

Working on a restricted budget, Elliot astutely captures a sadly realistic glimpse of the defensive shield those at society's fringes must assimilate as a given part of their daily lives that also highlights the dichotomy between city life and rural living. As such, it is an effective snapshot of contemporary Australia. Aided by costume designers Lizzy Gardiner and Tim Chappell, whose brace of awards including an Academy Award, a BAFTA and an AFI (Australian Film Institute), the director also infuses the film with an impressive and distinctly Felliniesque panache. This is perhaps most evident in a Verdi sequence, in which Weaving, standing on top of the bus as it ploughs through the desert, mimes along to *La Traviata*, his 50-foot silver train trailing in the breeze behind him.

Dir: Stephan Elliot; **Prod**: Al Clark, Michael Hamlyn; **Scr**: Stephan Elliot; **DOP**: Brian Breheny; **Edit**: Sue Blainey; **Score**: Guy Cross; **Principal Cast**: Terence Stamp, Hugo Weaving, Guy Pearce, Bill Hunter, Sarah Chadwick.

Badlands
US, 1973 – 94 mins
Terrence Malick

Arguably the most lyrical and artistic directors of the auteur-friendly US cinema of the 1970s, Malick's exquisite self-written and produced debut was compared by David Thomson with *Citizen Kane* (1941) in terms of its originality and enduring influence. Ostensibly a rural lovers-on-the-run gangster film in the tradition of Nicholas Ray's *They Live by Night* (1948), the independently made *Badlands* is distinguished by the oblique approach Malick takes to his familiar material. This is perhaps most evident in the enigmatic attitude towards the psychological motivations of its characters, a pair of murderous juveniles in search of release from the banality of their existence in the American Midwest of the late 1950s.

Loosely based on the true story of nineteen-year-old Charles Starkweather who murdered the family of his thirteen-year-old lover Caril Ann Fugate before embarking with her on a killing spree through Nebraska and Wyoming, *Badlands* relocates events to Fort Dupre, South Dakota. Garbage-man and James Dean look-alike Kit (Sheen) begins courting Holly (Spacek), a fifteen-year-old immersed in trashy, celebrity-fixated magazines. Holly's father (Oates) forbids the relationship and kills his daughter's dog as punishment when she disobeys him. As Holly impassively stands by, Kit shoots her father dead. Pursued robbing and killing across the Dakota badlands, Holly's affections for Kit wither and she turns herself in. Kit, however, is seduced by the celebrity status the media bestows upon him and is arrested only after stopping to build a monument to himself during a high-speed chase. Having played no part in the killings, Holly receives a lengthy prison term; Kit is sentenced to execution.

Presenting the narrative elements from contrasting perspectives, Malick offers an at times mysterious and yet eloquent dissection of disaffection and the role the media plays in offering unsustainable alternatives to the commonplace. Self-obsessive and self-mythologising, Kit regards himself as a heroic non-conformist whose good looks and affability will mark him out as worthy of remembrance. This conviction blinds him to the gravity of his actions (and indeed to Holly's growing disinterest in him) but is in effect fulfilled by the esteem in which his pursuers hold him. Contrastingly, the film is narrated in the dispassionate, listless voice of Holly, whose description of mundane

Shooting for fame and glory: Martin Sheen as Kit in Malick's visually assured *Badlands*

events is nonetheless littered with vocabulary from the romantic magazines in which she is constantly immersed. The disparity is furthered by the sensory perfection of the film and Malick's evocative combining of Carl Orff's ethereal music and Tak Fujimoto's painterly cinematography. Organically merging psychological and physical landscapes, *Badlands* has a mythic, iconic quality that recurs throughout Malick's hermitic career, as does the director's interest in man's capacity for destruction and the interaction of the characters, from whom we are purposefully distanced, with the natural world around them.

Acquired by Warner Bros. following its reception at the 1973 New York Film Festival, *Badlands* marked the emergence of a skilled perfectionist with little regard for the dictates of commercial film-making. Malick is regularly cited as an inspiration by successive generations of American directors too numerous to mention, of whom David Gordon Green is perhaps among the most notable recent film-makers to bear his indelible mark.

Dir: Terrence Malick; **Prod**: Terrence Malick; **Scr**: Terrence Malick; **DOP**: Tak Fujimoto; **Edit**: Robert Estrin; **Score**: Carl Orff; **Principal Cast**: Martin Sheen, Sissy Spacek, Warren Oates, Ramon Bieri.

Bombón el perro
Spain, 2004 – 98 mins
Carlos Sorin

Cut from a similar cloth to Sorin's earlier *Minimal Stories* (2002), *Bombón el perro* is ostensibly an amiable shaggy-dog tale that became a significant success in Europe and the US. However, despite the film's whimsical nature and humorous, self-effacing charm, it is a more complex and perhaps polemical work than initially appears, its ability to entertain and enthral concealing a number of incisive observations on the travails of the working class in a country still coming to terms with economic collapse.

Juan (Villegas), or 'Coco' to his friends, is a likeable, slightly vacant middle-aged man who has spent his entire life working in a Patagonian service station. When it closes, he finds himself out of work, unemployable and in a desperate fix. Unable to find work as a mechanic

A shaggy-dog tale: Bombón and Juan (Juan Villegas) in *Bombón el perro*

elsewhere, Coco drives around the countryside trying to sell ornate knives, doing odd jobs and struggling, until in exchange for mending her broken-down car, a woman gives him a pure-bred perro Argentino and informs him that Bombón has the potential to be a successful show dog. Proving a staunch companion, Bombón brings his new owner some fiscal good fortune (including employment as a security guard) and so before long, Coco decides to try his luck at the country's canine beauty pageants. Inexperienced in such matters, he joins forces with a carefree dog trainer (Donado) and the unlikely trio hit the dog-show circuit.

The sense of hardship is indelibly etched both into the narrative and into the rolling, dusty, Patagonian desert plains, which are boldly rendered by Sorin's regular cinematographer, Hugo Colace. It is also there in the weather-beaten brows of the largely non-professional cast that Sorin has drawn together, casting from the environs in which the film is set. However, Sorin frequently underplays the sense of disenfranchisement and struggle, his tendency towards naturalism eliciting a delicious understatement and frequently absurdist humour. This is evident not only in a number of repeated visual set-pieces, the best of which involves a comically morose Bombón in the front seat of Coco's van, but is also demonstrated by Coco's various by-the-way interactions with a number of strangers on the road, including a policeman to whom he fails to sell a knife but then must bribe to avoid arrest. It is also there in the relatively minimal and matter-of-fact exchanges of dialogue, such as Coco's comment that he is unable to get employment working on a petrol station forecourt because 'Now they use a pretty girl'. The comment, an accurate reflection of market forces, is uttered entirely without bitterness or malice.

Coco and his canine companion are revealed as having more in common than their respective backgrounds as proletariat worker and thoroughbred would initially appear. Much in demand after claiming competition prizes, Bombón is hired by a breeder to act as a stud on his farm. Unable to perform, his value is greatly diminished and the duo's future suddenly less secure. It is one of the film's many bittersweet moments, with Coco ultimately extending a sense of commitment and devotion that he was himself denied. An insightful glimpse into the plight of a man who never really had a direction in life but is suddenly forced into finding one, this is a story of humility and grace.

Dir: Carlos Sorin; **Prod**: Óscar Kramer, José María Morales; **Scr**: Santiago Calori, Salvador Roselli, Carlos Sorin; **DOP**: Hugo Colace; **Edit**: Mohamed Rajid; **Score**: Nicolas Sorin; **Principal Cast**: Juan Villegas, Walter Donado, Micol Estévez, Kita Ca, Pascual Condito, Claudina Fazzini.

Bonnie and Clyde
US, 1967 – 111 mins
Arthur Penn

A Benton and Newman-scripted project that was originally destined for Godard or Truffaut, *Bonnie and Clyde* marked a pivotal moment in American cinema. The canny merging of a staple American genre with dynamic young leads, a no-holds barred attitude towards sex and violence, and a contemporary social relevance, ensnared the counter-culture audience of the late 1960s and directly led to the creative freedom the studios accorded the 'New Hollywood' film-makers of the 1970s.

Based loosely on the 1930s exploits of Clyde Barrow and Bonnie Parker, the film begins as Clyde (Beatty) tries to steal the car of Bonnie Parker's mother. Bonnie (Dunaway) is excited by Clyde's outlaw demeanour, and he further stimulates her by robbing a store in her presence. Clyde steals a car, with Bonnie in tow, and their legendary crime spree begins. The two move from town to town, pulling off petty heists, until they join up with Clyde's brother Buck (Hackman), his shrill wife Blanche (Estelle Parsons) and a slow-witted gas-station attendant, C. W. (Pollard). The new gang robs a bank and Clyde is soon painted in the press as a Depression-era Robin Hood when he allows one customer to hold onto his money. With the police on their tail, the gang are constantly on the run, their fugitive status intensified after they kidnap a Texas Ranger. The act comes back to haunt them when the Ranger returns to lead a raid on the gang that leaves Buck dying, Blanche captured and both Clyde and Bonnie injured. The ever-loyal C. W. takes them to his disapproving father's house and ultimately into a police trap that ends with one of the bloodiest deaths in cinematic history.

Originally inciting critical revulsion for refusing to assert a clear morality and no small degree of fear in Warner Bros., the studio under whose aegis it was reluctantly made after much hectoring by producer-star Beatty, the film became a genuine social phenomenon after it was re-released (again at the behest of Beatty) and went on to gross over $20 million. The portrayal of Bonnie and Clyde as rebels who stood shoulder to shoulder with the poor working folks of the 1930s struck a chord with young American audiences, convincing the studios of their importance in generating box-office hits. The critical tide also turned, landing *Bonnie and Clyde* on the cover of *Time* as cultural commentators gradually found favour in the film's redefining of violence and the recasting of its criminal protagonists as pin-up anti-heroes. Viewed retrospectively in terms of Penn's subsequent career, crudely defined as a series of subsequent highs followed by an irreversible decline, the film also marked the clearest realisation of the director's interest in the tension between oppression and vitality.

The charismatic Beatty and sultry Dunaway aside, the brightest stars in the film's brimming firmament include Theodora Van Runkle's trendsetting costumes, Dean Tavoularis' historically authentic art direction and Burnett Guffey's cinematography. One of only two victories among ten Academy Award nominations (Parsons was the other), Guffey emphasises the muted colours and tones of the period to give the impression, the many ambiguities aside, that we may be watching a historical document.

Dir: Arthur Penn; **Prod**: Warren Beatty; **Scr**: David Newman, Robert Benton; **DOP**: Burnett Guffey; **Edit**: Dede Allen; **Score**: Charles Strouse; **Principal Cast**: Warren Beatty, Faye Dunaway, Michael J. Pollard, Gene Hackman.

Boys on the Side
US, 1995 – 117 mins
Herbert Ross

Returning to the terrain of his earlier *Steel Magnolias* (1989) with its subject of female bonding and solidarity in the face of physical and emotional crises, Herbert Ross' *Boys on the Side* is popularly considered something of a feminist road movie for its examination of how three women from different walks of life find comfort in each other through tragedy.

Parker plays Robin, an HIV-positive real-estate executive who meets Jane (Goldberg), an out-of-work lesbian lounge singer on her way to the West Coast. Jane, who has a habit of falling for straight women, needs a driver and Robin finds herself volunteering for the job. En route, they stop in Pittsburgh to visit Jane's pregnant friend Holly (Barrymore), whose pattern of picking abusive men has not diminished. In an attempt to save Holly, all three decide to head West together to begin a new life. But they only get as far as Arizona before Robin falls ill and the trio are forced to learn to rely on one another for growth and emotional sustenance. Jane, though concerned about Robin's condition, finds herself harbouring a romantic interest in her ailing companion, while Holly confronts her need to be with violent partners. Robin, meanwhile, slowly comes to grips with her fear of being alone and the realisation of her impending death.

That the terribly titled *Boys on the Side* manages to rise above its TV movie-of-the-week origins is largely due to an offbeat and engaging script by writer/executive producer and future director Don Roos (*The Opposite of Sex*, 1998). Cruising along as an entertaining if less than inspirational sisterhood road movie, complete with bonding in-car sing-along sessions, iconic landmarks, travelling shots and various asides about the feckless nature of the male species, Roos' trademark humour hints at a certain sense of the subversive and he competently navigates a potentially tricky switch into more poignant and emotionally resonant territory as Robin's health deteriorates. Perhaps ironically, given its road movie status and inclusion here, the film undoubtedly becomes of greater interest once it stops moving, exiting the interstate to become stationary in Arizona.

Bearing numerous similarities to Ridley Scott's *Thelma & Louise* (1991), which *Boys on the Side* in fact playfully references when one character quips that she won't be driving over any cliffs in support of her companions, this latter work is similarly marked by a combination of good intent, charismatic performances (Parker is terrific and Goldberg, atypically restrained, seldom better) and a tendency towards oversimplification, overt sentiment and moments of undoubted cliché.

Dir: Herbert Ross; **Prod**: Arnon Milchan, Steven Reuther, Herbert Ross; **Scr**: Don Roos; **DOP**: Donald Thorin; **Edit**: Michael R. Miller; **Score**: David Newman; **Principal Cast**: Whoopi Goldberg, Mary-Louise Parker, Drew Barrymore, Matthew McConaughey, James Remar.

Bring Me the Head of Alfredo Garcia
US/Mexico, 1974 – 112 mins.
Sam Peckinpah

Reflecting Peckinpah's deep love of Mexico, a country where numerous visionary film-makers from Eisenstein to Buñuel found a spiritual home, *Bring Me the Head of Alfredo Garcia* is also one of the most uncompromising and remarkable entries in the director's filmography. Combining the fascination with death and mortality from the previous year's *Pat Garrett and Billy the Kid* (1973) with an almost primordial concern with the subject of virility and sexual potency, the film can also be read as an allegory for Peckinpah's own experiences in Hollywood.

Wealthy Mexican industrialist El Jefe (Fernández) puts a bounty on the head of local stud Alfredo Garcia, who has seduced, impregnated and then abandoned Fernandez' daughter. Trouble is, unbeknown to the powerful patriarch, Alfredo Garcia is already dead and buried. Washed-up American bar-room pianist Bennie (Oates) and prostitute Elita (Vega) travel to the small town in whose cemetery Garcia is interred, planning to dig up the body, recover the head and claim the reward. Attacked by a shadowy Mexican clan, Elita is murdered and Garcia's body stolen. Hell-bent on revenge, Bennie joins El Jefe's henchmen Quill (Young) and Sapensy (Robert Webber) in killing off the Mexican murderers, before turning his gun against them. Finally delivering the head of Alfredo Garcia to an expectant El Jefe, Bennie decides to pull off one last blood-spattered act of carnage.

Blending gritty sadism, machismo and pitch-black comedy in equal doses as it depicts Bennie's increasingly violent, tequila-driven and surreal odyssey across Mexico, Alex Phillips' stunning and meditative cinematography reflects both the local colour and topography – from the expansive landscapes and the shanty towns with their local cantinas – and the film's connection of the inextricable links between sex, death and violence. The cast is exceptional, Peckinpah drawing on a rich well of Mexican acting talent, from the renowned Vega, who made her name with a series of uncompromising 1960s Mexican dramas such as *Las pecadoras* (1968), to the veteran Fernández, a Mexican Nationalist synonymous with Mexico's Golden Era (*El cine de oro*) of the 1940s and early 50s. Peckinpah had previously cast Fernández in both *The Wild Bunch* and *Pat Garrett and Billy the Kid*. It is the venerable Oates' movie, however, the actor charting a remarkable transition from nervous, washed-up drunk to avenging angel with characteristic intensity.

Among the orgy of violence and alcohol, there are moments of poetic contemplation, most of which are filtered through Bennie's increasingly close and vocalised relationship to the severed head that lies next to him on his front seat. Initially viewing Alfredo's head purely as his ticket out of a personal hell and determined, even at the cost of exposing the nakedness of his greed to protect it at all costs, Bennie slowly comes to realise that they have things in common: both have loved the same woman (Elita was a shared former flame) and both are being destroyed by a member of a social strata of which they can never be a part.

Dir: Sam Peckinpah; **Prod**: Martin Baum; **Scr**: Gordon Dawson, Sam Peckinpah; **DOP**: Alex Phillips; **Edit**: Gareth Craven; **Score**: Jerry Fielding; **Principal Cast**: Warren Oates, Isela Vega, Gig Young, Emilio Fernández, Kris Kristofferson.

Broken Flowers
US, 2005 – 105 mins
Jim Jarmusch

Though its creator was quick to demur, *Broken Flowers*, self-consciously or not, seemed an attempt to nudge American independent auteur Jim Jarmusch a little closure to the mainstream. It succeeded, attaining a crossover appeal and level of commercial success that had largely eluded the Ohio-born writer-director. However, the film's success was very much on Jarmusch's own terms, standing it alongside *Dead Man*, the director's notional 1995 Western, and existential hitman thriller *Ghost Dog: The Way of the Samurai* (1999) as an identifiable genre film filtered through Jarmusch's determinedly offbeat and melancholic sensibility. Like all of Jarmusch's movies, this pithy, charming road-comedy fable concerning a latter-day Don Juan could be described as existing in a self-contained world all of its very own.

Wealthy Don Johnston (Murray, impassive) has just been dumped by his latest lover, Sherry (Julie Delpy). Resigned to being alone, he is instead compelled to reflect on his past when he receives by mail a mysterious pink letter from an anonymous former lover. Untraceable due to the lack of a postmark, the letter informs Don that he has a nineteen-year-old son who may now be looking for his father. Don is urged to investigate this 'mystery' by his closest friend and neighbour, Winston (Wright), an amateur sleuth and family man. Hesitant to travel at all, Don nonetheless embarks on a cross-country odyssey in search of clues from four former flames. Unannounced visits to each of these unique women hold new surprises for Don as he haphazardly confronts both his past and, consequently, his present.

Initially immobilised and framed, in a trademark Jarmusch composition, seated on his sofa, a slave to classical music and the movies shown on daytime TV, Don's eventual journey will not only eventually cover a lot of miles, but go some way to shaking him from his emotional apathy. The film's conclusion – offering only partial closure at best – in

Amateur sleuth Winston (Jeffrey Wright, left) peruses the letter that will send a reluctant Don Johnston (Bill Murray) out on the road to catch up with his former flames

which a young man Don believes to be his son is swiftly replaced by another, equally likely candidate is preceded by Johnston's announcement of a newly discovered philosophy of sorts. 'The past is gone. I know that. The future isn't here yet, whatever it may bring. All there is, is this.' It may not seem much, but for a man so previously disengaged from his own emotions and from society in general, it represents a considerable advance. Jarmusch has perhaps found his perfect actor in Murray, whose name and hangdog expression causes mirthful comparison to *Miami Vice* star Don Johnson during his prolonged trip. The rest of the cast excel too, Sharon Stone, Jessica Lange, Frances Conroy and an unrecognisable Tilda Swinton perfect in small but pivotal cameos as the exes. Wright threatens to run away with the film, commenting to Johnston with delicious irony 'only you can solve this mystery, because you understand women'.

Dedicated to Jean Eustache, whose *La Mamam et la putain* is a favourite of Jarmusch's, *Broken Flowers* may continue what Nick Roddick terms Jarmusch's presentation of his characters on 'a take-them-or-leave-them basis' (Roddick 2005, p. 18), but it is structurally very different from Eustache's masterwork. Interestingly, the geography of *Broken Flowers* is never fully mapped out. A mixture of the urban, the suburban and the wildly rural, we never actually find out where in America Don actually is. However, despite a characteristically freeform element to the riffing on personal disappointment, intimacy and the inability to ever really know one another, the film is quite tightly structured in terms of Don's journeying from one ex to the next and has a definable rhythm, a result in part of the superb score by Ethiopian jazz musician Mulatu Astatke.

Dir: Jim Jarmusch; **Prod**: Jon Kilik, Stacey Smith; **Scr**: Jim Jarmusch inspired by an idea from Bill Raden, Sara Driver; **DOP**: Frederick Elmes; **Edit**: Jay Rabinowitz; **Score**: Mulatu Astatke; **Principal Cast**: Bill Murray, Jeffrey Wright, Jessica Lange, Sharon Stone.

The Brown Bunny
US, 2003 – 119 mins
Vincent Gallo

Few films have polarised opinion as much as Gallo's follow-up to
Buffalo 66 (1997). Presented at the 2003 Cannes Film Festival in a cut
running at a little less than two hours, *The Brown Bunny* was greeted
with howls of derision, causing Gallo, the film's writer, producer,
editor, production designer and director of photography (and, lest we
forget, camera operator) to apologise for the film at a press
conference.

Bud Clay (writer, director, producer, editor and cinematographer Vincent Gallo) on *The
Brown Bunny*'s Bonneville Salt Flats

Gallo later denied issuing such an apology, but nonetheless licked his wounds in the cutting room, where he trimmed his much maligned film to a more manageable 93 minutes for its subsequent US release. Gallo then paid for expensive billboard ads out of his own pocket, to little effect, the film failing to make even the slightest commercial impression. There was, however, a certain critical revision, with a small number of the film's fiercest critics, including Roger Ebert, with whom Gallo became embroiled in a vindictive public spat, coming to admire its uncompromising portrait of masculinity in crisis. Shrouded in accusations of pretension, *The Brown Bunny* failed to find a theatrical release in the UK, but found favour with more discerning critics such as the *Daily Telegraph*'s Sukhdev Sandu, who defended the film, calling the original, and superior, Cannes cut 'a precious, self-indulgent, consistently exasperating near-masterpiece' (Sandu 2003).

Gallo plays motorcycle racer Bud Clay who has just lost a race in New Hampshire. Bud silently heads to his next contest in Southern California. The film closely follows Bud's every action on his journey, capturing him driving, pumping gas, visiting a pet shop, kissing and then abandoning an anonymous girl (Tiegs) and racing his bike on the Bonneville salt flats. Bud is also seemingly searching for the source of his happy memories, a former flame named Daisy Lemmon (Sevigny) who we see in idyllic flashbacks. Arriving in California, Bud chats with prostitutes but stops short of physical interaction. The film concludes on a note of revelation, Bud's emotional and sexual reuniting with Daisy in his Los Angeles motel room revealing why he remains impaled on the past.

An at times unapologetically tedious film in which for long periods very little happens – in Cannes the critics sarcastically applauded after Gallo stopped driving momentarily to change his shirt – *The Brown Bunny* is also cinema at its most brooding, intense and transcendental. Unfolding in unbroken, marathon-long takes, it is a self-mythologising road movie that parallels the laconic, existentialist spirit of 1970s titles like *Five Easy Pieces* (1970) and *Two-Lane Blacktop* (1971) in its dealing with the theme of paralysis-in-motion. Most of the film is shot with a static camera through Bud's dirty, bug-splattered windscreen, 'the freeways he drives along leached of the reckless excitement found in cult road movies such as *Easy Rider* (1969)' (Sandu 2003).

Gallo is undoubtedly one of cinema's great narcissists, but in a central performance of understated if preening complexity, he also lays himself pretty bare, revealing himself to be defenceless and frequently uncomfortable. The final and very graphic sex scene between the two real-life ex-lovers attracted accusations of misogyny and exploitation, but is actually affecting and rather tenderly played, serving to further highlight Clay's suffocating vulnerability. An unjustly maligned work that is one of the most valuable modern additions to the genre.

Dir: Vincent Gallo; **Prod**: Vincent Gallo; **Scr**: Vincent Gallo; **DOP**: Vincent Gallo; **Edit**: Vincent Gallo; **Score**: Ted Curson, Jeff Alexander, Gordon Lightfoot, Jackson C. Franck; **Principal Cast**: Vincent Gallo, Chloë Sevigny, Cheryl Tiegs.

Butterfly Kiss
UK, 1995 – 88 mins
Michael Winterbottom

The debut feature from prolific, genre-hopping British director Michael Winterbottom, and the first fruit of his and long-standing producer Andre Eaton's Revolution Films, *Butterfly Kiss* marked an early foray into road-movie terrain. It was a terrain that the director would later revisit in refugee drama *In This World* (2002) and the dystopian sci-fi *Code 46* (2003).

An unsettling and provocative variation on *Thelma & Louise* (1991) that merges black comedy with a macabre lesbian love story, *Butterfly Kiss* concerns two female misfits who journey across England on a killing spree. Eunice (Plummer) is a tattooed, sociopathic drifter wandering in search of her recently departed lover, Judith. But when she meets Miriam (Reeves), another gas-station assistant who longs for love, attention and escape from her mother's apron strings, sparks fly. Strangely captivated by the eccentric woman, the introverted Miriam spends the night with Eunice and falls under her peculiar charm. Calling each other 'Eu' and 'Mi', they hit the road, where they murder anyone who gets in their way. Both women sense that their actions will ultimately bring about a tragic end, but their dedication to their cause – rebelling against men who trivialise and demean women everywhere – and their love for one another drives them forward.

Building on his adventurous television work, Winterbottom makes few concessions to the commercial consensus in this spiky drama that remains somehow emphatically English while being clearly indebted to the American road movie. Tracking the two protagonists as they journey on a road that will patently take them nowhere, Winterbottom and regular writer of choice Frank Cottrell-Boyce replace the iconography of the picturesque highways of, say, *Badlands* (1973) with northern Britain's dreary, incessantly grey geography. As such, good visual mileage is drawn from endless motorways, monotonous car parks, Happy Eaters and dead-end motels. There are no evocative sunsets here, merely rain-lashed vistas. *Butterfly Kiss* also corresponds to genre tropes through its use of popular music, bolting, somewhat uncomfortably, songs by New Order (an ironic 'World in Motion' to signify Eunice's schizoid worldview), Björk and P. J. Harvey to John Harle's more subtle and understated score.

Foreshadowing a subsequent career in which she has been regularly called upon to play high-volume unhinged, Plummer gives an uneven but authentically raw and edgy performance. In a less showy role, Reeves provides the film's anchor as Eunice's beguiled accomplice and would-be redeemer. Frequently touching as the anorak-clad, puzzle-loving Miriam, Reeves is especially impressive in a black-and-white flashback story coda.

Filmed, the director attests, in six unpaid weeks with 'a very small crew on the edge of the M6' (Bedell 2004), the film was submitted to

Eunice (Amanda Plummer, left) and Miriam (Saskia Reeves) in search of love and affection in Michael Winterbottom's *Butterfly Kiss*

the Berlin Film Festival. The significant overseas sales that it achieved there were enough to put Revolution and Winterbottom firmly on the film-making map.

Dir: Michael Winterbottom; **Prod**: Julie Baines; **Scr**: Frank Cottrell-Boyce; **DOP**: Seamus McGarvey; **Edit**: Trevor Waite, Rupert Miles; **Score**: John Harle; **Principal Cast**: Amanda Plummer, Saskia Reeves, Kathy Jamieson, Des McAleer, Lisa Jane Riley, Freda Dowie.

Bye Bye Brasil
Brazil/France, 1979 – 100 mins
Carlos Diegues

One of the fathers of Brazil's 'Cinema Novo', a group of young film-makers who turned away from conventional film forms in the 1960s to start a cinema more responsive to the country's political and social needs, Carlos Diegues' low-key follow-up to *Xica da Silva* (1978) is a surprisingly conventional and temperate affair. One of the most popular and successful imports of late 1970s and early 80s South American cinema, it is far from being entirely without substance, adopting the guise of an introspective ensemble drama about a shabby circus crawling from small town to small town through the Brazilian backwaters, to offer, as the film's title implies, a farewell to a country rendered increasingly unrecognisable by seismic industrial and economic development. In the midst of this change, all ties with tradition and the past are in danger of being severed, astutely represented by the lack of interest afforded the film's anachronistic band of travelling players. Theo Angelopoulos' *The Travelling Players* (1975) is an obvious influence.

Led by its somewhat menacing medicine-show-like leader, Lorde Cigano (Wilker), and featuring the erotically charged, raven-haired dancer Salome (Faria), 'Queen of the Rumba', and the deaf-mute strongman Swallow (Principe Nabor), who also doubles as a fire-breather, *Bye Bye Brasil*'s Carnival Rolidei provides the locals with entertainment and the exotica of contact with the outside world. The performers initially captivate their audience, dazzling them with magical realism despite the threadbare sets and financial fragility of the company. However, as the troupe travels on, adding the strapping young accordion player Cico (Júnior) to their ranks, they encounter increasing competition. In one village it is a television, in another it is a movie projector. The further they travel, the more the performers recognise the industrialisation of their homeland and the inescapable inevitability of the Carnival Rolidei's demise. Finally fetching up in San Paulo, Lorde Cigano is forced to prostitute the female performers so that the troupe does not starve.

Digues' meditative and gently quizzical view of advancing modernity is not without moments of wry humour. In one neat sight gag, the director assembles a town of some 3,000 inhabitants as if they were a cinema crowd expectantly waiting the main feature to start, only to reveal in fact that they are gathered around a 12-inch TV screen. A portent of the increasing role home-entertainment technology would play on a national and international scale, the moment also feels eerily prophetic in terms of its accurate if gently humorous predictions concerning the loss of cinema audiences to television.

The Golden Palm-nominated writer-director also offers a perceptive take on the internal dynamics of the travelling group (all well played by an experienced cast), capturing their passions and simmering romances and festering hostilities as they inch their way from poverty-stricken northern Brazil, across the jungles on the trans-Amazonian highway to Brasilia and points in between in their decrepit truck. Complementing Digues' interest in the dwindling connection between the past and the present is Lauro Escorel's cinematography. Escorel demonstrates why she would go on to become a much in-demand figure in Brazilian film-making, effectively contrasting the film's verdant early section with the endless highways and muted urban landscapes of its final third.

Dir: Carlos Diegues; **Prod**: Luis Carlos Barreto; **Scr**: Carlos Diegues; **DOP**: Lauro Escorel; **Edit**: Mair Tavares; **Score**: Chico Buarque, Roberto Menescal, Dominguinhos; **Principal Cast**: Betty Faria, José Wilker, Fábio Júnior, Zaira Zambelli.

Le Camion (*The Truck*)
France, 1977 – 80 mins
Marguerite Duras

A writer widely considered to be one of the leading exponents of the
nouveau roman, Marguerite Duras abandoned many of the conventions
of the novel form. Characteristically mixing the themes of eroticism and
death, Duras' work often emphasises the existential moments in the lives
of her protagonists. Initially making her mark in cinema with her
screenplay for Alan Resnais' *Hiroshima, mon amour* (1959), Duras turned
to directing in the mid-1960s because of her dissatisfaction with the
cinematic adaptations others made of her texts.

Perhaps Duras' most experimental and challenging work as a
director, *Le Camion* is a favourite of John Waters, who made reference
to it in *Polyester* (1981) in a scene involving a Marguerite Duras drive-in
triple bill. Apparently, during the shooting of Waters' film, people
actually turned up to see the advertised attraction, expecting *The Truck*
(the film's American release title) to be an action movie. Introducing the
film at an Alliance Française event in New York in February 2006,
Waters praised the film for its provocative structure and refusal to make
even the slightest concession to commerciality. The participation of
Depardieu notwithstanding (the actor had just completed Bertolucci's
1900 (1976) and had previously collaborated with Duras on *Nathalie
Granger* (1972)), Waters is characteristically on the money. Though
punctuated with a number of insert shots of a blue truck driving
through industrial sectors of the French suburbs, *Le Camion* almost
exclusively consists of Duras and Depardieu doing an on-camera read-
through of a script by Duras (never actually shot) concerning a
communist male truck driver who picks up an older, female hitchhiker;
the pair then engaging in a series of political, humanitarian and
philosophical dialogues during their journey along endless highways and
byways. A single shot of the truck's interior offers the only other visual
distraction.

Duras once claimed to have approached cinema with the intention of murdering it, and in *Le Camion* she assiduously works to deny any sense of spectacle. Initially describing the script as concerning a woman possessed of 'the *noblesse* of banality', Duras grows increasingly snappy and belligerent as the read-through progresses, at various points railing bitterly at communism's failed ideals. Chain-smoking throughout, Duras does provide some background on the motivations of the characters, claiming that the truck driver is 'exercising his profession', and the initially blank slate of a woman is 'transported by him'. Depardieu initially asks questions but is haughtily dismissed, Duras at one point exclaiming 'I'm talking' when asked to provide clarification. Depardieu's interest seems to visibly shrink.

An exacting, austere and determinedly 'difficult' work that will infuriate many, *Le Camion* does, however, gradually assert a trance-like fascination. Frequently wrong-footing the spectator and defying categorisation, the film's somewhat stern hectoring is a refreshing riposte to traditional audience expectations regarding verisimilitude and enjoyment.

Dir: Marguerite Duras; **Prod**: François Barat, Pierre Barat; **Scr**: Marguerite Duras; **DOP**: Bruno Nuytten; **Edit**: Dominique Auvray; **Score**: non-original music by Ludwig Van Beethoven; **Principal Cast**: Marguerite Duras, Gérard Depardieu.

Candy Mountain
Canada/France/Switzerland, 1987 – 92 mins
Robert Frank, Rudy Wurlitzer

A co-production that begins in New York before meandering cross-country and concluding in Canada, *Candy Mountain* is nonetheless described as a resolutely American film by its two well-matched collaborators. An acclaimed photographer whose 1958 book *The Americans* depicted American iconography and the mythic allure of the road in a more downbeat light, Robert Frank segued into film-making, establishing his reputation with the Jack Kerouac-scripted Beat classic *Pull My Daisy* (1959). Combining a passion for the road-movie genre, as evidenced by his work on Monte Hellman's seminal *Two-Lane Blacktop* (1971), scriptwriter Rudy Wurlitzer further mined the tarnished mythology of America in Peckinpah's *Pat Garrett and Billy the Kid* (1973).

Informed by Wenders' *Kings of the Road* (1976), *Candy Mountain* tracks the dispiriting personal odyssey of ambitious but untalented New York musician Julius (O'Connor), whose quest for glory leads him to feigning an association with Elmore Silk (Yulin), the J. D. Salinger of guitar-making. Charged with luring the legendary craftsman from hiding and retirement, Julius initially contacts Elmore's brother Al (Waits). Financially lighter (he is repeatedly sold cars that he either trades or crashes, signifying problems with travel and mobility), Julius again takes to the road and heads for the Canadian border and the remote home of Silk's former French lover (Ogier), who redirects him to a barren seaboard town. There, Julius finally tracks Silk down only to discover that in return for a lifetime of security and freedom he has signed an exclusive deal with a Japanese businesswoman (Kazuko Oshima). A helpless bystander as Silk destroys his remaining guitars, a tired, broke and disillusioned Julius attempts to hitch a ride home.

Wurlitzer draws upon Frank's background, specifically the dichotomy between art and commerce; the pressures of fame; journeys towards selfhood (a recurring road-movie motif) and the defining importance of music (Frank directed the seminal *Cocksucker Blues*, 1972) for the third celluloid collaboration between the pair. In part developing from the practical imperative of having to satisfy the demands of the various international financiers, Frank/Wurlitzer also tapped into Frank's desire to make a film about a journey from the centre of one culture to the margins of another. In turn, the pair also debunk the romantic notion of the open road as a symbol of freedom; *Candy Mountain* certainly strikes a sobering note and can perhaps be seen as providing the natural conclusion to the American road movie.

Pio Corradi's photography – redolent of Frank's own – imbues the shifting landscapes and their weird, cranky and frequently lonely populace with a timelessness and distinctly iconic quality. Corradi's absorbing attention to detail further heightens the pervading malaise. In a key moment, a toothless van driver warns the initially optimistic Julius that 'life ain't no candy mountain' before, like so many others, smartly ripping him off. Coordinated by Hal Wilner, the music, provided by luminaries such as Arto Lindsay and Marc Ribot, is essential, intelligently foregrounding both character and action. Endorsing the film's endearing, counter-culture sensibility, the film-makers' cast from an esoteric pool of musicians and are repaid with accomplished and entertaining turns from the likes of Tom Waits, Dr John, David Johansen and Joe Strummer. The 'regular' actors aren't bad either, especially O'Connor as the bowed but not quite beaten Kerouac-lite hero.

Dir: Robert Frank, Rudy Wurlitzer; **Prod**: Ruth Waldburger; **Scr**: Robert Frank, Rudy Wurlitzer; **DOP**: Pio Corradi; **Edit**: Jennifer Auge; **Score Coordinator**: Hal Wilner; **Principal Cast**: Kevin J. O'Connor, Harris Yulin, Tom Waits, Bulle Ogier.

The Cannonball Run
US, 1980 – 95 mins
Hal Needham

Included as representative of the cycle of late-1970s and early 80s cross-country car race movies that began with *The Gumball Rally* (1976) and the *Smokey and the Bandit* series (1977, also directed by Needham and starring Reynolds), *The Cannonball Run* beefed up the already successful recipe for box-office success by adding a cavalcade of stars in walk-on cameos. The film became the fifth highest-grossing film of its year and spawned the inevitable sequel, 1983's *Cannonball Run II*.

Based around an illegal race from Connecticut to California, Reynolds stars as J. J. McClure, a speed-loving racer disguised as an ambulance driver to outsmart the police. J. J.'s dim-witted sidekick is Victor (Dom DeLuise), who in moments of extreme trouble dons a suit and transforms himself into Captain Chaos. Rat Packers Dean Martin and Sammy Davis Jr join the line-up as Ferrari-driving priests, while martial-arts expert Jackie Chan takes on one of his first American film roles driving a souped-up Subaru. Roger Moore offers a less than hilarious parody of 007, driving a car complete with secret devices and weapons, and Farrah Fawcett provides the love interest and the buffer for J. J.'s charm and patter of witty one-liners. For good measure, there's also a deranged Islamic sheik, played by Jamie Farr, while Needham himself cameos (hey, everyone cameos) as a patient in J. J.'s ambulance, and Peter Fonda appears as an *Easy Rider* (1969)-style chopper-riding biker.

Sounding a rare note of authenticity in that it was scripted by Brock Yates, who allegedly sponsored an illegal, real-life coast-to-coast race, Yates also appears as the Cannonball Baker Sea-To-Shining-Sea Dash organiser. From thereon in, however, any attempt at realism is firmly eschewed in favour of lowest-common-denominator comedy and broad slapstick. Just about skirting by on Reynolds' charisma and irrepressible charm, the characterisation is two-dimensional at best, and only a couple of the cameos pass muster: Davis Jr and Martin offering a touch of class as the priests who turn out to be criminals.

A former stunt coordinator whose first break was doing stunts for a young Reynolds on *Gunsmoke* (1962–5), Needham does manage to pull off some impressive chases and crashes. Funnier than the entirety of the film itself and a device that has since been adopted many times (not least by Jackie Chan), the final few minutes are a series of outtakes and ad libs revealing that the stars certainly had a lot of fun making the movie.

Dir: Hal Needham; **Prod**: Albert S. Ruddy; **Scr**: Brock Yates; **DOP**: Michael Butler; **Edit**: Donn Cambern; **Score**: Al Capps; **Principal Cast**: Burt Reynolds, Roger Moore, Farrah Fawcett, Dean Martin, Sammy Davis Jr.

Catch Us If You Can (aka *Having a Wild Weekend*)
UK, 1965 – 91 mins
John Boorman

Inspired by the critical and commercial success of Richard Lester's self-reflexive and endlessly inventive *A Hard Day's Night* (1964), producer David Deutsch envisioned a similar vehicle for the Dave Clark Five, at that point considered serious rivals to The Fab Four's international pop crown. Impressed by Boorman's innovative documentaries for the BBC during the gold-rush era of British television (particularly the groundbreaking *Citizen 63* and the influential arts programme *Monitor*), Deutsch approached the fledgling director and playwright Peter Nichols about replicating Lester's success. With Warner Bros. sold on the film in the US, effectively covering the budget, Boorman, keen to make a break into features, was further persuaded by being given carte blanche on the project. 'As long as Dave and the band were in it, I could make whatever film I wanted' (Boorman 2003, p. 111).

Dinah (Ferris, in a role originally intended for Marianne Faithful), a famous pretty blonde model, is bored with her career and life in the limelight. While shooting a commercial for meat ('Meat For Go'), she meets a stuntman, Steve (Dave Clark), and the pair strike up an immediate rapport, deciding to flee across England to escape. Accompanying them are Steve's musical friends (the rest of the Dave Clark Five), but before long Dinah is reported as having been kidnapped by her manager (Lodge) and a frantic search for her whereabouts ensues. With their flight already proving anything but tranquil, the pair encounter a swathe of 1960s types, lose their car and are picked up by a strange Somerset couple (Bailey and Joyce) before the frantic chase resumes. Making for an apparently idyllic island off the coast of Devon, the film ends on a note of disillusionment when the low tide reveals that it is not an island at all. Their dreams shattered, the pair part; Dinah returning to her ad, Dave to his male cohorts.

Working from loose fragments of a story Boorman and Nichols discussed in an initial meeting with a less than enthusiastic Dave Clark (the singer's sole input was a request that his character be a stuntman), the director fashioned an original and satirical jaunt across a jaundiced English landscape beautifully photographed by Manny Wynn. A sequence shot in the snow on the Quantock Hills is especially memorable. Boorman describes the shoot as a nightmare. The crew were inexperienced and though for many of them it also signalled their first feature work, they were scornful of the director's TV background. A number of on-set clashes with a surly Clark hardly helped morale, the singer coming to blows with Deutsch's assistant Alex Jacobs over the costumes designed by Alex's wife, Sally. Viewed retrospectively, the clothes the characters wear are ahead of their time, especially Dinah's striped rugby jerseys. To round off a miserable production, Boorman made the mistake in a press interview of stating that he did not view *Catch Us If You Can* as a great film. The wrath of American movie moguls came down on his head.

Like Lester, Boorman would of course go on to bigger and better things, but the patent lack of chemistry between the two leads aside, his self-criticism of the film is largely unfounded. Making evident the band's relative lack of talent, the film's cynicism concerning manufactured commodities is impressive in the extreme. It also scores highly in terms of drawing a raw portrait of a materialistic society controlled and manipulated by advertising.

Dir: John Boorman; **Prod**: David Deutsch; **Scr**: Peter Nichols; **DOP**: Manny Wynn; **Edit**: Gordon Pilkington; **Score**: Dave Clark; **Principal Cast**: the Dave Clark Five, Barbara Ferris, David Lodge, Robin Bailey, Yootha Joyce.

Cold Fever
Iceland/US, 1995 – 95 mins
Fridrik Thór Fridriksson

Staking a claim as Iceland's first road movie, Fridrik Thór Fridriksson's *Cold Fever* offers a distinctive and suitably chilly take on road-movie conventions. Evoking the films of Aki Kaurismäki and Jim Jarmusch, right down to borrowing *Mystery Train*'s (1989) lead actor and producer, the first partly English-language feature from Iceland's premier director begins from the perspective of a personal odyssey made under the duress of the dictates of Japanese tradition. To this premise, a familiar road-movie foundation, a delightfully droll comic travelogue evolves, as

Atsushi Hirata (Masatoshi Nagese) feels the chill in the delightfully droll *Cold Fever*

taciturn Japanese culture merges with Iceland's unpredictable terrain and some of its more eccentric and singular inhabitants.

Bound for Hawaii on a golfing holiday, Tokyo businessman Atsushi Hirata's (Nagase) plans deviate when his grandfather reminds him that he should go to Iceland, where his geologist parents died seven years ago, and perform a ceremony at the site of their deaths. According to Japanese custom, in order to find peace, the spirits of the drowned must be comforted and fed by the surviving family members. So, after a brief inner struggle, Hirata heads for the cold and snowy wastes of Iceland and a bizarre trek from Reykjavik to the remote river where his parents met their end. Along the way, Hirata endures a number of surreal and offbeat encounters, including a young woman who sells him a temperamental old car after his previous travel arrangements go askew, another woman obsessed with funerals, and a pair of American hitchhikers (Taylor and Stevens) with designs on becoming Iceland's Bonnie and Clyde.

The first film to be shot during an Icelandic winter, leading to a fraught production marred by lost days due to adverse weather and acute continuity problems, *Cold Fever*'s delightful sense of the absurd is equalled by its visual beauty. With opening scenes shot in Japan to accentuate Iceland's vast white expanses, Ari Kristinsson's cinematography ravishingly captures the frequently strange and frankly awe-inspiring natural habitat, taking in enticing hot springs, abstract volcanic rock formations and furious, swirling blizzards. Hirata, portrayed with skilful understatement by Nagase, stoically bears all that the hostile elements can throw at him, the various idiosyncratic interludes he encounters along the road providing welcome relief and respite. During one particularly memorable encounter with an irascible local (Halldórsson), he even learns how to drink the potent local brew.

The car our intrepid traveller acquires is also worthy of mention. Boasting only one working handle and a radio that can be tuned only to a single station, it is a worthy edition to the catalogue of colourful road-movie vehicles. And yet for all its undeniable quirks and entertaining diversions, *Cold Fever* finally reveals a very clear destination, concluding with a poignant spiritual affirmation. As Hirata asserts, 'sometimes a journey can take you to a place that's not on any map'. A suitable mantra for any broad-minded traveller.

Dir: Fridrik Thór Fridriksson; **Prod**: Jim Stark; **Scr**: Jim Stark, Fridrik Thór Fridriksson; **DOP**: Ari Kristinsson; **Edit**: Steingrímur Karlsson; **Score**: Hilmar Örn Hilmarsson; **Principal Cast**: Masatoshi Nagase, Lili Taylor, Fisher Stevens, Gísli Halldórsson.

Dear Diary (*Caro diario*)
Italy, 1994 – 100 mins
Nanni Moretti

Nanni Moretti's intimate and hilarious film diary, which follows the
idiosyncratic Italian director's personal experiences over eighteen months,
was received rapturously at Cannes where it won the Best Director
Award. Moretti was already a cult figure in Italy and elsewhere in
Europe, and *Dear Diary* gave audiences further afield a chance to
discover his deliciously offbeat and irresistible appeal.

 The film, an effortless blend of blend of documentary and fiction
that is part road movie, part sociological satire and part polemical
reminiscence, is divided into three chapters. In the first, we follow
Moretti on his Vespa as he journeys through the streets of Rome. This
section is perhaps the most purely enjoyable as we see Moretti mingling
with the disparate characters he meets in the Roman suburbs. What
most clearly emerges is Moretti's love of cinema, as evidenced when he
enjoys a whimsical encounter with *Flashdance* star Jennifer Beals and her
husband, film-maker Alexandre Rockwell. Moretti then moves on to
observe that during the summer, the cinemas in Rome show films
saturated in violence and pornography. This gives rise to a humorous
fantasy interlude in which Moretti confronts a critic who dared to give
John McNaughton's *Henry: Portrait of a Serial Killer* (1986) a rave
review. At the end of this first section, and to conclude Moretti's
wandering meditation on cinema, the director visits the barren urban
wasteland where Pier Paolo Pasolini was murdered in 1975. A scene
conducted in near silence, Moretti forces the spectator to merely look
and observe.

 The film's second section travels to the beautiful Aeolian Islands off
Sicily, where Moretti hooks up with a friend who claims to have never
watched TV. All too soon, however, Moretti's companion has cultivated
an addiction to American soap operas and is unable to talk of anything
else, even while walking in the splendour of the islands' mountains. This

segment offers a telling reflection on the destructive and debilitating effects of mass media and consumer culture.

The film's final episode is undoubtedly the most poignant and overtly personal as Moretti deals with the aftermath of the discovery of a skin rash and the peculiarities of the Italian health system. We accompany him through his dealings with conventional and alternative doctors and his subjection to one ineffective treatment after another, including

Director and star Nanni Moretti searching for the answer to life's bigger questions in the intimate and idiosyncratic *Dear Diary*

massage, diet, herbs and electro-acupuncture, before the source of the problem is revealed to be a spot on his lung. Diagnosed as Hodgkin's lymphoma, Moretti, who never for a single moment lapses into mawkishness or attempts to use his camera to elicit sympathy, is told that there is a possibility that he may not survive the cancer.

Despite its quirks, this relaxed, leisurely and quietly modest personal odyssey ultimately offers a revealing and quite complex portrait of contemporary Italy, its seemingly fractured structure adding up to a surprisingly coherent and infectiously charming whole. The relative success of the film outside his native Italy earned Moretti somewhat lazy and fatuous comparisons with Woody Allen in regard to the autobiographical nature of their examinations of life and death.

Dir: Nanni Moretti; **Prod**: Nanni Moretti, Angelo Barbagallo, Nella Banfi; **Scr**: Nanni Moretti; **DOP**: Giuseppe Lanci; **Edit**: Mirco Garrone; **Score**: Nicola Piovani; **Principal Cast**: Nanni Moretti, Renato Carpentieri, Antonio Neiwiller, Jennifer Beals, Alexandre Rockwell.

Detour
US, 1945 – 68 mins
Edgar G. Ulmer

Edgar G. Ulmer was one of the relatively few film-makers to carve out a distinctive and personal style while working with the most meagre of budgets. A set and production designer and co-director for the likes of Max Reinhardt, F. W. Murnau, Fritz Lang and Ernst Lubitsch in the 1920s, Ulmer joined the parade of émigrés from the Viennese high-art community who came to America and helped change its artistic landscape. After making the Universal horror classic *The Black Cat* in 1934, Ulmer suffered a change in fortune and found himself toiling in the depths of poverty row, knocking out bargain-basement B-movie Westerns. Subsequently hired by the unglamorous PRC, Inc, headed by Leon Fromkess, Ulmer's frustration at the lack of studio funds was tempered by his being accorded complete creative freedom. Ulmer produced several notable films for the studio, arguably the best of which is *Detour*, a compelling Martin Goldsmith-scripted combination of 'the sinister and the mobile' (Williams 1982, p. 47).

Downtrodden New York pianist Al Roberts (Neal) decides to hitchhike to Los Angeles where his girlfriend, Sue (Drake), is a waitress. En route, Roberts accepts a ride from affable playboy Charles Haskell Jr (MacDonald), who after imbibing some pills asks Roberts to take over at the wheel. When Haskell suffers a fatal heart attack, Roberts, afraid that he will be accused of murder, disposes of the body, takes the man's clothes and wallet, and begins driving the car himself. He picks up beautiful but embittered Vera (Savage), who suddenly breaks the silence by asking, 'What did you do with the body?' It turns out that Vera had earlier accepted a ride from Haskell and has immediately spotted Roberts as a ringer. Holding the threat of summoning the police over his head, Vera forces Roberts to continue his pose so that he can collect a legacy from Haskell's millionaire father, who has not seen his son in years.

Shot in a mere six days and hampered by shoddy, minimalist sets and clumsy, in-camera optical effects, *Detour* nonetheless offers ample proof that few film-makers were able to do more with less. Clocking in at an economical 68 minutes, it is a thrillingly nihilistic tale in which Ulmer taps into a deep well of bitterness to combine road-movie and film-noir conventions (the femme fatale, greed, the road as a descent into peril and degradation, chance encounters) with bold compositional framings and a distinctive visual style. Utilising both flashback, extended voiceover (a world-weary Neal), changes of identity and a cross-country trek, even for a film noir *Detour*'s plot is highly convoluted and yet Ulmer drives the film along with an exhilarating, manic zeal. The performances act as further propellants, Savage excelling as the evil, self-interested 'dame with claws'.

A bleak and cynical view of post-war America that surveys the psychological wrecks that litter its lost highways, *Detour* has since acquired a bona fide cult status. Initially founded on the grisly life-imitating-art dictum that saw Neal sentenced to prison for killing his third wife, the film's reputation is now more properly regarded as evidence of Ulmer's visual expressiveness and ability to transcend economic stricture.

Dir: Edgar G. Ulmer; **Prod**: Leon Fromkess; **Scr**: Martin Goldsmith; **DOP**: Benjamin Kline; **Edit**: George McGuire; **Score**: Leo Erdody; **Principal Cast**: Tom Neal, Ann Savage, Claudia Drake, Edmund MacDonald.

Drugstore Cowboy
US, 1989 – 101 mins
Gus Van Sant

Though minimising actual road travel as a central drive of the narrative, Gus Van Sant's second feature bears many of the hallmarks of post-modern 1980s road movies such as *Paris, Texas* and *Stranger Than Paradise* (both 1984). Such films emerged in a decade in which the road-movie genre was resuscitated by a thriving independent scene in America, modifying the genre's modernist impulse to exaggerate 'irony and cynicism through stylized spectacles of sex, violence, or simple tongue-in-cheek cool' (Laderman 2002, p. 133). Set, like *Mala noche* (1985), in the director's hometown of Portland, Oregon, *Drugstore Cowboy* transposes the gay milieu of his improvisatory black-and-white debut for a more linear and outwardly conventional tale involving a quartet of pharmacy-robbing junkies. Also of note is the film's portrayal of alienation and aimlessness, and the sense that its rebellious central characters are adrift from society, ensnared in a state of permanent transience.

Led by the charismatic and paranoiacally superstitious Bob Hughes (former teen idol Dillon in a career-resurrecting performance), the young, makeshift surrogate family of outlaws – a defining road-movie type – is completed by Bob's long-term girlfriend Dianne (Lynch) and fellow couple Rich (Le Gros) and Nadine (Graham). Supporting their habit by knocking off pharmaceuticals and money from drug stores in a series of increasingly perilous raids, the gang are pursued by a cop (John Kelly) and frequently forced to skip town. Cue the engagement of the classic road-movie montage of driving shots and road motifs. Events take a more sombre turn when Nadine overdoses causing Bob to re-evaluate his life, checking into a rehabilitation programme in an attempt to straighten himself out. Set during the early 1970s (the authentic outfits and attentive production design are superb), it is narrated in flashback by a fatally wounded Hughes – who we later learn is the victim of a vicious attack by an amoral junkie – as he is being transported to hospital. It is worth noting that Hughes' injuries are sustained at the juncture when he decides to take stock and stand still.

Adapted by Van Sant and Daniel Yost from an unpublished autobiographical novel by convicted felon James Fogle, the film offers further evidence of the director's ability to respond with empathy to both environment and the failings and foibles of his characters. Resisting adopting a judgmental and sanctimonious tone towards chemical addiction, perceptively revealed in Bob's post-rehab refusal to condemn the actions of his former 'family', Van Sant presents the activities of his wandering protagonists as a reaction to the numbing boredom of lower-middle-class suburbia and the oppression of everyday existence. As with *Bonnie and Clyde* (1967), *Badlands* (1973) and other outlaw road movies, life on the road is a risk and a game of chance, the danger of which offers less cause for concern than the mundane, constricting forces of conformity. Contributing a cameo as a junkie ex-priest, counter-culture icon William Burroughs, whose *The Discipline of D. E.* formed the basis for one of Van Sant's earliest shorts, lends *Drugstore Cowboy* further resonance and authenticity in regard to the subculture it depicts.

Robert Yeoman's understated cinematography lends the film a gritty realism, but as in 1991's more determinedly surreal *My Own Private Idaho*, in which Mike (River Phoenix), a gay hustler, takes to the road in search of his mother, Van Sant also punctuates proceedings with a series of stylishly exuberant interludes to replicate Bob's superstitious paranoia – he harbours a fear of dogs and red hats – and descent into a chemical haze. Many of these interludes occur when Bob is shooting up in the back seat of the gang's beat-up Cadillac, fusing the notions of the drug trip and the road trip.

Dir: Gus Van Sant; **Prod**: Nick Wechsler, Karen Murphy; **Scr**: Gus Van Sant, Daniel Yost; **DOP**: Robert Yeoman; **Edit**: Curtiss Clayton, Mary Bauer; **Score**: Elliot Goldenthal; **Principal Cast**: Matt Dillon, Kelly Lynch, James Le Gros, Heather Graham.

Duel
US, 1971 – 90 mins
Steven Spielberg

A travelling salesman and a mysterious truck that pursues him are the
only ingredients in this minimalist story that marked Steven Spielberg's
first major directorial feature. Conceived by author and former Corman
cohort Richard Matheson after a similarly hair-raising experience with a
reckless trucker, Matheson's story originally appeared in *Playboy*
magazine, where it caught the eye of the producers of the ABC Movie of
the Week. To direct they selected a twenty-three-year-old who had
shown promise and an ability to work at speed and on budget on fare
such as *Night Gallery* and *Colombo*.

David Mann (Weaver) is a businessman on a long-distance car
journey to his next appointment. Driving down a deserted Southern
California highway at a safe and sane fifty-five miles per hour, Mann
steps on the pedal to pass a large gas trailer truck. The truck driver takes
umbrage and moments later is back, dangerously tailgating Weaver
before abruptly cutting him off. Mann briefly composes himself before
continuing, but the truck remains hell-bent on pursuit, its driver – whom,
to add to the sense of menace and mystery, we never see – intent on
engaging Mann in a motorised duel to the death.

A synthesis of horror, monster picture and road movie, in essence
the film is a cat-and-mouse car-chase concept that is simplicity itself.
Originally broadcast on 18 December 1971, *Duel* proved so popular that
a longer version with added violence was later prepared for theatrical
release in Europe in the 1970s. With Spielberg having become a
household name, the film finally found its way into American cinemas in
1983. Filmed entirely on location in dusty Soledad Canyon, the film's
fledgling director's approach to a minimal budget and restrictive shooting
schedule was precision and military planning and organisation. The
action sequences, of which the film is a ninety-minute series punctuated
by Weaver's weary interior monologue in which he references a middle-

class malaise including discord with his wife and a broken hose on his brand-new car, were all story boarded to the smallest detail. Spielberg, in what would become a trademark approach, shot the film in sequence.

In tandem with his facelessness and relentlessness, it is the lack of motive of his persecutor that heightens the allegorically named Mann's terrifying ordeal. The film's almost grinding sense of repetition develops its own hypnotic rhythm, suggesting a Kafkaesque world in which seemingly random and inescapable acts of psychological torture flourish and thrive. Mann's conservative Plymouth Valiant and his general nervous and needy demeanour exist in stark contrast to the bulky, formidable truck, and the film has fun suggesting that its panicky protagonist is enduring a particularly gruelling test of his masculinity, or indeed lack of it.

The confrontation between the two vehicles is expertly choreographed by the estimable Cary Loftin, with Spielberg showing flourishes beyond his experience by pitching the roar of the duelling engines at an uncomfortable volume. The playing of bland country music on Mann's radio in a sequence when his life is most in danger is another moment of inspiration.

Dir: Steven Spielberg; **Prod**: George Eckstein; **Scr**: Richard Matheson; **DOP**: Jack Marta; **Edit**: Frank Moriss; **Score**: Billy Goldenberg; **Principal Cast**: Dennis Weaver, Jacqueline Scott, Eddie Firestone, Lou Frizzell.

Easy Rider
US, 1969 – 95 mins
Dennis Hopper

Originating from an idea by Peter Fonda expanded into a loose story outline by Fonda and Dennis Hopper, *Easy Rider* began life as *The Loners*. With Fonda producing and the live wire Hopper slated to direct, financing for the project was in a state of flux until a chance meeting with Bob Rafelson's and Bert Schneider's independent Raybert company provided the required $360,000 to make a picture Fonda promised would challenge the rules of film-making and traditional screen representations of contemporary American society.

Born to be wild: Dennis Hopper (bottom left), Jack Nicholson (centre) and Peter Fonda in the pioneering *Easy Rider*

Easy Rider tells the story of anti-authoritarian bikers Wyatt 'Captain America' Earp (Fonda) and Billy (Hopper) who, buoyed by the proceeds of a cocaine deal and with alcoholic, part-time lawyer George Hanson (a star-making turn from Nicholson) in tow, 'went looking for America and couldn't find it anywhere'. Dealing with male camaraderie, the quest for freedom and America's pioneering spirit, the film offered a rebellious riposte to Establishment ideologies. László Kovác's sweeping cinematography of iconic national landmarks such as Monument Valley lends the film a mythic symbolism, but this is undercut by both the indolence and drug dependency of the protagonists and the depiction of the country as populated by narrow-minded bigots. Admitting that they 'blew it', the film closes with Earp and Billy being slain by a group of vicious rednecks.

Though in places technically raw and riddled with imperfections (Hopper cited underground film-making and the immediacy of the French New Wave as inspirations), the film saw Hopper crowned Best New Director at the 1969 Cannes Film Festival. The subsequent critical and commercial reaction to both the film and its huge-selling rock-orientated soundtrack was phenomenal: *Easy Rider* grossed over $50 million during its initial release, allegedly making its money back in one week and in one theatre, putting the film and its film-makers at the forefront of the industry and contemporary counter-culture politics. The film is also retrospectively viewed as establishing the road movie as a key post-1960s genre.

Perhaps most importantly, the film precipitated in Hollywood a move towards pictures dealing with the counter-culture, revealing among studios and major companies (*Easy Rider* was distributed by an initially wary Columbia) an ever-evolving opportunistic hunger to cash in on the latest fad. By extension, the independent nature of the film and its refusal to adhere to pre-subscribed formulas were enough to grant independent producers and artists a new autonomy, ushering in a period of relative artistic freedom and experimentation. Described as the 'New Hollywood' directors, figures such as Peckinpah, Altman and

Bogdanovich found themselves comfortably accommodated within the confines of the mainstream.

Moreover, this general erring towards risk-taking and the favouring of a looser, less consequential narrative structure led more by character than plot found in *Easy Rider* and its immediate progeny has much in common with what we today traditionally regard as key aesthetics in American independent films and film-making practices.

Dir: Dennis Hopper; **Prod**: Peter Fonda; **Scr**: Peter Fonda, Dennis Hopper, Terry Southern; **DOP**: László Kovács; **Edit**: Donn Cambern; **Score**: Hoyt Axton, Mars Bonfire, Roger McGuinn; **Principal Cast**: Peter Fonda, Dennis Hopper, Jack Nicholson, Antonio Mendoza.

Exils (*Exiles*)
France, 2004 – 103 mins
Tony Gatlif

A direct descendant from French-Algerian film-maker Tony Gatlif's earlier *Gadjo dilo* (1997), *Exils* is a more pessimistic but no less enthralling voyage of discovery that reinforces the director's interest in music, travel, life, love and people. Actor Romain Duris, fresh from breakthrough success in *The Beat that My Heart Skipped* (2004), also links the two pictures.

Zano (Duris) and Naïma (Azabal) are a pair of footloose bohemian lovers living in Paris who decide to pull up roots and travel to Algeria, even though they don't know the language and are unfamiliar with the cultural traditions. They take the scenic route, travelling from town to town along the way by train, by bus or foot, depending on their mood and financial circumstances. En route they encounter Leila (Makhlouf) and Habib (Cheik), an Algerian couple journeying in the other direction. Amused by Zano and Naïma's naiveté, Leila charitably gives them a letter of introduction to her family, and after a long passage Zano and Naïma eventually arrive in Algeria, where they are befriended by Leila's brother, Said (Zouhir Gacem). With Said in tow, the pilgrim pair explore the city and at once discover a land that fascinates them even as they realise just how far away from its culture they truly are.

Echoing his own family history in the story, Gatlif has fashioned a picaresque tale that poignantly deals with social and cultural displacement. It is made clear throughout, and this contributes to the tone of solitude that clouds the film's moments of joyful abandon (it takes on a darker hue once it touches down on African shores), that the name Naïma may be Arabic in origin but the character is herself almost entirely rootless. These moments of abandon certainly come thick and fast once the two protagonists initially take to the road, Gatlif's passion for his characters and for the vitality of life coming to the fore in a fruit-picking exercise that becomes erotic foreplay. Significant to the film's success as a picturesque travelogue is Céline Bozon's ravishing cinematography that both emphasises the relationship between characters and their environment and indulges in some original road-movie iconography (characters interestingly framed in cars and trucks etc.).

Gatlif operates in an almost anthropological fashion and his instinctiveness for disparate cultures is characteristically reflected in the score co-composed with Delphine Mantoulet. Essential to the film's narrative thread and taking in everything from techno and Andalusian flamenco, it is eclectic in the extreme, coming prominently to the fore in a climactic Sufi ceremony that suggests Zano and Naïma's spiritual awakening.

Dir: Tony Gatlif; **Prod**: Tony Gatlif; **Scr**: Tony Gatlif; **DOP**: Céline Bozon; **Edit**: Monique Dartonne; **Score**: Tony Gatlif, Delphine Mantoulet; **Principal Cast**: Romain Duris, Lubna Azabal, Leïla Makhlouf, Habib Cheik.

Familia rodante
Argentina, 2004 – 103 mins
Pablo Trapero

A popular audience favourite at festivals including Venice and Toronto, *Familia rodante* leaves far behind the brutal world of police corruption Argentinian writer/director Pablo Trapero previously explored in *El bonaerense* (2002). An amiably sour and bittersweet road movie, and another entry to the continued excellence in New Argentine cinema, *Familia rodante* adopts a fly-on-the-wall documentary approach to capture four generations of a Latina family confined in a temperamental, gas-guzzling camper van. Produced by Trapero's own Matanza films, the film, which translates as 'rolling family', was shot entirely in sequence and on location in Argentina, significantly contributing to the picture's suitably fraught and naturalistic feel.

Providing a fascinating insight into director Pablo Trapero's Argentinian homeland, *Familia rodante* captures four generations of a Latina family confined in a temperamental, gas-guzzling camper van

Celebrating her eighty-fourth birthday with her extended family, Emilia (Chironi) gets a phone call from her sister back home in Misiones asking her to be her niece's matron-of-honour. Emilia promptly declares that the whole family is going to the wedding. Son Oscar (Bernardo Forteza) dusts off his home-made motor home, and twelve family members pile in for the two-day journey from Buenos Aires to the coast. Along the way, they are interrupted by various dramas, road obstacles (including, somewhat surreally, a carnival and inquisitive ostriches), numerous vehicle breakdowns and illicit romances; and as Emilia heads home after a whole lifetime in the capital, she begins to put her life into perspective.

Buoyed by the spirited central performance of Chironi, a non-professional actor and Trapero's real-life grandmother, Trapero's observations of this feisty, chattering, emotionally chaotic family are so authentic as to be unnerving. Examining with wit and insight the various expectations, regrets, jealousies of the group, this affecting rites-of-passage tale assiduously avoids any hint of contrived sentiment, emerging as colourful, perceptive and utterly refreshing. Beginning with Chironi leafing through a family album to stress the importance of family and the extent to which we are prisoners of memory and the past, Trapero avoids individual introductions to the family members and gives no indication as to their lives in the city. The film begins with crowded group shots and snatches of conversation, inviting the spectator to share in their lives and the seemingly single, unified action of a collective, 1,000-kilometre journey. The cramped discomfort and simmering tension is authentically replicated by Trapero's aesthetic approach, an effective combination of restless handheld camera and intense, tight framing.

In a similar vein to Alfonso Cuarón's *Y tu mamá también* (2001), the journey provides a fascinating insight into its creator's homeland. As the family travel further north and the landscapes grow more lush and fertile, there are strategic references to Argentina's identity and heritage. These include the gauchos that roam the open roads, accompanied by traditional accordion music, to the stop-off at the birthplace of San

Martín, the country's liberator and national hero. The rolling family of the title can also be interpreted as a metaphor for the wider Argentinian society, overcoming various seemingly insurmountable obstacles and mounting economic crisis through a combination of resourcefulness and simply sticking together.

Dir: Pablo Trapero; **Prod**: Pablo Trapero, Donald Ranvaud, Robert Bevan; **Scr**: Pablo Trapero; **DOP**: Guillermo Nieto; **Edit**: Nicolás Goldbart; **Score**: León Gieco, Hugo Díaz, Juanjo Soza; **Principal Cast**: Graciana Chironi, Liliana Capuro, Ruth Dobel, Federico Esquerro.

Five Easy Pieces
US, 1970 – 98 mins
Bob Rafelson

Arguably among the best of the cycle of American road movies of the 1960s and early 70s and a key moment in the flowering of the American New Wave, *Five Easy Pieces* followed *Head* (1968) to mark the second film in what would become a long and productive partnership between director Rafelson and actor Nicholson. The film that helped propel Nicholson to stardom, it is also the role that defined his alienated, anti-Establishment persona.

A disaffected pianist from a family of classical musicians, Bobby Eroica Dupea (Nicholson) has forsaken his background of privilege to lead a humdrum, blue-collar existence as an oil rigger. Shacked up with the emotionally demanding Rayette (Black), recreation largely involves drinking, bowling and brawling with their friends Elton (Green Bush) and Stoney (Fannie Flagg). Suffocated by Rayette, Bobby seeks out his sister, Tita (Smith), and, discovering that his father is gravely ill, reluctantly heads back to the family estate in Puget Sound, Washington State, with a pregnant Rayette in tow. After an eventful road trip featuring a harangue from a pair of hitchhikers about filth, Bobby tucks Rayette away in a humdrum motel before heading to the house. There, Bobby seduces his uptight brother Carl's cultured fiancé, Catherine (Anspach), before Rayette arrives to unbalance the equilibrium with her apparent crassness. After failing to reconcile with his mute father, Bobby once again takes to the road, leaving Rayette stranded at a truck-stop after hitching a ride to an unspecified destination.

Less a film about the undertaking of a journey as it is a film about flight, *Five Easy Pieces* reduces the fantasy of rebellion and the desire for independence to the act of merely running away and absconding from any emotional attachment or wider sense of responsibility. A fascinating character study of a man embroiled in a crisis of the self, whose inability to find comfort either with the Establishment or society's working-class substrata is leading him to weave a trail of destruction and regret, the film is fondly remembered for a scene in which Bobby tries and fails to order a variant on a chicken salad in an interstate diner. Undeniably funny, the moment is apt evidence of the complexity of Nicholson's startling performance, his character's surplus of wit and charm insufficiently masking a torrent of loathing and frustration.

Influenced by European cinema, especially in its use of long takes, digressive narrative trajectory and complex sense of characterisation, and photographed by László Kovács in muted, out-of-season greys, browns and greens, *Five Easy Pieces* was instrumental in breaking down the divisions between art and commerce in American cinema. Though shot on a modest budget and defined by its resolutely low-key, minimalist aesthetic, the film was marketed to a mass audience and found commercial favour with 1970s American audiences caught between Nixon's 'silent majority' and the troubled counter-culture. Perceptively scripted by Rafelson and Eastman (credited as Adrien Joyce), the film retains a timeless quality and the ability to astound on repeated viewings. The conclusion, with a cold and jacketless Bobby hopping aboard an outbound rig as an unsuspecting Rayette nervously paces the petrol station forecourt, still packs a remarkable punch.

Dir: Bob Rafelson; **Prod**: Bob Rafelson, Richard Weschler; **Scr**: Adrien Joyce (Carole Eastman); **DOP**: László Kovács; **Edit**: Christopher Holmes, Gerald Sheppard; **Score**: N/A; **Principal Cast**: Jack Nicholson, Karen Black, Lois Smith, Susan Anspach, Billy Green Bush.

Gallivant
UK, 1996 – 100 mins
Andrew Kötting

Artist and film-maker Andrew Kötting is one of the most restless and searchingly innovative directors working in Britain today. He mines much the same psycho-geographic terrain as documentary-maker Patrick Keiller and writer Iain Sinclair, but in a more playful, idiosyncratic fashion. Gareth Evans has called him 'the only contemporary film maker who could be said to have taken the spirit of visionary curiosity and hybrid creativity exemplified by the late Derek Jarman' (Artists' newsletter).

Gallivant, Kötting's best-known work, is a travelogue like no other and a valuable addition to the British road-movie tradition. Kötting claims not to have been directly influenced by road-movie tropes, but does profess an affinity with Ross McElwee's *Sherman's March* (1985). In *Gallivant*, the director embarks on a coastal trip around Britain with his octogenarian grandmother and his young daughter, Eden, who suffers

Andrew Kötting and daughter Eden in *Gallivant*, a very British travelogue

from Joubert's Syndrome, a condition that restricts communication. This freeform journey, which involves various encounters with the flotsam and jetsam of the British public, is at once larky and epic, becomes part skewed homage to national eccentricity and identity, and part emotional voyage around the ties that bind Kötting's family.

A rare hybrid of avant-garde travelogue and family adventure movie, *Gallivant*'s tender meditation on the frailties and strengths of the human spirit ensure that the film manages both to evoke a strong sense of what differentiates and unifies three generations, while offering us a curiously effective travelogue of Britain's coastline, at times seemingly caught somewhere in the 1950s. It is also a more general look at the state of the UK today. Having studied at the Slade School of Fine Art under Chris Welsby, Kötting's work is shaped by his art-school training – the director describes his approach as sculptural – and here he employs an avant-garde visual repertoire, including found footage and time-lapse photography. The film's sound design is also striking. Landscape and its effect on the individual has remained a recurring preoccupation for Kötting, who mined similar terrain in 2001's down and dirty *This Filthy Earth*. Indeed, the artist and director has continued to offer reports on the lives of those closest to him in a series of various ongoing projects, the online diary and moving-image piece *Mapping Perception* updating us on Eden's continuing interaction with the world around her.

Strangely uplifting, surprisingly touching and a uniquely personal work of both humour and heart, *Gallivant* offers rare proof that innovation and entertainment in film need not be strangers.

Dir: Andrew Kötting; **Prod**: Ben Woolford; **Scr**: Andrew Kötting; **DOP**: Nick Gordon-Smith; **Edit**: Clifford West; **Score**: David Burnand; **Principal Cast**: Andrew Kötting, Gladys Morris, Eden Kötting.

Get on the Bus
US, 1996 – 122 mins
Spike Lee

Released one year to the day after Louis Farrakhan's 1995 Million Man March, in which a million African-American men marched peacefully in Washington, DC, in a bid for greater unity and understanding, Spike Lee's *Get on the Bus* follows a group of black men who take a charter bus from South Central LA to the rally in the nation's capital and watches as they interact and air their personal issues and concerns.

George (Dutton) is the organiser of the trip and de facto leader. Evan Thomas (Jefferson Byrd) is a truck driver who travels to the march with his son (Bonds) chained to his belt by court order after the boy was arrested for theft. Kyle (Isaiah Washington) and Randall (Harry Lennix) are gay lovers who take no small amount of abuse from their fellow passengers. Gary (Roger Guenveur Smith) is the product of a mixed-race marriage who could pass for white but sees himself as black; he's also a cop, which does little to endear him to his peers. Flip (Braugher) is an actor who seems more concerned with getting his next film role than the larger issues of the rally. Jamal (Casseus) is a good-natured young Muslim trying to lead a righteous life to make up for his violent past as a gang member. A film student (Hill Harper) is capturing the trip on videotape, and Jeremiah (Lee veteran Ossie Davis) sits in the back, reflecting on the struggles of African-Americans in the past and present.

One of Spike Lee's most cogent works, *Get on the Bus* was completed under arduous circumstances, the director working on a meagre budget and a tight schedule to ensure that the film was ready for release for the anniversary of the event. Going the route of his *Malcolm X* (1992) biopic, Lee felt that the subject matter necessitated strictly African-American finance, and raised $2.5 million of investment from a private group of fifteen black Americans, among them Wesley Snipes, Danny Glover and Lee himself. *Get on the Bus* speaks less of a single political goal than of the need for black men to set aside their

Heading in the right direction: Spike Lee's *Get on the Bus*

differences to work for their common good. While the film falls short of openly criticising Million Man March organiser Louis Farrakhan, it does present debate, much of it originating from the improvised dialogue of the cast, about Farrakhan's ideals and statements (and particularly his anti-Semitism), ultimately coming to the conclusion that whoever brought this group together is less important than the fact that they came together in peace and brotherhood.

Filmed in a documentary style, a dictate of the running and gunning production, *Get on the Bus* is cited as a landmark work by David Laderman. A road movie with a specific destination in which the narrative is driven by and focuses almost exclusively on black characters, 'as opposed to just putting blacks behind the wheel for a politically innocuous joyride, as in 1998's *Ride*' (Laderman 2002, p. 218), the film also displays several well-executed references to the tropes of the genre, including police harassment, an unexpected stop-off following a mechanical breakdown, numerous visits to iconic roadside diners and the use of music-as-movement – James Brown in this instance. Clearly re-politicising the genre from a black perspective, the film was of huge personal significance to its director. Though mishandled by its US distributor – who, unsure of how to present it, pitched it as a documentary – the film made its money back, its on-schedule US opening coinciding with Lee personally sending out cheques to the film's initial investors.

Dir: Spike Lee; Prod: Reuben Cannon, Bill Borden, Barry Rosenbush; Scr: Reggie Rock Blythewood; DOP: Elliot Davis; Edit: Leander T. Sales; Score: Terence Blanchard; Principal Cast: Richard Belzer, DeAundre Bonds, Andre Braugher, Thomas Jefferson Byrd, Charles S. Dutton, Gabriel Casseus, Albert Hall.

The Goalkeeper's Fear of the Penalty Kick (*Die Angst des Tormanns beim Elfmeter*)
Germany, 1971 – 101 mins
Wim Wenders

In terms of contemporary European film-makers, Wim Wenders is perhaps the one most closely aligned with the road movie. Many of Wenders' films reflect a fascination with the genre, and with American culture in general, while also seeking to establish his own identity and film-making aesthetic. For this reason, I feel that a brief background is necessary.

Wenders graduated from the Hochschule für Fernsehen and Film (HFF, Graduate School of Film and Television) with a feature-length film *Summer in the City* (*Dedicated to the Kinks*, 1970), shot on 16mm and black and white for the budget of the half-hour 35mm film he was expected to deliver. In 1971, together with a group of fourteen other German film-makers including Hark Bohm and Uwe Brandner, Wenders started a production and distribution cooperative called Filmverlag der Autoren. That company became the nucleus of the New German Cinema and Wenders one of its most recognisable and influential figures. After subsequently founding Wim Wenders Produktion in 1974, the company mutated to the Berlin-located Road Movies Filmproduktion Inc. Over the ensuing years, Road Movies would produce the majority of Wenders' subsequent films, including the seminal *Paris, Texas* (1984).

The beginning of Wenders' professional career, *The Goalkeeper's Fear of the Penalty Kick* was based on the novel of the same name by Wenders' friend and collaborator Peter Handke. Existing in the missing-narrative tradition favoured by the 'New Sensibility' (*Sensibilisten*), a movement that had sprung up around the HFF, the film follows a goalkeeper, Joseph Bloch (Brauss), who lets a penalty kick past him without making any effort to save it, thus revealing his passive disposition. Sent off for arguing with the referee, Bloch trudges away without a word, getting changed before heading into Vienna to pick up girls. Wandering by a local cinema (local cinemas becoming a recurring motif in Wenders' work), Bloch picks up the pretty cashier (Pluhar) and the two spend the night together. Inexplicably strangling her in the morning, the seemingly unaffected Bloch leaves Vienna by bus to a Burgenland village on the Austro-Hungarian border. While the village is preoccupied by the disappearance of a mute schoolboy (later found drowned), Bloch spends his days flirting with his hotel maid (Schwarz) and with a former girlfriend (Fischer). Making little attempt to escape, even when a composite drawing of Bloch circulates around the village, the emotionally estranged man seemingly waits for the net to tighten.

A deconstructed thriller in which no motive is given either for the crime or more generally for Bloch's listlessness, the film is very much reflective of the road-movie protagonists found in European and American movies of the period. The sense of a man who has grown too old for his vocation and whose inability to communicate (another abiding Wenders theme) and remoteness is expressive of a man almost entirely devoid of human feelings is remarkably conveyed by Bloch's hangdog facial expression. *The Goalkeeeper's Fear of the Penalty Kick* is also a key work in the Wenders canon for the inflated importance ascribed to objects, which here, and in Handke's original novel, is an indication of Bloch's mental instability. Frequently absorbed in objects and their function, this sense is beautifully realised in a scene in which Bloch becomes fascinated by the act of records mechanically dropping down in a jukebox. This moment also conveys the importance of music to Wenders and his own fascination with American culture and ephemera.

Like Wenders, Bloch becomes caught up in his interest in all things American (there are various references to Coke and gum), and in the film there is an awareness that 'As a European he [Wenders] was unable to fall back totally on the American style of film-making he admired so much' (Geist 1988, p. 26). Reaching back to his short works, Wenders shot the film's many travelling passages in a distinctive fashion, the camera remaining focused on something of interest after it has passed.

A film in which the nucleus of his creative team for many years to come was established, Wenders' use of high- and low-angle camera positioning is another idiosyncratic contribution to the grammar of road-movie style.

Dir: Wim Wenders; **Prod**: Peter Genée; **Scr**: Wim Wenders; **DOP**: Robby Müller, assisted by Martin Schäffer; **Edit**: Peter Przygodda; **Score**: Jürgen Knieper; **Principal Cast**: Arthur Brauss, Erika Pluhar, Kai Fischer, Libgart Schwarz.

Le Grand Voyage
France/Morocco, 2004 – 107 mins
Ismaël Ferroukhi

A labour of love six years in the making, the feature debut of Moroccan-born Ismaël Ferroukhi was conceived as a spiritual, rather than religious or political work. Earning praise for capturing the soul of the world at a difficult time, the former Cédric Kahn collaborator cited his intention as making a film that would 'rehumanise a community whose reputation is smeared by an extreme minority using religion for political ends' (Jaafar 2005, p. 66). Ferroukhi's source of inspiration was an epic overland road journey undertaken by his own father.

Fast-rising star Cazalé plays French teenager Reda, whose stern, dominating Muslim Moroccan father (Majd) speaks only Arabic. The pair become uneasy travelling companions when Reda's father forces him to drive him to Mecca in a battered old car so that he can undertake his final pilgrimage – or hajj – before he dies. Though reluctant to leave behind his French girlfriend, Reda finally acquiesces and the pair embark on an arduous 3,000-mile road trip that will take them across Europe. The father, whose name we never learn, further emphasising the generational and cultural gulf that exists, justifies the choice of car over plane by explaining that a pilgrimage must be accompanied by hardship. Eventually arriving in Saudi Arabia to join the massed throng of other pilgrims, the father ultimately recognises Reda's right to express his individual beliefs, rewarding him with an understated but heartfelt 'God bless you' for his efforts and patience. The ailing elder enters Mecca but sadly dies, leaving a distraught Reda to return home by plane alone.

A road movie with genuine geographical and emotional scope, the deftly performed *Le Grand Voyage* movingly captures the intricacies of parent–children relationships in a globalised world. In this regard, Ferroukhi adopts a familiar road-movie conceit, that of the ill-suited travelling companions, and drolly explores its dramatic and comic potential to observe the intricate interplay between two people who set out with little understanding of each other, but incrementally acquire respect as the shared kilometres rack up. Perhaps most impressively, the writer-director guards against sentimentality, the temporary truce denied full resolution by the death of Reda's father.

The geographical scope of the film allows for the adoption of another traditional road-movie motif: the incorporation of scenes depicting memorable encounters with disparate strangers. As with directors such as Aki Kaurismäki or Nanni Moretti's *Dear Diary* (1994), these skilfully, perfectly woven interludes in *Le Grand Voyage* stress the unknowingness of road travel. There is an unsmiling, elderly woman in the Balkans who demands safe passage before being left marooned at a restaurant, and an incident with a belly dancer that raises a great line about forgiveness in religion. The vagaries of the Bulgarian public-health system are also revealed when Reda's father is taken ill and treated in hospital, and an incident in Turkey involving Mustapha (Nercessian), an outwardly helpful young Turk later suspected of plundering the pair's ebbing coffers.

Featuring breathtaking scenery, such as father and son atop a sand dune, alongside more mundane images of road travel, such as customs checkpoints and queues of stationary vehicles, Ferroukhi's film is especially impressive in the Mecca sequences, capturing from above and at ground level the mass of pilgrims during the Kaaba. Keeping backstory to a minimum and stripped of all extraneous dialogue – another reason, perhaps, why we never learn the father's name – *Le Grand Voyage* is a heartfelt, wholly accessible and ultimately deeply compassionate picture that offers an all too rare insight into both traditional and contemporary attitudes towards Islamic identity. It leaves an unmistakable impression.

Dir: Ismaël Ferroukhi; **Prod**: Humbert Balsan; **Scr**: Ismaël Ferroukhi; **DOP**: Katell Djian, Nicolas Duchesne; **Edit**: Tina Baz; **Score**: Fowzi Guerdjou; **Principal Cast**: Nicolas Cazalé, Mohamed Majd, Jacky Nercessian, Ghina Ognianova.

The Grapes of Wrath
US, 1940 – 129 mins
John Ford

The road movie evolved from the long-standing literary tradition of the journey as narrative, and similarly retains the device of using mobility to offer social and cultural critique. Stretching back to Homer's *The Odyssey*, Mark Twain and Joseph Conrad are two other writers whose key personal-passage works, *The Adventures of Huckleberry Finn* and *Heart of Darkness* respectively, offer comment on a civilisation undergoing a process of modernisation. Another key author in this regard is John Steinbeck, whose *The Grapes of Wrath* particularly examines America's depressed economic classes and the socio-political causes that produce them. Undoubtedly the writer's finest treatment of

Mobility as social and cultural critique: John Ford's adaptation of John Steinbeck's *The Grapes of Wrath*, a key work that makes clear the genre's literary origins

these themes, the novel takes the form of a desperate family struggle for survival on the road during the Depression.

Marking an important transition towards the contemporary road movie in its suggestion that 'road travel has the potential for revelation' (Laderman 2002, p. 28), Ford's adaptation of Steinbeck's Pulitzer Prize winner is a rare example of a film that is equal to its source. Possessing an epic mythic quality, due to its subject matter, Gregg Toland's astonishing chiaroscuro cinematography and Ford's association with the Western (which the film closely resembles in theme and structure), *The Grapes of Wrath* also stands alongside Mervyn LeRoy's *I Am a Fugitive from a Chain Gang* (1932) in terms of the wider influence exerted by Depression-era Hollywood on the road movie.

Tom Joad (Fonda, solidifying his image as an upstanding hero) returns to his Oklahoma home after serving time for manslaughter. En route, he meets a family friend and former preacher (Carradine) who warns that dust storms, crop failures and new agricultural methods have financially decimated the once prosperous farmland. At the homestead, Joad is greeted by his mother (Darwell) and informed that the family is migrating to the 'promised land' of California. Their first stop is a wretched camp full of starving children and surrounded by armed guards. Further down the road, the Joads drive into an idyllic government facility, with clean lodging, indoor plumbing and a self-governing clientele. Having witnessed an America ravaged by human cruelty, corruption and greed, Joad feels compelled to keep moving, and bids his family farewell to embark on a life of unattached transience. Newly politicised, Joad moves off with the immortal lines: 'Wherever there's a fight so hungry people can eat . . . Whenever there's a cop beating a guy, I'll be there . . . And when the people are eatin' the stuff they raise and livin' in the houses they build. I'll be there too.'

Eloquently representing the Depression and the mass exodus following the Dust Bowl crisis, Ford's film differs from more established notions of the genre in that it has an extended family on the road as opposed to the more traditional fugitive couple. In this regard, it can be popularly viewed as having precipitated what Leslie Dick (1997) in an article in *Sight and Sound* dubbed an interesting subgenre, frequently termed the bus movie, in which a family or a band of people travel together. Subsequent examples include *Magical Mystery Tour* (1967), *Familia rodante* (2004) and the recent *Little Miss Sunshine* (2006).

Ford's film also played a significant part in the founding of a number of key road-movie aesthetics. These include the non-narrative travel montages comprising the ebb and flow of vehicles, frequently shot from a low-angle camera, and the explicit connection between man and machine through the reflection of faces in windscreens and rear-view mirrors. Most notably, and now very much part of road-movie iconography, is the mounting of the camera on a car, bringing new meaning to the travelling shot and allowing the spectator to experience motion from the most intimate point of view.

Dir: John Ford; **Prod**: Darryl F. Zanuck; **Scr**: Nunnally Johnson; **DOP**: Gregg Toland; **Edit**: Robert Simpson; **Score**: Alfred Newman; **Principal Cast**: Henry Fonda, Jane Darwell, John Carradine, Russell Simpson.

Guantanamera
Cuba, 1995 – 105 mins
Tomás Gutiérrez Alea

Widely regarded as Cuba's greatest film-maker, the work of Tomás
Gutiérrez Alea centred on the revolution and its effects on Cuban
society. Retaining a sophisticated balance between a dedication to the
revolution and a critical judgment of when its ideals had been betrayed,
the films of Alea, of which the internationally renowned *Memories of
Underdevelopment* (1968) is perhaps the best known, also provide a
thematic and artistic trajectory for Cuban cinema, from early cinéma
vérité and radical experimentalism, through to neo-realist drama and
social comedy.

    Alea's final film, the satirical *Guantanamera*, belongs in the latter
camp but still maintains an intelligent and critical discourse regarding
economic conditions and contemporary politics in modern-day Cuba.
Yoyita (Conchita Brando), a well-known singer living in Havana, travels
with her niece Georgina (Ibarra), a college professor, to the village of her
birth, where Yoyita is reunited with Candido (Eguren), whom she loved
as a young woman. When Yoyita and Candido meet for the first time in
fifty years, they are thrilled to discover that the flame of passion still
burns; unfortunately, Yoyita is so thrilled that she suffers a fatal heart
attack. Yoyita's body must be transported back to Havana for burial, but
while logic would dictate that Georgina should simply hire a hearse to
make the journey, her husband Adolfo (Cruz), a bureaucrat with more
enthusiasm than common sense, has another idea – by transferring the
body from one vehicle to another at the border of each province, the
cost of fuel will be distributed more evenly along the route. Georgina,
Candido and Adolfo begin a long, slow incident-strewn journey back to
Havana, sharing their thoughts on faith, politics and love.

    With Alea dying of cancer before shooting was finished,
Guantanamera (taken from the popular ballad of the same name) was
completed under the supervision of Alea's frequent co-writer, Juan

Carlos Tabio (*Strawberry and Chocolate/Fresa y chocolate*, 1993). The visions of a Cuba run by petty bureaucrats and the cynical asides on the failings of socialism, particularly on an economic level, are, however, undoubtedly Alea's own. In a telling detail, it is revealed that fruit is worth as much if not more than the national currency, and behind the American dollar is the preferred tender with which to trade and barter on the thriving black market. Perhaps the film's most astute observation, hitting its target precisely because of its road-movie structure, is the fact that people own plush Russian sedans, but are unable to afford the petrol to put in them.

Taking in numerous plot digressions, most of which involve the two resourceful and amorous truck drivers charged with transporting the coffin and the increasingly frustrated Georgina's fling with an old suitor, Alea's bitterness and disappointment is tempered, rather successfully, by a graceful and engaging blend of romance and magical realism. The use of traditional songs to comment on the narrative – and the motivations and sensibilities of the colourful characters – is another successful device, with Hans Burmann's accomplished cinematography equally capturing both the beauty and the idiosyncrasies of the country.

Dir: Tomás Gutiérrez Alea, Juan Carlos Tabio; **Prod**: Gerardo Herrero; **Scr**: Eliseo Alberto De Diego Garcia Marroz, Tomás Gutiérrez Alea, Juan Carlos Tabio; **DOP**: Hans Burmann; **Edit**: Carmen Frias; **Score**: José Nieto; **Principal Cast**: Carlos Cruz, Mirtha Ibarra, Raúl Eguren, Jorge Perugorria.

Gun Crazy (aka *Deadly is the Female*)
US, 1949 – 87 mins
Joseph H. Lewis

While often compared to *Bonnie and Clyde* (1967), which it preceded by nearly twenty years, *Gun Crazy* is in many ways a more daring work. While the leads lack the charisma of Warren Beatty and Faye Dunaway, and the picture is sometimes betrayed by its meagre budget, director Joseph H. Lewis gives his story a subversive sexual economy that is more provocative than Arthur Penn's later variation. A high-octane thriller that also contains the very essence of film noir, the film's doomed romanticism achieves an intense poetry eloquently expressive of the dark side of the American Dream.

Bart Tare (Dall) is a timorous kid with an obsession with guns: playing target practice in the woods, stealing a revolver out of a hardware store and even bringing a handgun to school. But when he shoots a baby chick with his BB gun, he swears he'll never kill again. That is, until the adult Bart meets Annie Star (Cummins), an expert markswoman performing in a travelling carnival. When Bart beats Annie in a shooting competition, there's no question that these two are going to pair up and hit the road together. But the honeymoon period is short-lived for the sharp-shooting sweethearts. When the money runs out and nights on the town fade, Annie reveals that her only desire is for bigger and better kicks, and if Bart can't keep the action coming, she'll hook up with another man who can. Bart finds himself pressured into a cross-country crime spree as the lovers on the lam rob gas stations, liquor stores, jack the occasional car and generally cause mayhem wherever they go. With every job, Annie's admiration for and commitment to Bart grows, as does Bart's confidence, until the quest for the quintessential last big score brings predictably tragic results.

Rising eloquently above the modesty of its means, *Gun Crazy*'s origins lie in the poverty-row operation of the King Brothers, who gained the film wider exposure than its intended Monogram release by securing a distribution deal with United Artists. Originally based on a magazine article by MacKinlay Kantor, blacklisted writer Dalton Trumbo disingenuously mastered the restrictions of the Production Code, crafting a violent, lustful and unrepentantly bloody tale. Trumbo's dialogue is hard-boiled in the extreme, lines such as 'Take the baby, they'll be less likely to shoot at us' depicting a desperate society running short on morality. Lewis and his co-contributors skilfully locate the film in a rain-slicked, after-hours world, while also offering a brutal analysis of the post-war American society that gave birth to it.

A film-maker with a gift for creatively overcoming frugality, Joseph H. Lewis' direction is excellent throughout, expertly ratcheting up the tension in a number of audaciously executed on-road pursuits and set-pieces. There is a striking on-foot chase through a warehouse of hanging cow carcasses, but the film's most talked about scene is a bank job shot in real time from the back seat of the protagonists' getaway car in which the audience is whisked along for the ride on Bart and Annie's fatalistic fast track to damnation.

Dir: Joseph H. Lewis; **Prod**: Maurice King, Frank King; **Scr**: Mackinlay Kantor, Millard Kaufman; **DOP**: Russell Harlan; **Edit**: Harry Gerstad; **Score**: Victor Young; **Principal Cast**: Peggy Cummins, John Dall, Berry Kroeger, Morris Carnovsky, Annabel Shaw.

The Hit
UK, 1984 – 98 mins
Stephen Frears

Having made his feature-film debut in 1971 with *Gumshoe*, Stephen
Frears made an immediate return to television, working on the BBC's
Play for Today and *Play of the Week* slots. After venturing into bigger-
budgeted small-screen works with: *Bloody Kids* (1980), co-written by
Stephen Poliakoff; *Walter* (1982), the first *Film on Four*, and its sequel,
Walter & June (1983); and *Saigon: Year of the Cat* (1983), Frears once
again tackled a feature with the modestly budgeted, offbeat crime
thriller *The Hit*.

Willie Parker (Stamp), an English mobster-turned-informant with a
new identity, has been living in a small, isolated village in Spain for ten
years. Unfortunately for Parker, the men he has betrayed have
ascertained his whereabouts and send Braddock (Hurt), a professional
hitman, and his apprentice Myron (Roth) to bring Parker to Paris where
his ex-associates await. After kidnapping Parker, nothing goes as
planned. Followed through the Spanish countryside by a Spanish
policeman (Fernando Rey) who seems to anticipate their every move,
they are also burdened by Maggie (del Sol), the mistress of a fellow
mobster they were forced to kill. What should have been a routine hit
becomes a psychological battle between all the participants, as Parker,
in a fight for time and for his life, plays one against the other.

With a resurgent Stamp exuding the rakish charm with which he
made his name in the 1960s, Hurt radiating thinly concealed malice and
menace, and Roth, in his film debut, immediately impressing as the
rookie thug with a buried conscience, the performances in *The Hit* are
uniformly excellent. Scripted by Peter Prince, with whom Frears had
collaborated on a number of his television plays, the film's strong
characterisation and interesting starting premise – Stamp's affable
cockney supergrass accepting his inevitable execution with apparent
good grace – are matched by a mordant black humour and skilfully

sustained tension once Parker, Braddock and Myron's journey to Paris becomes a tense cat-and-mouse pursuit through the bleak but beautiful Spanish countryside. There are various off-road incidents – many of which involve the feisty Maggie, a woman prepared to do what it takes to survive – and dangerous detours along the way, before Frears builds to a surprising conclusion in which the characters' true selves are revealed.

Given the combustible nature of the erstwhile travelling companions, it is no surprise that the film also features one of the most uncomfortable car journeys in history. Paco da Luca's memorable score (featuring Eric Clapton on guitar) provides some respite from the frequently nerve-shredding mind games that blend psychology and philosophy to offer up an enjoyable and enlightening meditation on mortality and courage.

Dir: Stephen Frears; **Prod**: Jeremy Thomas; **Scr**: Peter Prince; **DOP**: Mike Molloy; **Edit**: Mike Audsley; **Score**: Paco da Luca; **Principal Cast**: John Hurt, Terence Stamp, Tim Roth, Laura del Sol, Bill Hunter.

In This World
UK, 2002 – 90 mins
Michael Winterbottom

Prolific British film-maker Michael Winterbottom adds to his impressively eclectic and diverse filmography with this harrowing account of two Afghan refugees' passage to the West in search of a better life. A director who has worked across genres and styles, if there is a general thread tying the films of this restless maverick, it is perhaps his dedication to people and places, created largely on location and exploring a wide range of geographical and social settings.

Written by Tony Grisoni, *In This World* is a potent slice of cinematic realism exploring migration and movement. Opening at the Shamshatoo refugee camp in Peshawar, Pakistan, where Afghans have sought refuge in the wake of the US military campaign in their country following the 11 September terrorist attacks, the film follows the journey of orphaned fourteen-year-old Jamal (Udin Torabi) and his older cousin Enayat (Enayatullah) from the Pakistan–Afghanistan border. Travelling in the back of trucks, by bus and on foot, the two cross Central Asia in an arduous journey punctuated by encounters with hostile border guards and shady smugglers. Even more traumatic is the ocean voyage from Turkey to Italy, during which Jamal and Enayat are forced to hide in a shipping container with other asylum seekers, including a terrified infant. The film concludes in England, with scenes shot at Sangatte.

Shot with a tiny crew and non-professional actors and improvised dialogue vérité-style on digital video, the film's rapid cutting and general urgency reinforces the fact that we are watching two real people perilously undertaking an actual, albeit staged, journey. This approach also allows for the residual build-up of empathy with Jamal and Enayat as the film progresses. By the conclusion, the emotional engagement with their situation is almost unbearably acute. Winterbottom and young DOP Marcel Zyskind deviate from this 'in the moment' aesthetic only for a more stylised nighttime sequence revealing a mountainous border-crossing. Shot in almost pitch-black and highly pixelated, the moment achieves an almost surreal, abstract beauty.

Winterbottom's intimate methodology, resulting in hundreds of hours of footage, makes for gruelling and often traumatic viewing, none more so than when the two refugees are shown as tiny figures wedged beneath the wheels of an HGV heading for the UK. Strenuously resisting the labelling of the film as a documentary, Winterbottom has, however, achieved the feat of taking us into a world and characters infrequently represented on screen and drawn invaluable attention to the plight of refugees, displacement and the notion of people as currency. One of the director's finest and most vividly realised works, *In This World* won the Golden Bear at the 2003 Berlin Film Festival.

Dir: Michael Winterbottom; **Prod**: Andrew Eaton, Anita Overland; **Scr**: Tony Grisoni; **DOP**: Marcel Zyskind; **Edit**: Peter Christelis; **Score**: Dario Marianelli; **Principal Cast**: Jamal Udin Torabi, Enayatullah, Jamau.

Jizda (*The Ride*)
Czechoslovakia, 1994 – 88 mins
Jan Sverák

After having made one of the most ambitious and, at $1.5 million,
expensive productions ever undertaken by the Czech film industry with
his previous work, 1994's *Accumulator 1*, director Jan Sverák took an
entirely different approach for *Jizda*. Resourcefully shot in just twenty
days on a budget of $30,000, this gentle, Eastern European take on the
road movie incorporates everything from *Easy Rider* (1969) to *Thelma &
Louise* (1991).

Uninspired by their humdrum lives, two thirtysomething friends,
Radek (Pasternák, also the film's composer) and Frank (Spalek), buy a
cheap car, cut its roof off and head out of Prague to spend summer
touring the Czech countryside. Bored with his marriage, Frank appears to
be floundering in lieu of an alternative, his kinship with Radek at times
approaching an almost romantic attachment. Along the way, the pair
pick up Anne (Czech supermodel Geislerová), an initially forlorn,
subsequently strong-willed waif who has run out on her aggressively
possessive boyfriend. A sexual cat-and-mouse game subsequently ensues,
with Radek's efforts to come on to Anne being met with indifference,
vague encouragement or humiliating rejection. As Radek turns the tables
on her game-playing, Anne switches her attentions to Frank, but her
moves, made against the backdrop of her out-of-sight but fast-
approaching ex, come up against apparent imperviousness.

Sverák's regular cinematographer F. A. Brabec crisply captures the
rolling beauty of the Bohemian countryside, his beautiful images
frequently set to travelling montages of Czech pop sings. Sverák's
fondness for such sequences may seem overindulged, but alongside the
intriguing depiction of the sexual triangle, this is one of the film's main
avenues of pleasure for Czech viewers, many of whom openly sang
along with the film when it was screened at a season of Czech films
presented by the Czech Centre at London's Riverside Studios. A modest

domestic success, the high regard in which the film is held by Czechs is also partially because *Jizda* certainly reflected the contemporary mindset of a nation freely embracing democracy and revelling in the abandonment of convention.

If the film's fondness for visually arresting tracking shots and extended use of soundtrack music offers firm evidence of *Jizda*'s self-knowing awareness of the conventions of the road-movie genre, so too does the frisson that develops between the two male friends once a capricious female enters the equation. The road movie is frequently accused of being a predominantly male domain and here, as in works such as the aforementioned *Easy Rider* and *Two-Lane Blacktop* (1971), a traditional sexist hierarchy is retained that privileges the heterosexual male in terms of narrative and point of view. 'As in typical Hollywood films, the road movie tends to define the active impulse (here, to drive) as male, relegating women characters to passive passengers and/or erotic distractions' (Laderman 2002, p. 20). This could certainly said to be true of Anna, but of course this could also be part of Sverák's tactic of gently parodying a distinctly American genre.

Dir: Jan Sverák; **Prod**: Klara Bukovska, Marketa Hajkova; **Scr**: Jan Sverák, Martin Dorstal; **DOP**: Frantisek A. Brabec; **Edit**: Alois Fisarek; **Score**: Radek Pasternák; **Principal Cast**: Anna Geislerová, Radek Pasternák, Jakub Spalek.

Journey to the Sun (*Günese yolculuk*)
Turkey, 1999 – 105 mins
Yesim Ustaoglu

A director who initially trained as an architect, Yesim Ustaoglu found the
inspiration for this, her second feature, after reading newspaper reports
depicting the burned shells of evacuated villages in southeastern
Anatolia. A courageous work, especially given the levels of censorship
Ustaoglu faced, *Journey to the Sun* suggests a government bureaucracy
flirting with totalitarianism, where the least signs of dissidence are cause
for repression.

Turkish Mehmet (Newroz Baz) and Kurdish Berzan (Nazmi Qirix) are
two lonely souls trying to keep their heads above water in a huge
metropolis. The gentle-natured Mehmet comes from the west coast of
Turkey, while Berzan's village is far away in the southeast, near the Iraqi
border. They meet in the threatening urban environment of Istanbul,
where Mehmet is working for the water department and Berzan is selling
music cassettes on the street. Mehmet is in love with Arzu (Mizgin
Kapazan), a city girl who works in a laundrette, while Berzan carries the
photo of the sweetheart he left behind. Mehmet's hopes for a new life
come to an abrupt end when he is mistakenly arrested as a terrorist
suspect; his dark complexion raises suspicions that he might be a Kurd.
Tortured in police custody, and now without a job or a place to sleep, he
is sheltered by Berzan, who lives in a shanty town on the outskirts of the
city. However, when Berzan is tragically killed by the police, a new
journey begins for Mehmet when he resolves to return Berzan's remains
to his remote, stricken village in southeast Anatolia.

Using largely non-trained actors – who retain their real names –
Ustaoglu avoids commenting directly on the specific details of the
Kurdish conflict, instead skilfully evoking character and place and tracing
the fragile network of odd jobs and temporary shelters that serve as the
immigrant community in Istanbul's teaming and combustible metropolis.
Beautifully shot by Krzysztof Kieslowski's former cameraman Jacek

Petrycki, the film presents the capital as a place of surreal and disquieting dichotomies. The juxtaposition of prostitutes plying their trade in the shadow of ancient minarets is particularly striking. All the while, lives are easily lost or derailed amid sudden acts of terror and bursts of sporadic violence.

Of course, the central, initially tentative friendship and tenderness between Berzan and Mehmet is a suggestion of hope for the future, an optimistic note that continues to chime even after Berzan's sudden death. It is at this moment that Ustaoglu withdraws from the leitmotiv of the migration to the city and the struggles of traditional cultures to keep pace with modernity – recently returned to again in Nuri Bilge Ceylan's *Uzak* (2002) – as Mehmet takes to the road to undertake the epic task of returning his unlikely companion to his birth village. Moving through Turkey's often bleak, desolate but also frequently breathtakingly beautiful landscape, the film's gentle lyricism becomes more pronounced, its obvious and often unresolved political concerns (for example, how would Mehmet's love for the Kurdish Arzu play out?) meshing with an emotionally engaging tale about companionship, loss and identity in harsh and troubled environments.

Dir: Yesim Ustaoglu; **Prod**: Behrooz Hashemian; **Scr**: Yesim Ustaoglu; **DOP**: Jacek Petrycki; **Edit**: Nicolas Gaster; **Score**: Vlatko Stefanovski; **Principal Cast**: Nazmi Qirix, Newroz Baz, Mizgin Kapazan, Ara Güler, Lucia Marano.

Kalifornia
US, 1993 – 118 mins
Dominic Sena

This debut feature film from former music video director Dominic Sena is a violent serial-killer romp that explores the thin line between social convention and depravity, and between high art and low-life living. Unfolding in a landscape that is bleak and morally bankrupt in the extreme, *Kalifornia* looks back to *Badlands* (1973) and forward to Oliver Stone's *Natural Born Killers* (1994) in its portrayal of a celebrity-fixated society where murderers attract intense media interest bordering on celebrity status.

Hip photographer Carrie Laughlin (Forbes) wants to relocate to California for a fresh start. The idea also appeals to her boyfriend, Brian Kessler (Duchovny), a writer planning a travelogue on the locations of serial slayings. The pair make plans for a cross-country tour, with Brian writing the commentary and Carrie taking the pictures. But they need a couple to share the driving expenses: enter Grayce (Pitt) and his girlfriend, Adele (Lewis). Grayce is an ex-con looking to jump parole, while Adele is a childlike naïf. The quartet hit the road, with Brian and Carrie unaware just how close they are to their serial-killer subject. That is until the bodies begin piling up disturbingly behind them as they make their way across the country.

Blood-drenched and undoubtedly disturbing and uncomfortable to watch, Sena's intelligent script and relatively restrained direction ensure that *Kalifornia*, rather than just revelling in its violence, actually seeks to contextualise it, holding a mirror to a society where the culture of violence and the media obsession with it seem to be increasing in currency. On the evidence of the film, Sena certainly seemed to be a film-maker who actually had something to say, and the grasp of the medium to say it, so it is disappointing to note that his subsequent career has trailed off into monotonous action epics such as *Gone in Sixty Seconds* (2000). Though well received, *Kalifornia* was immediately overshadowed by director Oliver Stone mining a similar terrain the following year, the director's characteristic lack of subtlety and MTV aesthetic blunting his polemic.

Viewed retrospectively Lewis' credible performance also now seems a dry run for *Natural Born Killers*. Sexy, tacky and pitiable, innocent and yet manipulative, Lewis affectingly conveys the sense that Adele's complicity in the carnage is born of psychological damage and the direct result of her own experience with violence. In a more showy turn, Pitt also gives good value, his Method approach allegedly causing him to break a tooth opening beer bottles when preparing for the role. Grimy and foul-mouthed, Pitt's lascivious sneer is the most effective clue to his unsavoury activities.

Though undoubtedly pandering to the yuppies-in-peril scenario, the film is interesting for avoiding the routine thriller route and a standard cat-and-mouse pursuit once the supposedly cultivated couple become aware of the true nature of the people with whom they are travelling. Sena seems to suggest that Carrie and Brian's unhealthy fascination with depravity and celebration of it through art is dangerous and misjudged. That's pretty impressive for a film that arguably plays a similar card and whose commercial success will be predicated on the voyeuristic appetites of the cinemagoing public.

Dir: Dominic Sena; **Prod**: Steve Golin, Sigurjon Sighvatsson, Aristides McGarry; **Scr**: Tim Metcalfe; **DOP**: Bojan Bazelli; **Edit**: Martin Hunter; **Score**: Carter Burwell; **Principal Cast**: Brad Pitt, Juliette Lewis, David Duchovny, Michelle Forbes.

Kikujiro
Japan, 1999 – 122 mins
Takeshi Kitano

With his eighth feature, Japan's foremost contemporary film-maker took an interesting and worthwhile detour from the violent, hard-hitting Yakuza gangster films with which he was so inextricably associated. Named after Kitano's father, though the character is not based on him, *Kikujiro* is a delightful, picaresque road movie more evocative of Chaplin's *The Kid* (1921) than of previous Kitano pictures such as *Violent Cop* (1989).

Nine-year-old Masao (Sekiguchi) lives with his grandmother in Tokyo. With a lonely summer holiday looming, he stumbles across his mother's address and decides to journey to a distant coastal city to track her down. His companion, Kikujiro (Kitano), is a washed-up layabout, who reluctantly assists the boy under orders from his domineering wife. Before they even set off, they spend two days blowing their money at the racetrack, making the ensuing expedition a slow and difficult one. En route, Masao's demeanour and plight invite the intervention of a series of other eccentric characters, ranging from a poet in a camper van to a pair of effete Hell's Angels.

Despite hints that the indolent Kikujiro may have once been a Yakuza, the most significant being his revealing of an elaborate tattoo, the film is undoubtedly marked by the almost complete absence of Kitano's signature, stylised violence. The one instant in which the spectator expects retribution to explode, a scene in which Masao, beautifully portrayed by Sekiguchi in a near-wordless performance, is almost abducted by a paedophile, passes with nary a blow traded. When questioned about this more contemplative direction and sedate pacing, Kitano, recently recovered from a life-threatening road accident,

(*Opposite page*) Previously known for his violent Yakuza pictures, Takeshi 'Beat' Kitano (pictured with child actor Yusuke Sekiguchi) makes a welcome detour with the beguiling *Kikujiro*

commented that the lack of violence was far from a conscious decision; it simply wasn't in the script. Kitano also perceptively asserted that the emotional detachment and the mentality of the characters in fact closely echoed those of his previous films.

Kikujiro unfolds as a series of deliberately drawn-out scenes, conveying a sense of endless time, juxtaposed with comic workouts featuring quirky jump-cuts and Chaplinesque visual slapstick. Watching the film, one instantly recalls that Kitano began his career as a very physical, stand-up comedian. Windows on Masao's inner world are opened through subjective viewpoint shots and the extraordinary dream sequences use the imagery and choreography of traditional Japanese theatre. Kitano often likes to augment his narrative structure with idiosyncratic visual flourishes – the paintings in *Hana-Bi* (1997), or the scenes in *Sonatine* (1993) of people larking around on the beach – and *Kikujiro* shows the same level of invention.

Kitano delicately mines the somewhat formulaic narrative conceit, avoiding its potential for sentimentality by imbuing his character with mood swings, inept social skills and an almost insatiable capacity for incompetence. Brash and loud, the opportunistic Kikujiro also does little to conceal his lack of fondness for children. Inevitably, over the course of their incident-packed journey, during which progress is made incrementally through Masao's skill cadging lifts, adult and child discover that they have rather more in common than they expected. At a press junket in Cannes, Kitano described *The Wizard of Oz* (1939) as his role model when making the film, beginning this bewitching, shaggy-dog tale with the sound of an angel bell tinkling in a nod to *Oz*'s more fantastical, fairytale elements.

Dir: Takeshi Kitano; **Prod**: Masayuki Mori, Takio Yoshida; **Scr**: Takeshi Kitano; **DOP**: Katsumi Yanagishima; **Edit**: Takeshi Kitano; **Score**: Joe Hisaishi; **Principal Cast**: Takeshi 'Beat' Kitano, Yusuke Sekiguchi, Kayoko Kishimoto, Akaji Maro.

Kings of the Road (*Im Lauf der Zeit*)
Germany, 1976 – 176 mins
Wim Wenders

Beginning as a self-funded itinerary of small towns with ailing movie theatres on the border of East and West Germany, Wenders took to the road with a handful of actors, a small crew and a few completed script pages. He worked on the dialogue overnight, but if his inspiration didn't flow, then the crew didn't shoot the next day. Forming part of a loose

Robert (Hanns Zischler) attempts to take flight in *Kings of the Road*, one of several notable road movies from German director Wim Wenders

trilogy comprising *Alice in the Cities* (1973) and the more static,
dialogue-driven *Wrong Move* (1974), in conjunction with 1971's *The
Goalkeeper's Fear of the Penalty Kick*, the three films exemplify Wenders'
combination of the American road movie with the *Bildungsroman*, the
German literary tradition in which a young man travels to find his true
being or purpose in life.

Originating with the premise of a self-sufficient projector repairer
servicing the rural cinemas whose existence is under threat from the
dominance of American cinema, *Kings of the Road* evolved into an
analysis of the relationship that develops between the repairman, Bruno
(Wenders regular Vogler), and a suicidal linguist, Robert (Zischler), as they
travel in Bruno's truck along the dusty border roads. Lonely and
introspective, the pair tentatively bond over their love of pop records, but
are unable to totally escape their longing for the company of women.
Representative of the Germany of the time, Bruno and Robert are
uncertain about their place in the scheme of things, and worried about
the future. By the end of their journey, which concludes in a deserted
American border-patrol hut, the pair seemingly derive comfort from the
fact that 'in the course of time' (the film's German title) their lives may
take on some shape and significance: Robert's goodbye note to Bruno
states 'Everything must change'; Bruno finally tears up his itinerary.

Combining the look and feel of a documentary – Wenders visited
several cinemas and opens with an interview with a cinema owner – with
the leisurely pacing of a John Ford Western, *Kings of the Road* typically
eschews psychological motivation, suspense and dramatic tension. A
lyrical work visually defined by Müller's sumptuous black-and-white
photography, the film's attentiveness to the capturing of real time
passing on screen also reflects Wenders' admiration for the films of
Yasujiro Ozu.

Many of the themes Wenders had pursued in his first five features
find their culmination in *Kings of the Road*. These include pop music ('My
life was saved by rock and roll' reads some graffiti), language, the
dominance of American culture (the film is littered with US iconography

and boasts the immortal line, 'The yanks have colonised our subconscious') and the failure of communication between men, and, more importantly, women. Any interaction is almost silent and frequently achieved through gesture rather than dialogue. The male/female dichotomy finds particular purchase here: Robert is estranged from his wife and children, while Bruno claims to have 'never felt anything but loneliness in a woman'.

The commentary on the state of German cinema is astute and linked to a wider analysis of German history. The cinema industry, and the forgotten borderlands between East and West Germany, has been irreparably wounded by the residual decline of German culture, with one theatre owner preferring to close her cinema rather than show mindless violence. Several others are reduced to screening pornography. It is initially through film that Wenders journeys back into Germany's painful past. An elderly man explains that he was not allowed to run his theatre because of his former Nazi Party membership; then, in a comic moment, Bruno and Pauline (Kreuzer), a local woman he picks up, discover a lighter in the form of Hitler's head. The scene is juxtaposed with Robert attempting to discuss with his father, now the owner of a provincial newspaper, his tyrannical past. Wenders seems to suggest that only by embracing history can Germany collectively journey towards the future.

Dir: Wim Wenders; **Prod**: Wim Wenders; **Scr**: Wim Wenders; **Dop**: Robby Müller; **Edit**: Peter Przygodda; **Score**: Axel Linstädt; **Principal Cast**: Rüdiger Vogler, Hanns Zischler, Lisa Kreuzer, Rudolf Schündler.

Koktebel
Russia, 2003 – 102 mins
Boris Khlebnikov, Alexei Popogrebsky

An award-winning first feature by Russian film-makers, Boris Khlebnikov
and Alexei Popogrebsky, *Koktebel* emerged shortly after the release of
another equally remarkable Russian road movie, Andrei Zvyagintsev's
The Return (2003). The films placed their creators at the vanguard of a
Russian New Wave of young directors, in which travel, the search for
identity, generational angst and the intrinsic relationship between a
country and its people formed the central thrust.

After his wife's death and the loss of his job, an aerodynamics
engineer (Chernevich) sets off from Moscow with his eleven-year-old son
(Puskepalis) for his sister's house in Koktebel by the Black Sea. With no
money or means of transport, they drift through the expansive and
mesmeric landscapes at the mercy of chance. The father is content to
drag his feet, stopping occasionally for the odd job to raise money, while
the son impatiently dreams of reaching the coastal resort to see gliders
fly in the wind. For the father, the journey is an attempt to restore self-
respect, to piece together his broken life and win back the trust of his
son. For the boy, the mythic coastal town holds the key to a new life and
emancipation. They come across many hurdles but the last encounter is
with a beautiful young doctor (Steklova) who tends to the father's
physical and emotional wounds. As she is single and lonely, they begin
to fall for each other. The son, who sees her as an intrusion on the only
loving relationship in his life, sets off to complete the journey by
himself . . .

The relationship between father and son is genuinely expressed
through illuminating details and nuanced performances. A simple plot,
gracefully composed with stunning lyrical visuals, spaced-out dreamy
shots and a loving eye for natural beauty, recalls vintage Terrence Malick
and Tarkovsky. An enigmatic and often charming riddle, *Koktebel* is a
hypnotic road movie that has a balance between an earthly realism and a

parable open to symbolism and interpretation. It is also the wry and gently melancholic story of the Russian landscape and the people living in the countryside.

First conceived as a project in 1995, a first draft of the film was completed in 1998. In May 2000, writers/directors Khlebnikov and Popogrebsky and director of photography Berkeshi set off on an expedition along the protagonists' route from Moscow to the eponymous town at the Crimean peninsula in order to gather additional material and search for locations. Covering 4,000 kilometres of country roads and sleeping in a tent, they took pictures of the landscapes and people of rural Russia and Ukraine. Two more expeditions followed in 2001 and 2002. The result, beautifully set to Chick Corea's *Children's Songs*, both romanticises the Motherland while authentically exposing some of its deep-rooted socio-economic problems.

At script stage, the film won the European Pitch Point event in Berlin in 2001 before going on to claim the Grand Prize at the 2003 Moscow Film Festival.

Dir: Boris Khlebnikov, Alexei Popogrebsky; **Prod**: Roman Borisevich; **Scr**: Boris Khlebnikov, Alexei Popogrebsky; **DOP**: Shandor Berkeshi; **Edit**: Ivan Lebedev; **Score**: Chick Corea; **Principal Cast**: Gleb Puskepalis, Igor Chernevich, Vladimir Kucherenko, Agrippina Steklova.

Landscape in the Mist
Greece/France/Italy, 1988 – 124 mins
Theo Angelopoulos

The final film following *Voyage to Cythera* (1984) and *The Beekeeper*
(1986) in Angelopoulos' Trilogy of Silence, *Landscape in the Mist*
continued the Greek director's attempts to capture the human toll of the
tragic legacy of twentieth-century Greek history. Viewed cumulatively,
the trilogy represents a series of haunting, incisive, intimate and deeply
moving odysseys that navigate through consciousness, myth and
memory.

'In the beginning was the darkness. And then there was light . . .'
Every evening, Voula (Palaiologou) begins to tell her younger brother,
Alexander (Zeke), the same bedtime tale – the story of creation – and is
invariably interrupted by the approach of their mother. It is an
appropriate preface for the children's own unresolved story of their
origin, as they attempt to unravel the mystery of their father's identity.
Each day, they walk to the railway station and attempt to stow away on
a train to reunite with their unknown father who, their mother explains,
lives in Germany. A failed attempt to board the train leads them via the
police to an uncle, who reveals that their father is non-existent, an
invention devised by their mother, to give them false hope. However,
Voula refuses to accept this explanation and so the pair once again take
to the road, drifting from one desolate, wintry town to another, en route
crossing paths with various characters, including a brutish trucker and a
cheery itinerant actor whose willingness to act in a paternal manner is
lent a melancholic bent by the fact that he is on his own forlorn journey
towards military service.

To emphasise the film's preoccupation with the human struggle for
connection and the seemingly inevitable extinction of Greek cultural
identity, Angelopoulos briefly revisits the wandering, world-weary family
of actors from *The Travelling Players* (1975), who are still, without
success, attempting to perform 'Golfo the Shepherdess' in an

uncomprehending and largely disinterested modern world. To further augment this theme, there are also sequences of astonishing originality and austere beauty, such as the children's surreal observation of a large, spinning, disembodied stone hand with a missing index finger rising from the sea, and the image of a horse dying in the snow. Such moments are beautifully rendered by Angelopoulos' regular cinematographer, Yorgos Arvanitis – the pair have worked together since the director's multi-award-winning first feature, *Reconstruction* (1970) – but *Landscape in the Mist* also shows contemporary Greece in all its industrial, rain-sodden ugliness. In this regard, Arvanitis' cinematography again superbly evokes the mood of loneliness and disillusionment.

A poignant and allegorical fable that won its director a Venice Silver Lion, the overall tone of brutality – the film features a particularly upsetting rape – and profound despair at the forlorn futility of human experience is tempered by the enchanting performances of the two young leads and a number of lighter interludes, including a joyous wedding celebration. Such moments, in tandem with the film's final scene in which Voula and Alexander embrace a surrogate connection to their ancestral history, provide an enduring symbol of nature and life and offer tentative gestures towards the prospect of hope and personal and national reconciliation.

Dir: Theo Angelopoulos; **Prod**: Theo Angelopoulos; **Scr**: Theo Angelopoulos, Tonino Guerra, Thanassis Valtinos; **DOP**: Yorgos Arvanitis; **Edit**: Yannis Tsitsopoulos; **Score**: Eleni Karaindrou; **Principal Cast**: Tania Palaiologou, Michalis Zeke, Stratos Tzortzoglou, Nadia Mourouzi.

The Last Detail
US, 1973 – 104 mins
Hal Ashby

Hal Ashby's follow-up to the now legendary *Harold and Maude* (1971) is a similarly anti-authoritarian fable that emphatically chimes with America's profound sense of post-Vietnam disillusionment. Funny, profane and achingly melancholic, the film, brilliantly scripted by Robert Towne, is an engaging and ultimately pessimistic combination of improvised road movie and homoerotic buddy tale.

'Badass' Buddusky (Nicholson) and 'Mule' Mulhall (Young) are assigned to escort a naïve new Navy recruit from their Virginia base to a New England military prison where the recruit, Meadows (a young Quaid), will serve an eight-year sentence for attempting to swipe church funds raised for charity by the commanding officer's wife. Buddusky thinks that the sentence is a waste of Meadows' formative years, and convinces a sceptical Mulhall to show the hapless Meadows a good time by partying on their per diem for the rest of the detail's allotted week. As they journey north, the comically posturing Buddusky leads Meadows through the masculine rituals of getting drunk, getting in a fight and visiting a whorehouse to get laid. In fact, Buddusky teaches Meadows to stand up for himself so well that he finally tries to escape. Ultimately, and despite his self-proclaimed 'badass' reputation, Buddusky is, as Mulhall tells him, 'a lifer', and the two ultimately carry out their orders, delivering Meadows to his unforgiving detention centre to serve out his harsh sentence.

Taking full advantage of the new ratings system, Towne adapted the Darryl Ponicsan novel with a keen ear for the dialect of hardened, embittered blue-collar servicemen, allowing Nicholson free rein with his expletives. And yet, despite a number of grandstanding scenes, not least his trashing of a hotel room in an attempt to rouse Meadows' anger and resentment at his impending incarceration, Nicholson delivers one of his very finest and most nuanced performances. Winning the Best Actor prize at Cannes and earning himself an Academy Award nomination, Nicholson, who throughout the decade was to make the role of the would-be non-conformist his own, skilfully captures the tormented psyche of his generation, and his loathing and yet fierce loyalty to the rigid authoritarianism of the military.

Ashby, a reclusive but talented director whose star shined brightly before being all but snuffed out by Hollywood, deserves much credit for keeping Nicholson's histrionics to the minimum and for ensuring that his performance never overshadows those of Young and Quaid (who beat John Travolta to the part), both of whom are equally accomplished. In fact, the direction is often inspired, Ashby employing the picaresque structure of the standard World War II-era service comedy while also frequently undercutting its clichéd devices at every turn to pass comment on a war that represented one of the darkest moments in American history. This is evident in two key moments. In the first, an inebriated Nicholson tries to impress partygoers with anachronistic tales of on-duty heroism only for them to drift away bored. A second such occasion occurs when Buddusky attempts to teach Meadows to be a signalman, with Ashby drowning out their dialogue with the sounds of gunfire emanating from the war film playing on the hotel room TV.

Columbia, wary of the film's obscenity and dour tone, initially refused to release *The Last Detail*, finally buckling under the pressure of rave reviews and a plethora of awards and nominations. By this time, however, it was all too late, and the film resolutely failed to find an audience. Ashby's days were already numbered.

Dir: Hal Ashby; **Prod**: Gerald Ayres; **Scr**: Robert Towne; **DOP**: Michael Chapman; **Edit**: Robert C. Jones; **Score**: Johnny Mandel; **Principal Cast**: Jack Nicholson, Otis Young, Randy Quaid, Clifton James, Carol Kane.

Last Orders
UK, 2001 – 110 mins
Fred Schepisi

Australian Fred Schepisi may have initially seemed an odd choice to adapt Graham Swift's 1996 Booker Prize-winning novel, but the writer-director faithfully recreates the camaraderie, recriminations and drinking culture of London working-class life in a handsome and poignant production. Avoiding the potential pitfalls of sentimentality, Schepisi explores the lives of Bermondsey Londoners with intelligence and affection, aided by a sextet of iconic British actors in excellent form.

A group of old friends gather together following the death of charismatic butcher Jack Dodds (Caine), whose last wish was for them all to go on a road trip from south London to Margate to scatter his ashes off the pier. Margate was the scene of happy memories for Jack, being the location of his honeymoon in 1939, on the eve of World War II. As the sentimental journey progresses, their emotional histories and heartbreaks unfold as they reminisce the loss of their dearly departed mucker. Ray (Hoskins), a dodgy bookie, Lenny (Hemmings), an ex-boxer, Vic (Courtenay), a serene undertaker and Vince (Winstone), Jack's son, recollect the group's younger days, shedding light on their relationships and suppressed secrets. As the foursome speed across the Kent countryside via various welcoming hostelries in an especially selected, top-of-the-range Mercedes from Vince's used-car dealership (the interior of which becomes increasingly claustrophobic), Jack's widow, Amy (Mirren, the film's moral centre), undertakes her own significant journey to visit their mentally handicapped daughter, June (Laura Morelli), whose existence Jack refused to acknowledge.

Sober and elegiac in tone, the film fleshes out in full these Londoners' lives by the accumulation of detail, history and context, replicating Swift's time-spanning tome by using continual and rather complex flashbacks to show significant scenes from the lives of the principals, their wives and their families. These include youthful hop-picking escapades in 1930s Kent, through World War II, to earning a crust in the late 1980s while enjoying a jar or four in the local Coach and Horses. The focal point for the group and a largely exclusively male domain, the pub is also the source of a continual running joke about never leaving or going anywhere. As such, it acts as an apt metaphor for the group, whose lives appear to be slowly winding down.

Elegantly shot in CinemaScope by Brian Tufano – and scored with admirable restraint by Paul Grabowsky – *Last Orders* achieves the difficult feat of operating on a grand scale in terms of its themes and concerns while also retaining a genuine intimacy. Key to this, and the foundation on which the successful integration of the many flashbacks are built, is the excellent casting by Patsy Pollock and Shaheen Baig, who find a series of talented newcomers to play the characters' younger selves. South Londoners will be especially enamoured of the film's locations – Peckham features heavily – and Schepisi's film must

(From left) Michael Caine, Bob Hoskins, Tom Courtenay and David Hemmings enjoy a jar in the forever stationary Coach and Horses in Fred Schepisi's *Last Orders*

be one of the few roads movies to feature the Old Kent Road, Caine's old stamping ground. Strangely, the traffic on it appears to be moving.

Dir: Fred Schepisi; **Prod**: Fred Schepisi, Elisabeth Robinson; **Scr**: Fred Schepisi; **DOP**: Brian Tufano; **Edit**: Kate Williams; **Score**: Paul Grabowsky; **Principal Cast**: Michael Caine, Tom Courtenay, David Hemmings, Helen Mirren, Ray Winstone, Bob Hoskins.

The Last Run
US, 1971 – 99 mins
Richard Fleischer

A project that was originally to have been directed by John Huston, a series of fierce confrontations with star George C. Scott saw Houston exit the picture, to be replaced by Richard Fleischer. This may perhaps account for *The Last Run*'s slight unevenness in tone and its relative failure to capitalise fully on the nuances and cynicism of Alan Sharp's intelligent and brooding script.

Whatever his temper, Scott is in superlative form as Harry Garmes, an ageing, semi-retired gangster who used to drive Chicago hoods back in the day. Garmes is coaxed from retirement to drive an escape car for Paul Rickard (Musante), who brings along his girlfriend, Claudia (Van Devere). Rickard is double-crossed by the people who have sprung him, leaving Garmes and his female passenger on the run. While they are running, their relationship develops and a tentative love between them flourishes. However, their flight is clouded by Garmes' premonitions concerning his own demise, and these portents come to fruition when Garmes is mercilessly gunned down at the film's climax.

The conclusion of *The Last Run* is incredible in its suggestion of the meshing of man and car. As Garmes lies dying on a beach, Fleischer cuts to his car and a Spanish cop turning off the ignition key. The film then cuts back to Scott, who breathes his last as the engine expires. Rarely has the link between man and his machine, even within the road-movie genre, been rendered so indelible: 'With the demise of one, the other is rendered lifeless' (Williams 1982, p. 78). The bond between the lead actor and his mode of transport was pretty strong in real life too, Scott being so taken with his rare 1956 BMW 503 convertible that he went out and purchased one directly after shooting wrapped.

The car chases are expertly executed, foreshadowing Walter Hill's similarly themed *The Driver* (1978) in their disarming combination of pulse-quickening excitement and relative matter-of-factness; Garmes is presented as highly skilled behind a steering wheel, but the film's clear inference, in keeping with the generally morose and understated tone, is that this is simply what he does. The film is notable also for its arresting cinematography by Bergman's regular DOP Sven Nykvist, and trivia lovers will find interest in the fact that while Scott's then current wife Trish Van Devere took the part of Claudia, Scott's former wife, Colleen Dewhurst, also features.

Dir: Richard Fleischer; **Prod**: Carter De Haven Jr; **Scr**: Alan Sharp; **DOP**: Sven Nykvist; **Edit**: Russell Lloyd; **Score**: Jerry Goldsmith; **Principal Cast**: George C. Scott, Tony Musante, Trish Van Devere, Colleen Dewhurst, Aldo Sambrell.

The Leather Boys
UK, 1964 – 108 mins
Sidney J. Furie

Based on Gillian Freeman's novel, Sidney J. Furie's *The Leather Boys* is perhaps most notable for offering one of the earliest sympathetic depictions of a gay working-class man. Upon its release, the book's publicity promised a 'strange, twisted love'; the film's poster more coyly claimed to depict 'three lives torn savagely apart'. A hybrid of biker movie and kitchen-sink realism, the film's treatment of homosexuality saw it embraced by the gay movement in the UK, and the film was recently resuscitated for the 2006 London Lesbian and Gay Film Festival.

Sixteen-year-old Dot (Tushingham) and her boyfriend Reggie (Campbell) are the happiest couple among their biker peers, a relatively harmless gang who hang around the Ace Café, admire each other's bikes and gun off down the motorway in packs. They all get by and seem relatively unconcerned about their futures. Dot, however, is ready to tie the knot, and so with the grudging approval of both sets of parents, the lovebirds are quickly married in a fun if low-rent ceremony. The honeymoon is not as jolly. Trapped in a cramped room at a tacky seaside resort during several days of rain, the pair constantly bicker and scrap. Within days of their return to London, Reggie has moved out of their one-room flat and gone back to his grandmother's. He has given his room there to his best friend, the easygoing Pete (Sutton), but they agree to share the space, their relationship flourishing due to their common interest in bikes. Dot and Reggie are reconciled after the trio compete in a motorbike race to Edinburgh, but the old cracks quickly reappear and Reggie turns to Pete for sympathy and support. Seemingly oblivious to Pete's signals for a relationship that extends beyond the platonic, the pair make plans to set sail for a new life in America. However, an incident at Southampton docks clears up any confusion about Pete's sexuality and having sold his bike to fund the trip, Reggie finds himself marooned and alone.

The Wild One (1953) had been banned in the UK eleven years earlier because of fears that it would be a bad influence on the young, and *The Leather Boys* presents a similar portrait of juvenile delinquency, with the film's interest in sexuality lending it added spice. Arrestingly shot in stark black and white with plenty of fog and rain – the juxtaposition between the freedom suggested by the Scottish moors in contrast to the dingy and oppressive south London streets is particularly effective – the film is also an valuable melodrama about the frustrations of a young British generation still trying to find their feet in a pre-Beatles, pre-swingin' London.

Though very much of its age, the film certainly has credibility, both in terms of capturing the intrinsic Englishness of its characters and as a biker flick. Aficionado Mark Williams compares the film favourably to *The Wild One*, admiring the actual riding sequences for reeking 'of burning oil and ton-up bravura' (Williams 1982, p. 79). Smiths fans will, of course, already know that excerpts of the film were edited together for the music video for the band's 1987 single 'Girlfriend in a Coma'.

Dir: Sidney J. Furie; **Prod**: Raymond Stross; **Scr**: Gillian Freeman; **DOP**: Gerald Gibbs; **Edit**: Reginald Beck; **Score**: Bill Mcguffie; **Principal Cast**: Rita Tushingham, Colin Campbell, Dudley Sutton, Gladys Henson, Lockwood West, Dandy Nichols.

Leningrad Cowboys Go America
Finland/Sweden, 1989 – 79 mins
Aki Kaurismäki

Resembling what a hybrid between *The Blues Brothers* (1980) and *This is Spinal Tap* (1983) may have looked like if Jim Jarmusch – who memorably cameos here as a used-car dealer – had directed them, Finnish director Aki Kaurismäki's breakthrough picture (it was the first of his films to receive a US release) is a uniquely memorable viewing experience that merrily defies convention.

Two members of the Finnish band Leningrad Cowboys get ready to conquer the US in *Leningrad Cowboys Go America*

Unable to make it big in their native Finland, a band of Pogues-like musicians of questionable talent but extreme dedication are advised by a record producer to seek success in America. To ensure that they are under no illusion, the producer makes it clear that any success will be predicated on the fact that 'they'll swallow any shit there'. Arriving dressed in sunglasses, fur coats, pointy-toed shoes and sporting enormous quiffs so as to resemble their impression of hipster musicians, the band arrive in New York and immediately encounter a wise guy who sends them off to Mexico to play at his cousin's wedding; the wise guy obviously does not like his cousin. Travelling in their newly acquired Cadillac, the troupe hit the 'hamburger nation' with a vengeance, undergoing numerous bizarre encounters with the police, a gang of bikers and various oddballs and eccentrics, earning a crust and perfecting their idiosyncratic sound for the Mexican finale by picking up bookings at one seedy venue after another. Needless to say, blue-collar America has no idea what to make of these self-styled Finnish cowboys.

Filmed on location in a jumble of Finnish and English dialogue, this characteristically deadpan rock and road movie is infused with Kaurismäki's dry wit and the favouring of subtle irony and oblique nuances over narrative thrust. Generosity of spirit towards its characters and stylised dialogue aside, the film's distinctive visual aesthetic also owes much to Jarmusch, with the film unfolding in unhurried long takes and embracing any number of frequently inconsequential but never less than enjoyable plot digressions. Employing a determinedly minimalist approach and a similarly subdued palette, Kaurismäki also reveals what would become an abiding interest in the flotsam and jetsam of human life, the underdogs and underachievers whose seemingly minor personal quests somehow prove to be strangely monumental.

Quite apart from the stupendous running sight gags, including the fact that the band's deceased bass player is frozen in a coffin that accompanies them everywhere, the film also offers the kind of astute observations on America that could only come from the perspective of an outsider. Herzog's equally astonishing *Stroszek* (1977) comes to mind.

The Jarmusch comparisons made here should in no way detract from the sheer originality on display in *Leningrad Cowboys Go America*. The film, especially when viewed in conjunction with the Finn's subsequent output, exists in a wonderful and wilfully obtuse universe of its very own. To make it even better, the featured band actually exists and still regularly performs and releases records.

Dir: Aki Kaurismäki; **Prod**: Klas Oloffson, Katinka Farago; **Scr**: Aki Kaurismäki; **DOP**: Timo Salminen; **Edit**: Raija Talvio; **Score**: Mauri Sumén; **Principal Cast**: Matti Pellonpää, Nicky Tesco, Kari Väänänen, Jim Jarmusch, Sakke Järvenpää.

The Living End
US, 1992 – 84 mins
Gregg Araki

Having previously taught a course entitled 'Independent-Guerrilla-Underground-American New Wave-Neo Realist Cinema' at the University of California, Santa Barbara, Gregg Araki put his punkish and political sensibilities firmly in the driving seat with *The Living End*, a seminal moment in the emerging New Queer Cinema movement of the early 1990s. Made with equipment loaned by the intensely independent Jon Jost and less burdened by the suffocating claustrophobia of Araki's micro-budget features *Three Bewildered People in the Night* (1987) and *The Long Weekend (O'Despair)* (1989), the uncompromising and hard-hitting *The Living End* also revitalised and re-politicised the road-movie genre.

Proudly dubbed 'irresponsible' by the director and playing hard and fast with the conventions of the nihilistic outlaw couple on the run, the spunky and energetic film wears its cine-literacy proudly, evoking the spirit of Derek Jarman and more overtly referencing Godard's *Pierrot le fou* (1965). Godard's influence on the film is profound, both in terms of its diverse counter-culture aesthetics and mimicking of mainstream film-making practices, and in Araki's deconstruction of sound-bite culture.

Confrontational, savagely funny (in places the film resembles a screwball comedy) and frequently just savage, *The Living End* tells the story of rebels with a cause Luke (Dytri), a gay hustler prone to outbursts of brutal violence, and Jon (Gilmore), a disenchanted Los Angeles movie critic. Both HIV-positive and fiercely attracted to each other, the pair are forced to flee the patently plastic LA environment when Luke carelessly shoots a cop. To the accompaniment of a jagged score from the likes of Braindead Sound Machine, KMFDM and Coil, a fucking and *Badlands*-style killing rampage through the wastelands of Middle America ensues. At one point, Jon questions their ultimate destination: 'What difference does it make?' retorts Luke, making manifest the ennui of road-movie travel while also reinforcing the infected pair's status as total social outcasts.

Shot with a raw intensity and featuring extreme close-ups during the driving sequences through open landscapes to emphasise Jon and Luke's cramped enclosure in the car, and by extension their oppression by patriarchal society, *The Living End* daringly and with heartfelt conviction confronts America's fear of AIDS. In this, it exists in stark contrast to Hollywood-sanctioned pictures on the subject, such as Demme's *Philadelphia*, released the following year. Araki's rage and indignation is evident in the film's dedication to 'the hundreds of thousands who've died and the hundreds of thousands more who will die because of a big white house full of Republican Fuckheads'. In typically antagonistic fashion, Araki even takes a swipe at his US indie peers with a sequence in which Luke murders two gay bashers wearing *Drugstore Cowboy* and *sex, lies and videotape* T-shirts.

Like Todd Haynes and Tom Kalin, Araki also refuses to offer positive, sanitised representations of gay characters and, perhaps as a result, *The Living End* – part of a 'teen apocalypse trilogy' completed by *Totally F***ed Up* (1993) and *The Doom Generation* (1995) – received a largely muted response from gay critics. Feminists also found fault with the stereotypical depiction of female characters, and particularly the film's two inept lesbian serial killers. The film can also be seen as precipitating the subsequent rush of amoral, spree-killer-couples-on-the-road movies of the 1990s, to which *True Romance* (Tony Scott, 1993), *Kalifornia* (1993) and *Natural Born Killers* (1994) certainly belong.

Dir: Gregg Araki; **Prod**: Marcus Hu, Jon Gerrans; **Scr**: Gregg Araki; **DOP**: Gregg Araki; **Edit**: Gregg Araki; **Music**: Cole Coonce; **Principal Cast**: Craig Gilmore, Mike Dytri, Darcy Marta, Mary Woronov.

Lost in America
US, 1985 – 91 mins
Albert Brooks

Retaining the core team of co-writer Monica Johnson, director of photography Eric Saarinen and editor David Finfer from his earlier director outings, *Real Life* (1979) and *Modern Romance* (1981), Albert Brooks really hit his stride, crafting a film that perfectly chimed with the urban impulse to chuck the rat race and hit the open road. A skilled and cerebral satirist frequently labelled the West Coast Woody Allen, Brooks opted for a more sobering account of the consequences of pursuing dreams and exploring America, delivering a meticulous observation on self-delusion.

Bored with their cushy suburban existence, disillusioned yuppy David (Brooks) talks his wife, Linda (Hagerty), into selling everything they own and hitting the road in a Winnebago to 'see America'. Having liquidated all their assets, David promises Linda that 'We'll be like *Easy Rider* . . . with a nest egg'. As a starting-over gesture, David and Linda are romantically remarried in Las Vegas – which, ironically, proves to be the beginning of the end of their idyll. They travel cross-country, lurching from one disaster to another, losing their life savings and watching their marriage almost implode at the Hoover Dam. Ultimately reduced to taking menial blue-collar jobs in a dead-end Arizona town, the pair discover that the American Dream and irresponsible fantasies taste less sweet when you are flipping hamburgers and working as a school-crossing guard.

Though undeniably weakened by a compromised denouement, *Lost in America* offers a chastening and blackly comic look at the quest for freedom in a nation brought to its knees by consumer culture and capitalist greed. Offering a wicked parody of the Me Generation, with Brooks' protagonists a dark reflection of the idealism that suffered such a hard death after the 1960s, it is apt that David and Linda choose to roam the interstates in a gas-guzzling SV, waxing lyrical about the comfort that their considerable savings provide. Brooks' horror and disgust at America's shallow, materialistic nature is palpable – especially in the Las Vegas sequences – and as the ground disappears from under David and Linda and they sink ever deeper into a mire of woe, misery and financial hardship, the gleeful sense of *schadenfreude* for the spectator almost threatens to become too delightful to endure.

Performed with distinction and delicious understatement by a fine ensemble cast, comedian Garry Marshall particularly impresses as the bone-dry Desert Inn Casino manager, and with America's striking landscapes and national monuments seeming to mock the increasingly desperate husband-and-wife duo still further, the film's real trump card, however, is its mercilessly sarcastic dialogue. Pontificating endlessly about their need to go out and find themselves and the essence of their country, David and Linda speak of their desire to 'Go out and touch some Indians'.

Dir: Albert Brooks; **Prod**: Mary Katz; **Scr**: Albert Brooks, Monica Johnson; **DOP**: Eric Saarinen; **Edit**: David Finfer; **Score**: Arthur B. Rubenstein; **Principal Cast**: Albert Brooks, Julie Hagerty, Michael Green, Tom Tarpey, Raynold Gideon.

(*Mad Max 2*) *The Road Warrior*
Australia, 1981 – 96 mins
George Miller

Director-writer George Miller's follow-up to 1979's *Mad Max* is proof
that not all sequels are inferior. Made on a vastly increased budget, the
film turned Gibson, playing the leather-clad loner in monosyllabic Clint
Eastwood mode, into an international star. Savage, kinetic and
underpinned by a cruel Australian humour, *The Road Warrior* unfolds as
one savage encounter after another, careering towards an impressively
staged chase sequence that lasts for the entirety of the last third of the
film.

In the post-apocalyptic Australian wasteland, former Highway Patrol
officer Max Rockatansky (Gibson) has become a drifter, scavenging for

The Road Warrior's post-apocalyptic vision: George Miller's savage and arguably superior
follow-up to *Mad Max*

petrol in an outback that has fallen into tribal warfare. An encounter with the Gyro Captain (Spence) leads Max to a bric-a-brac fortress where an idealistic tribe led by Pappagallo (Mike Preston) is refining oil and planning to start a new life 'up north'. Surrounding their camp is an army of grotesque desert warriors led by Humungus (Kjell Nilsson) and his crazed henchman Wez (Wells). His tribe's defences weakening, Pappagallo agrees to pay Max in petrol upon delivery of a semi-trailer rig capable of transporting the precious 'gold'. As the battle intensifies, Max reluctantly agrees to help Pappagallo's people make a safe escape to the coast.

There is a distinct element of existentialism to *The Road Warrior*, and not just in its introverted anti-hero, a less than original composite of Western, film noir and *2000 AD* types. Trapped in a battle to stay alive, the majority of the characters, and certainly the marauding biker barbarians, spend their time looking for gasoline so that they can continue to trek across the desert in search of more gasoline. The premise distils one of the central motifs of the road movie to its purest essence: moving purely for the sake of moving.

Miller's access to increased funds allows him and his production team to create a fairly impressive post-industrial world, predicated on ritual, violence and terror. It is an environment that suggests the future – and the director's vision concerning the extent to which fuel would become such an important economic commodity is eerily prophetic – while also being tethered to the past. The cars and motorcycles are familiar from the highways of the early 1980s but have been given DIY makeovers to better equip them for the crime-ravaged present, and, it would seem, the even more dystopian future. The most fearsome vehicle has two steel posts on its front to which enemies can be strapped so that if the car crashes, they are the first to die.

Exquisitely executed, the breakneck race for the coast chase sequence in which the oil tanker, flanked by various defending vehicles, runs the gauntlet of everything the pursuing pack of murderers can throw at it is undoubtedly one of the tensest and most dynamic on-road pursuits in modern cinema. Miller stated his desire to invoke the speeding locomotive scenario of Buster Keaton's *The General* (1926), with its endless possibilities of devastation and collision. A tall order, but Miller comes very close with his superlatively coordinated stunt work.

Dir: George Miller; **Prod**: Byron Kennedy; **Scr**: Terry Hayes, George Miller, Brian Hannant; **DOP**: Dean Semler; **Edit**: David Stiven, Tim Wellburn, Michael Chirgwin; **Score**: Brian May; **Principal Cast**: Mel Gibson, Bruce Spence, Vernon Wells, Emil Minty.

Merci la vie (*Thank You, Life*)
France, 1991 – 118 mins
Bertrand Blier

Ever perverse, Bertrand Blier decided to follow up the uncharacteristically romantic *Trop belle pour toi* (1989), the most successful film of his career, with a retread of *Les Valseuses*, his anarchic and controversial 1973 road movie about a pair of amoral misogynists fucking their way across France. *Merci la vie* reverses the gender of its protagonists, following two young women who get together after discovering sufficient provocations in their lives to deliberately set out to wreak havoc on the wider world.

Joëlle (Grinberg) has just been thrown out of a moving car by her abusive boyfriend when Camille (Gainsbourg) first encounters her. Embarking on a cross-country rampage, the pair pick up and seduce men before abandoning them and destroying their cars. Eventually, they set their sights on a higher goal and decide to bring to its knees an entire town. Meanwhile, it transpires that a sinister medical researcher (Blier regular Depardieu) has infected Camille with a sexually transmitted disease that he formulated with the intent of making him rich and famous by discovering its cure. Slowly but surely the promiscuous Joëlle disperses the virus among the menfolk, ultimately incurring their wrath and hunger for revenge.

A frequently surrealist romp that also incorporates a number of complex flashbacks and a film-within-a-film structure (the cast talk direct to camera and an assistant director offers Brechtian comments on the proceedings and the likely reaction of critics), Blier goes to some lengths to ensure that the women are every bit as predatory as the men from *Les Valseuses*. The spectre of HIV, of course, looms large, with the director also offering strong comment on the abusive role women are forced to adopt within contemporary society. Punished both physically and morally, the sexual shenanigans of Joëlle and Camille lead not to liberation, but to enslavement and degradation. The film, which is almost entirely pessimistic in its outlook and at times shockingly violent, concludes with the pair pulled apart: Camille is left seeking refuge in a bombed-out house, while Joëlle is put aboard a train heading for a Nazi-style concentration camp. The cycle of male-on-female abuse is perhaps the axis on which the film rotates, with Camille being molested by a man who reveals that he also sexually assaults his daughter.

A confrontational and challenging work, *Merci la vie*'s various provocations are matched by a disorientating but nonetheless impressive visual aesthetic. Liberally moving between fantasy and reality – the film's final twist is a surprise best not revealed here – the freewheeling Blier both blurs and highlights the distinction, merging low-key black-and-white photography and verité effects with Philippe Rousselot's ravishing cinematography.

Dir: Bertrand Blier; **Prod**: Bernard Marescot; **Scr**: Bertrand Blier; **DOP**: Philippe Rousselot; **Edit**: Claudine Merlin; **Score**: Arno; **Principal Cast**: Charlotte Gainsbourg, Anouk Grinberg, Gérard Depardieu, Michel Blanc.

Messidor
Switzerland/France, 1978 – 123 mins
Alain Tanner

One of the leading lights of Swiss cinema, a movement influenced by
Brecht, Bresson and the French New Wave, Alain Tanner's *Messidor*
deals with alienation and the paradoxical nature of freedom. A
disturbing and original work in which liberty from the confines of
society, when carried to its absolute, becomes a kind of imprisonment,
the film is widely considered a precursor to Ridley Scott's *Thelma &
Louise* (1991).

Jeanne (Amouroux), a history student from Geneva, and Marie
(Rétoré), a store clerk from Moudon in France, are two women from very
different backgrounds. The pair meet while hitchhiking: Jeanne claims
that she is trying to escape from the noise of the city, while Marie is
returning home after visiting her father in Lausanne. Though little is
revealed of their backgrounds, it soon becomes clear that, apart from a
physical attraction, the pair also share a sense that their lives lack
context, giving rise to a feeling of exclusion from society. Travelling
together with no particular destination, they decide to play a game in
which they survive without money. The adventure takes a wrong turn
when Marie is forced to thwart an attempted rape, gravely injuring the
assailant. Stealing a gun from the glove compartment of a Swiss Army
officer for protection, the pair continue their journey, engaging in
haphazard and unmotivated acts that defy society's rules. Their antics
lead to TV coverage and ultimately police pursuit and mounting
desperation.

In considering Jeanne and Marie's wanderings through a
meaningless existence, or what Jeanne describes as a game in which they
'Move through empty spaces', Tanner remains objective, refusing to pass
comment on the increasingly violent actions of his protagonists (whose
self-christened Messidor moniker comes from an ancient calendar
signifying privilege and luck), while making clear that any transgressor

must understand the rules of freedom. The view of society seems in fact as dispassionate as that expressed by Harry Lime in the Ferris wheel in *The Third Man* (1949). 'All people look alike', Jeanne comments while surveying the comings and goings from a car park in a pretty Swiss village, 'it's as if they didn't really exist.'

Liberty as imprisonment in Alain Tanner's *Messidor*, a haunting account of psychological collapse on an individual and collective level

Juxtaposing the endless lifts in nondescript cars with uninteresting people during which the conversation rarely rises above the monotonous, Tanner invests the film with a beautiful, dreamlike quality, capturing the picturesque villages and verdant alpine scenery in all its splendour. Evocative of Terrence Malick's *Badlands* (1973) in this regard, Tanner conveys the impression that each journey takes us nowhere in a landscape that possesses abundant surface beauty but little real substance. 'Where are we headed?' asks Marie early on, to which her cohort replies, 'The usual: straight ahead.'

A hauntingly personal work, *Messidor* offers an effective and intelligent account of psychological collapse. At one point, the women fire their gun into the sky at a passing plane, and later, hearing that a plane has crashed, believe that they have caused it. As with earlier Tanner films such as *Jonah, Who Will Be 25 in the Year 2000* (1975), it also deals with a more collective sense of dehumanisation and ennui in an increasingly conformist and patriarchal modern Swiss society.

Dir: Alain Tanner; **Prod**: Yves Gasser, Yves Peyrot; **Scr**: Alain Tanner; **DOP**: Renato Berta; **Edit**: Brigitte Sousselier, Laurent Uhler; **Score**: Arié Dzierlatka; **Principal Cast**: Clémentine Amouroux, Catherine Rétoré, Franziskus Abgottspon, Gérald Battiaz.

Midnight Run
US, 1988 – 126 mins
Martin Brest

Having failed to land the lead in *Big* (1988), De Niro was determined to
find a vehicle to showcase his comic talents. Luckily, Martin Brest had
just the thing, a wisecracking script mirroring *Beverley Hill's Cop*'s (1984)
successful comedy and action formula that also skilfully utilised De Niro's
taciturn loner persona. A descendant of Arthur Hiller's 1979 road
comedy *The In-Laws*, *Midnight Run* is one of the best buddy pictures of
the 1980s and one of its star's few truly successful comedy outings.

Accountant Jonathan 'The Duke' Mardukas (Grodin) has embezzled
$15 million from gangster Jimmy Serrano (Farina, exuding customary
menace) and skipped bail. Los Angeles bondsman Eddie Moscone
(Pantoliano) hires Jack Walsh (De Niro), a hard-bitten former cop, to
bring the accountant back to LA. 'It'll be a piece of cake, get in, get out.

Planes . . .

trains . . .

. . . and automobiles: Robert De Niro as bounty hunter Jack Walsh having a bad trip in *Midnight Run*

It's a midnight run.' To secure the $100,000 bounty, Walsh needs to get Mardukas, also wanted by the FBI, back before midnight, at which time Moscone forfeits the bail money he fronted. Serrano meanwhile knows that Mardukas has access to financial information that could lead to his conviction, and has no intention of allowing him to live long enough to give evidence. After tracing Mardukas to Manhattan, Walsh attempts to extradite his quarry to LA, but having failed to allow for the Duke's fear of various forms of travel, FBI roadblocks, mobster assassins and the attention of rival bounty hunters, he's in for one hell of a journey.

With shoot-outs and car chases galore, Brest certainly gives you bangs for your bucks, but the key ingredient is the delightful interplay and genuine chemistry between De Niro's blue-collar, no-nonsense bounty hunter and Grodin's neurotic, over-fussy white-collar embezzler. Brilliantly scripted by George Gallo, the quick-fire exchanges between the pair come thick and fast as Walsh attempts to meet his deadline using plane, train and automobile. When Mardukas tells the increasingly irascible Walsh that he is unable to fly due to a phobia, Walsh's response is to warn that 'fistophobia' will be Mardukas' next psychological condition.

Walsh's short fuse and quick resort to violence is one of the film's many recurring comic motifs, as is Mardukas' seeming obsession with his escort's diet and smoking habit. Think Jack Lemmon and Walter Matthau's chalk-and-cheese double act from *The Odd Couple* (1967), only with extended cussing. Given equally good mileage is Walsh's continual foxing of the FBI's humourless Special Agent Mosely (Kotto), a man whose glasses and identity Walsh steals as he merrily impersonates him up and down the land.

In line with road-movie tradition, the arduous cross-country journey takes in various obstacles to motion and scrapes with colourful backwater locals. By far the most enjoyable is a scam involving the confiscation of dollar bills from a rural bar owner, in which the hopelessly marooned Walsh is given expert schooling in duplicity and financial impropriety by his light-fingered companion. Aboard a subsequent freight train, the pair inevitably find common ground and bond, speeding towards Los Angeles and a relatively uncontrived, bittersweet happy ending.

Dir: Martin Brest; **Prod**: Martin Brest; **Scr**: George Gallo; **DOP**: Donald Thorin; **Edit**: Billy Weber, Chris Lebenzon, Michael Tronick; **Score**: Danny Elfman; **Principal Cast**: Robert De Niro, Charles Grodin, Yaphet Kotto, John Ashton, Dennis Farina, Joe Pantoliano.

Minimal Stories (*Historias minímas*)
Argentina, 2002 – 92 mins
Carlos Sorin

It may have been Argentinian director Carlos Sorin's later road movie *Bombón el perro* (2004) that really chimed with international audiences, but his fourth feature is an equally assured and similarly genial addition to the genre. Eschewing the road-movie tendency to give its protagonists a bumpy ride as they journey through uncharted territory encountering various obstacles and frequently unsavoury types, Sorin and writer Pablo Solarz are interested in a gentler excursion. Chronicling a trio of separate yet interweaving stories about ordinary people attempting to follow their dreams, the travellers of *Minimal Stories* encounter nothing but kindness throughout their quests in southern Patagonia.

Roberto (Lombardo), an obsessive travelling salesman, hopes to win the love of a young widow by driving a specially ordered birthday cake to her son. En route to San Juliàn, he encounters Don Just (Benedicti), an octogenarian travelling to the city to find redemption and his long-lost dog, Badface. Meanwhile, Maria Flores (Bravo), whose path Roberto and Don Just will also cross, is a young mother so poor that the prospect of winning a food processor on the gauche game show *Multicoloured Casino* compels her to travel two hundred miles to be a contestant.

Contrasting the epic Patagonian landscapes with the modesty of his characters' aspirations, Sorin crafts an appealing portrait of a beautiful if remote region where television provides the main link to the wider world. Through the interconnected, tripartite structure, a dominant feature of many recent films emanating from South and Latin America, Sorin gently probes the hopes and aspirations of his deftly drawn characters, offering deceptively astute observations both on a culture relatively unscathed by modernity and on contemporary Argentina itself.

As one of only two professional actors in the film, Lombardo excels, but his co-performers are equally assured, bringing a gentle humour and understated appeal to their roles. Played by a retired auto mechanic from

Montevideo, the character of Don Just is especially enduring: having handed over the running of his grocery store to his son and daughter-in-law, he now spends his days by entertaining passing local children by wiggling his ears at them. With fading eyesight preventing him from travelling, the elderly Don Just must journey by other means, and it is in this regard, as well as the film's merging of landscape and character and bittersweet evocation of encroaching modernity, that *Minimal Stories* most closely resembles David Lynch's *The Straight Story* (1999), cited by Sorin as one of the film's main inspirations.

Sorin and Solarz wanted the film to develop organically, and after spending one month travelling through Patagonia together, they returned with their performers for a nine-week shoot armed with only a very simple and rudimentary shooting script. Encouraging improvisation and frequently wrong-footing the cast by changing scenes and situations (in one such moment, Roberto orders changes to the cake, unaware that the baker he confronts is also a professional wrestler), this creative process paid dividends, authenticating the characters' slow but sure discovery of the virtues of on-the-road solidarity.

Dir: Carlos Sorin; **Prod**: Martin Bardi, Leticia Cristi, José María Morales; **Scr**: Pablo Solarz; **DOP**: Hugo Colace; **Edit**: Mohamed Rajid; **Score**: Nicolas Sorin; **Principal Cast**: Antonio Benedicti, Javiera Bravo, Javier Lombardo, Julia Solomonoff.

The Motorcycle Diaries
Argentina/Chile/Peru/US, 2004 – 126 mins
Walter Salles

Based on the journals of both Alberto Granado (*With Che through Latin America*) and Ernesto Guevara (*The Motorcycle Diaries*), the man who would later become 'El Che', Brazilian director Walter Salles follows a journey of self-discovery and traces the origins of a revolutionary heart. Described by Salles as also being about friendship, solidarity and finding one's place in the world, *The Motorcycle Diaries* is also perhaps the ultimate road movie.

In 1952, two young Argentines, Ernesto Guevara (García Bernal) and Alberto Granado (de la Serna), set out on a road trip to discover the real Latin America. Ernesto is a twenty-three-year-old medical student from a privileged background who specialises in leprology, and Alberto, twenty-nine, is a biochemist. The film follows the young men as they unveil the rich and complex human and social topography of the Latin American continent. With a highly romantic sense of adventure, the two friends leave their familiar Buenos Aires surroundings on a rickety 1939 Norton 500. Although the bike breaks down in the course of their eight-month journey, they press onwards, hitching rides along the way. As they begin to see a different Latin America in the people they meet on the road, the diverse geography they encounter begins to reflect their own shifting perspectives. They continue to the heights of Machu Picchu, where the majestic ruins and the extraordinary significance of the Inca heritage have a profound impact on the young men. Finally arriving at a leper colony deep in the Peruvian Amazon, the two are beginning to question the value of progress as defined by economic systems that leave so many people beyond their reach. Their experiences at the colony awaken within them the men they will later become, defining the ethical and political journey they will take in their lives.

Even disregarding for a moment the subtext of Ernesto 'Che' Guevara's political awakening, and *The Motorcycle Diaries* certainly has value as a historical document, Salles' follow-up to *O primeiro dia* (1998) still offers a vibrant window into the spirit of South America. The filmmaker – with Salles especially well served by DOP Eric Gautier and a superlative script by José Rivera – explores the changing vistas and alternating geographies of Argentina, Chile, Peru and Venezuela, giving a fascinating glimpse into the South American psyche. However, like most road movies, all roads lead inward and the film presents a remarkable portrayal of a personal epiphany and coming to consciousness. If there is

A journey of self-discovery: Ernesto Guevara (Gael García Bernal, far left), Alberto Granado (Rodrigo de la Serna) and 1939 Norton 500 in Walter Salles' *The Motorcycle Diaries*

one scene that most clearly illustrates the changes Guevara has undergone on his journey it is one of the closing moments at the colony when he overcomes his paralysing asthma to complete a night swim across a river. Struggling with every stroke, the moment chimes with Guevara's later pronouncement that 'In a revolution, one either triumphs or dies'.

Despite the film's verité aesthetic, achieved through the use of non-professional actors for the peasants and labourers Guevara and Granado encounter, and through Gautier's shooting on grainy Super-16 stock, Salles ensures that the film is as entertaining as it is enlightening. The trip is liberally peppered with numerous humorous and bawdy encounters as its two protagonists – excellently portrayed by García Bernal and de la Serna – resort to all manner of grifting to progress along the dusty roads. In one encounter, Guevara even goes so far as to brazenly seduce the wife of the mechanic who is kindly fixing their Norton. Such moments serve to heighten the profundity of the initially feckless Guevara's eventual growth.

Dir: Walter Salles; **Prod**: Michael Nozik, Edgard Tenembaum, Karen Tenkhoff; **Scr**: José Rivera; **DOP**: Eric Gautier; **Edit**: Daniel Rezende; **Score**: Gustavo Santaolalla; **Principal Cast**: Gael García Bernal, Rodrigo de la Serna, Miá Maestro, Mercedes Morán.

My Own Private Idaho
US, 1991 – 104 mins
Gus Van Sant

Emerging just prior to Gregg Araki's *The Living End* (1992), Van Sant's third feature marked a formative moment in the New Queer Cinema movement of the 1990s. Possessing an edgy, independent sensibility and frequently reaching back to the American cinema of the 1970s with its elliptical narrative and emphasis on psychological and emotional malaise, *My Own Private Idaho* refuels and re-politicises the road movie through its filtering of the exploration of mobility as rebellion and personal quest through a gay sensibility.

The film focuses on the friendship between two male hustlers in Portland, Oregon, who come from different sides of the tracks. Mike (Phoenix, from whose perspective the film is largely told) is a gay narcoleptic who, having been abandoned as a child, has grown obsessed with finding his mother. Scott (Reeves) is the rebellious son of a high-ranking family who hustles men and women mostly to embarrass his father, whose fortune he is soon to inherit. Though resolving to take care of his friend and help him in his quest to find his mother (a journey that will ultimately take them from the Pacific Northwest to Italy), Scott gently rebuffs Mike's declaration of affection. Surrounding Scott and Mike are the waifs and strays of Portland, who live out of an abandoned hotel with their spiritual leader Bob (Richert), an ex-thief and hustler. Believing that Scott's inheritance will benefit them all – when in reality he will probably use the money to escape his bleak existence – Scott is cast as Prince Hal to Bob's Falstaff.

With its stunning rendering of dawn and dust landscapes and the frequent use of extreme long shots of deserted highways (cars rarely feature here), the film is imbued with vintage visual road-movie iconography. In narrative terms, the use of intertitles including 'Idaho', 'Seattle', 'Portland' and 'Roma' emphasises the fact that the film is structured along the lines of travel from one place to another. However,

Van Sant also offers a number of new configurations. There are documentary-style inserts of interviews with actual Portland street kids (harshly contrasting with the film's trance-like quality), the playful references to Shakespeare, and dreamlike shots of the sky and fast-motion cloud photography, as often as not used to emphasise Mike's narcoleptic condition and his imminent drifting into unconsciousness. The film's surrealist bent includes shots of salmon leaping upstream (to suggest both imminent orgasm and, in the film's final montage, Mike alone on the road again) and houses crashing in *Zabriskie Point* (1970)-style slow motion onto an open road. Another ingenious touch is when the studs adorning the pages of gay porno magazines playfully come to life and address the spectator.

The death of Phoenix shortly after completing the film, united with Van Sant's surreal and ambient aesthetic, lends *My Own Private Idaho* the feel of an elegy for the aimlessness of youthful alienation. This is a subject to which the director would continually return, most fruitfully in post-studio pictures including *Gerry* (2002), *Elephant* (2003) and, most recently, *Last Days* (2005). In the director's most explicitly gay film since 1985's *Male noche*, the fact that his two protagonists were both social and sexual outlaws gave Van Sant dual spokesman-like status.

Dir: Gus Van Sant; **Prod**: Laurie Parker; **Scr**: Gus Van Sant; **DOP**: Eric Alan Edwards, John Campbell; **Edit**: Curtiss Clayton; **Score**: Bill Stafford; **Principal Cast**: River Phoenix, Keanu Reeves, James Russo, William Richert.

Natural Born Killers
US, 1994 – 119 mins
Oliver Stone

A frenetic look at the elevation to celebrity status of mass murderers by an unscrupulous and deviant American media, Oliver Stone's controversial film divided critics and audiences with its heady brew of over-the-top violence and bitter cultural satire. Viewed retrospectively, the film, though starting from an interesting if entirely unoriginal premise, rarely hits its target, its melange of visual styles proving crude and ineffective. Quentin Tarantino is one of the film's many writers, which perhaps goes some way to explaining its sledgehammer aesthetic.

Mickey (Harrelson) and Mallory (Lewis) are a young couple united by their desire for each other and their common love of violence. Together, they embark on a record-breaking, exceptionally gory killing spree that captivates the sensation-hungry tabloid media. Their fame is ensured by one newsman, Wayne Gale (Downey Jr), who reports on Mickey and Mallory for his show, 'American Maniacs'. Even the duo's eventual capture by the police, led by a twisted and perverted Tom Sizemore, only increases their notoriety, as Gale develops a plan for a Super Bowl Sunday interview that Mickey and Mallory twist to their own advantage.

Unfolding as a hallucinogenic nightmare, Stone switches, randomly it seems, between hyperkinetic cinematography, black-and-white documentary verité, surveillance video, garishly coloured psychedelia and even animation in an attempt to mirror the psychosis of the killers and the media-saturated culture that makes them popular heroes. The film's extreme and gory violence required copious edits to secure an R rating in America and became the focus for a heated debate as to whether *Natural Born Killers* glorified the activities of its protagonists, thus potentially inciting copycat incidents, or whether its shock tactics were an attempt to force the American media to acknowledge its responsibilities

Mallory (Juliette Lewis) and Mickey (Woody Harrelson) in *Natural Born Killers*, Oliver
Stone's kinetic attack on the American media

regarding its obsession with celebrity. Stone is undoubtedly well
intentioned in this regard, but the volume is turned up so high that the
film becomes an exercise in alienation, and ultimately as sensationalist as
the subject it seeks to address.

A dark and ultimately depressing (for reasons good and bad) trawl
across the contemporary American landscape, the film's technical
virtuosity – though poorly utilised – is matched by compelling
performances from Lewis and Harrelson. Tommy Lee Jones provides
much-needed light relief as Mickey and Mallory's prison warden. Drawn

from the same well as *Bonnie and Clyde* (1967) and *Badlands* (1973), the film sadly polluted the water, briefly inspiring a series of equally unedifying *Natural Born Killers* variants.

Dir: Oliver Stone; **Prod**: Jane Hamsher, Don Murphy, Clayton Townsend; **Scr**: David Veloz, Richard Rutowski, Oliver Stone; **DOP**: Robert Richardson; **Edit**: Hank Corwin, Brian Berdan; **Score**: Bud Carr; **Principal Cast**: Woody Harrelson, Juliette Lewis, Robert Downey Jr, Tommy Lee Jones, O-Lan Jones.

Near Dark
US, 1987 – 94 mins
Kathryn Bigelow

Giving the vampire yarn a much-needed transfusion, Kathryn Bigelow's stylish take on the genre is a wildly original and influential synthesis of horror, road movie, film noir and Western. In fact, *Near Dark*, co-written by Bigelow and Eric Red, who penned the similarly inventive *The Hitcher* (1986), was originally conceived as a Western project but Bigelow was forced to change tack when funding became impossible to secure.

Caleb (Pasdar), a restless young man from a small farm town, meets an alluring drifter named Mae (Wright). She reveals herself to be a vampire, who 'turns' Caleb into one of her kind rather than kill him. But the rest of her 'family' is slow to accept the newcomer. The ancient leader, Jesse (Henriksen), and his psychotic henchman, Severen (Paxton), lay down the law: Caleb has to carry his own weight or die. Caleb can't bring himself to kill, but wins the travelling gang's approval when he rescues them from certain death in a spectacular daytime motel shoot-out. However, when the vampires threaten Caleb's blood family, he's forced to make a difficult choice.

Revolutionising the modern perception of vampires, Bigelow does away with the traditional Gothic trappings of the vampire picture, relocating the creatures of the night to the parched and near-deserted highways of the American Midwest. Re-imagining her bloodthirsty protagonists as nocturnal nomads who dress and act like a motorcycle gang to terrorise unsuspecting locals, Bigelow, whose *The Loveless* (1981) was a fetishistic look at the accoutrements of biker culture, constructs a number of exceptional set-pieces to show the very physical destructive effects of sunlight. To achieve this, special-effects makeup artist Gordon Smith devised a prosthetic system in which tubes were concealed in the actors' clothes and faces and then connected to a smoking device. Those vampires unfortunate enough to be exposed to the unforgiving sunlight sizzle and burn before our eyes.

One of Bigelow's few concessions to existing vampire lore was the idea, present in Bram Stoker's *Dracula*, that a vampire can be returned to normal by a process Stoker called 'bloodletting'. Bigelow used this transfusion process involving moral blood as a central premise in *Near Dark*, infusing the material with an erotic charge, sexualising the violence through the exploration of 'interracial' relationships and those vampires who choose to give up the ability to live for ever in exchange for their previous mortality. A fascinating and brilliantly shot hybrid that spawned numerous inferior variants including *The Lost Boys* (1987) and *From Dusk till Dawn* (1995), *Near Dark*'s surprisingly effective makeover of vampires as modern gunslingers has them traversing the desolate highways while living their nocturnal lives to the full with drugs, sex and violence always on the menu. In this regard, the film sticks closely to the road movie's well-trodden terrain of cultural critique and rebellion.

Dir: Kathryn Bigelow; **Prod**: Steven-Charles Jaffe; **Scr**: Eric Red, Kathryn Bigelow; **DOP**: Adam Greenberg; **Edit**: Howard Smith; **Score**: Tangerine Dream; **Principal Cast**: Adrian Pasdar, Jenny Wright, Bill Paxton, Lance Henriksen.

North on Evers
US, 1992 – 87 mins
James Benning

Few film-makers are as fascinated by the geographical, historical and social aspects of the American national landscape as James Benning, who has been creating 16mm portraits of American spaces for four decades. A native of Milwaukee, Benning trained as a mathematician, a fact that probably partially accounts for his structuralism – exemplified in the organisation of his films according to a set number of shots, and the use of intertitles and layered text and images. Exploring the sound–image relationships of film-makers like Michael Snow and Hollis Frampton, Benning's work reveals only a tentative interest in narrative, and is driven instead by deep sensitivity to colour, light and landscape.

In many ways, the work of Benning is something of a paradox, much like the avant-garde tradition in which his films are often located. Personal yet implicitly political, Benning's formalism reveals the landscapes in which he shoots in the most naturalistic manner possible. First coming to attention with *8½ x 11* (1974) and *11 x 14* (1977), Benning's films are perhaps first and foremost identifiable through their use of long, exquisitely composed static shots that frequently last minutes at a time. Echoes of his compositional sense can be found in the work of such directors as Jim Jarmusch, Chantal Akerman and Rob Tregenza.

North on Evers was completed prior to Benning's permanent relocation to California in the mid-1990s and his embarking upon a series of experimental documentaries, beginning with 1995's *Deseret*, investigating the effects of history and politics on the American West. A mix of film footage, audio and handwritten text to chronicle a cross-country motorcycle voyage, the film perhaps contains Benning's most cohesive and accessible narrative structure. Constructed of three parallel threads – one pictorial, one aural and the third a handwritten text that runs continuously across the bottom of the frame – *North on Evers* charts

Benning's trip across the West, through the South, up the East coast and finally back to California. He chronicles a series of brief encounters with old friends, chance acquaintances, hitchhikers and one-night stands, visits such historical sites as the home of Medgar Evers and Robert Smithson's 'Spiral Jetty'. The text at the bottom of the frame is informative and playful, the following example proving particularly instructive in that it mentions the hometown of Richard Linklater, who considered Benning to be one of the most important American film-makers of the last twenty years:

> From there I went to Austin. I stayed with three friends and found an old *Life* magazine at their home. It was from 1966. The cover story was about Charles Whitman. A map marked the spots where he had picked off his victims from the University tower. I followed it down Guadalupe Street . . .

In *North on Evers*, Benning is no tourist; his travels are informed by a heightened awareness of the history that has taken place in his own time and by a powerful sense of the strangeness and alienation of everyday life in the world's great, crumbling centre of capitalism. Beautifully photographed and intensely felt, the film offers a disturbing portrait of contemporary America and is, alongside *Sherman's March* (1985) and *Gallivant* (1996), one of the most interesting, personal and yet radical selections in this volume.

Dir: James Benning; **Prod**: N/A; **Scr**: N/A; **DOP**: N/A; **Edit**: N/A; **Score**: N/A; **Principal Cast**: N/A.

One False Move
US, 1991 – 105 mins
Carl Franklin

A graduate of the Roger Corman school, for whom he directed three uninspiring quickie genre pictures, former actor Franklin turned to directing in frustration at the lack of decent parts available to black actors. Having cultivated under Corman's tutelage an appreciation for the structures of genre film-making, Franklin chose to studiously avoid the inner-city milieu and urban tales from the hood currently being mined by many of his African-American contemporaries such as Matty Rich, John Singleton and Albert and Allen Hughes. In its own measured and low-key way, *One False Move* is equally revealing about the consequences of violence and the social and economic realities of the African-American experience.

Cut from a similar cloth as that worn by hard-boiled pulp novelist Jim Thompson, *One False Move* begins with a murderous drugs heist in South Central LA involving femme fatale with a heart, Fantasia (Williams), her highly strung white boyfriend, Ray (Thornton), and his black partner, Pluto (Beach). Pluto's high IQ is matched only by his thirst for cold-bloodedly stabbing his victims. Pursued by the black and white detective duo Cole and McFeely, the gang is tagged as heading to Star City, Alabama, where Ray has an uncle; aspirant local police chief Dale 'Hurricane' Dixon (Paxton) is alerted to their imminent arrival (the film expertly cuts between Dixon and the group for maximum suspense). However, when a faxed report arrives revealing Fantasia's involvement in an en-route shooting of a traffic cop, Dixon recognises her as former local flame Lila Walker, with whom, unbeknown to him, he has spawned a mixed-race son. A charged and ultimately violent reunion ensues as Dixon wrestles with his duty and his conscience.

Intelligently adopting classical thriller conventions – with a dash of *High Noon* (1952) – and applying them within a racially charged setting that traces black and white conflict back to its roots in the American

South, Franklin avoids the excessive, bravura and somewhat sermonising approach common to a number of films associated with the 'gangsta' cinema movement of the period. Instead, the theme of race is accorded a subtler and sophisticated treatment that naturally evolves through the characters, environments and the numerous mixed-race relationships and dynamics *One False Move* authentically creates. Written by Billy Bob Thornton and Tom Epperson, the film is similarly perceptive on subjects such as small-town mores, sexual inequality and the interrelationships between race, ambition, money and power.

Newcomer Williams convinces in the complex central role on which the film's revelations and motifs crucially balance, and the performances are generally well judged. So too is the treatment of violence, which manages to be explicit, disturbing and thus pertinent by never descending to gratuity. An ultimately humanist and economically executed triumph of insight and import, the film – which suffered rejection by many major film festivals – gave evidence of the ability of African-American directors to escape ghetto stereotyping while also ushering in a new era of neo-noir pictures such as John Dahl's *The Last Seduction* (1992).

Dir: Carl Franklin; **Prod**: Jesse Beaton, Ben Myron; **Scr**: Billy Bob Thornton, Tom Epperson; **DOP**: James L. Carter; **Edit**: Carole Kravetz; **Score**: Peter Haycock, Derek Holt; **Principal Cast**: Bill Paxton, Cynda Williams, Billy Bob Thornton, Jim Metzler, Michael Beach.

Out to the World (Sae sang bakuro)
South Korea, 1994 – 98 mins
Yeo Kyun-dong

Out to the World emerged alongside Lee Jae-yong and Byun Hyuk's *Homo Videocus* (1991), Lee Min-yong's *A Hot Roof* (1996) and *Sechinku* (*Three Friends*, 1996), a surreal look at three young male losers, directed by Yim Soon-rye, to suggest an exciting new wave in South Korean cinema. A black comedy following the exploits of two bumbling fugitives, the film acted as an apt and tragicomic allegory for the country's recent political past.

As mismatched jail mates Mun Seung-keun and Yi Kyung-yong (the actors' real names) are being transferred to another prison, their bus is hijacked by hardened criminals and in the resulting scuffle, the two become unwitting escapees. Their plans to turn themselves in go astray when a flighty thrill-seeker (Hye-jin) dumps her tyrannical lover to team up with the luckless duo. Fancying herself as something of an outlaw, the woman convinces a reluctant Seung-keun and Kyung-yong to go to Seoul where they attempt to rob a bank. Of course, they fail miserably, but escape in an armoured truck, leaving a huge stash of cash untouched. Defeated by their own ineptness and embarrassed by their lack of skill, they head for the North Korean border under the illusion of hope for a new start.

A former assistant to leading Korean film-maker Park Kwang-su (*The Black Republic*, 1990), first-time director Kyun-dong has an eye on American fugitive road movies and mismatched buddy capers in this engaging and progressive political allegory about the loosening of the shackles of dictatorship. A phenomenal success in Kyun-dong's homeland, where the broad humour and subversive comments on the quest for freedom and the constrictive conspiracy were warmly embraced, the film also attracted international interest, appearing as part of an ICA season entitled *Seoul Rising*, curated by Asian cinema expert Tony Rayns.

Liberally sprinkled with the Korean pop tunes of the era – another reason for its domestic success – the film bounces along at a brisk and frenetic pace, the director rarely missing the opportunity to reference American movies from *Bonnie and Clyde* (1967) to *Butch Cassidy and the Sundance Kid* (1969). Unfolding in South Korea's vast expanses, *Out to the World* also makes arresting visual use of its frequently inhospitable surroundings, bringing the dichotomy between rural and urban values into sharp focus as it tracks its bumbling protagonists into Seoul's sprawling metropolis.

Dir: Yeo Kyun-dong; **Prod**: Sang-in Park; **Scr**: Yeo Kyun-dong; **DOP**: You Yong-kil; **Edit**: Kim Hyun; **Score**: Kim Jong-seo; **Principal Cast**: Mun Seung-keun, Yi Kyung-yong, Shim Hye-jin, Yang Hee-kyung, Myong Kue-nam.

Paper Moon
US, 1973 – 102 mins
Peter Bogdanovich

Undoubtedly Bogdanovich's best work after *Targets* (1968) and *The Last Picture Show* (1971), *Paper Moon* was an artistic and commercial success that placed the director in the firmament of a new wave of young American auteurs afforded unparalleled creative freedom following *Easy Rider* (1969) and *M*A*S*H* (1970). Bogdanovich, who was unable to sustain his career trajectory after suffering a number of personal and professional disasters, gazes wistfully back in his introduction to the Paramount Directors' Series DVD release, commenting, 'The studio did a wonderful thing. It got out of the way and let us make the picture the way we wanted.'

In Depression-era America, orphaned Addie Loggins (Tatum O'Neal) is left in the care of unethical travelling Bible salesman Moses Pray (Ryan O'Neal), who may or may not be her father. En route to Addie's relatives, Moses discovers that the nine-year-old is quite a handful: she smokes, cusses and is almost as devious and manipulative as he is. They join forces as swindlers, fleecing widows by informing them that their departed husbands recently purchased deluxe editions of the Bible but passed away before the balances could be paid. The relationship is such a success that Addie is averse to breaking up the team and so sabotages the burgeoning romance between Moses and good-time gal Trixie Delight (Kahn). Later, while attempting to square a $200 debt that Addie claims he owes her, Moses falls foul of a bootlegger (Hillerman) and is nearly beaten to death by the criminal's twin-brother sheriff. Painfully pulling himself together, Moses gets Addie to her relatives, whereupon she adamantly refuses to leave his side.

In essence a sentimental tale about a daughter finding, and then redeeming, her wayward father, in less capable hands this adaptation of Joe David Brown's novel may easily have fallen foul of the narrative's mawkishness. But Bogdanovich, working from Alvin Sargent's vinegary script, keeps such tendencies at bay, performing wonders with O'Neal's debutante daughter, Tatum, who was eight at the time of the film's making and would go on to win a Best Supporting Actress Academy Award in one of cinema's most memorable performances by a minor. 'You're not really a director unless you've directed a child', comments Bogdanovich in his DVD commentary, where he also expresses his fondness and admiration for O'Neal and her investment of spirit and defiance.

Photographed on location in Kansas and Missouri in high-contrast black and white by Hungarian cinematographer László Kovács, *Paper Moon*'s commanding rendering of the stark prairie landscapes with their flat horizons and overarching skies is a further guard against overt sentiment and a marker of period authenticity. Production designer Polly Platt is another vital contributor, exhibiting an acute eye (and ear) for detail, as superbly illustrated in a sequence in which Addie listens to a Jack Benny radio broadcast from the confines of the fading glamour of her hotel room.

A film-maker and later raconteur with an extensive appreciation of a pantheon of directors such as John Ford and Howard Hawks, Bogdanovich's picaresque tale respectfully references them both. The film's sense of camaraderie in testing times, rueful shifts of tone and straight-faced one liners are certainly Hawksian, while the austere visual iconography, period setting and theme of travel as a means of trying to outrun poverty offer a more direct homage to Ford's king of the road movie, *The Grapes of Wrath* (1940).

Dir: Peter Bogdanovich; **Prod**: Peter Bogdanovich; **Scr**: Alvin Sargent; **Dop**: László Kovács; **Edit**: Verna Fields; **Score**: N/A; **Principal Cast**: Ryan O'Neal, Tatum O'Neal, Madeline Khan, John Hillerman, P. J. Johnson, Randy Quaid.

The Passenger (*Professione: Reporter*)
Italy/France/Spain, 1975 – 125 mins
Michelangelo Antonioni

One of Michelangelo Antonioni's finest achievements, and alongside
Blow Up (1966) the best of his English-language films, *The Passenger*
signalled a glorious return to form after the visually impressive but flawed
and largely incoherent *Zabriskie Point* (1970). Derek Malcolm (2000)
described what is ostensibly an existential road-movie odyssey with a
huge Hollywood star at its centre as resembling 'a heavily intellectualised
Graham Greene story, partly because of its screenplay, and partly
because Antonioni was concerned with spiritual values'.

Jack Nicholson as reporter David Locke in *The Passenger*, Antonioni's existential road-
movie odyssey

Nicholson gives one of his finest and certainly most understated performances as David Locke, a deeply disillusioned television journalist covering current affairs in Africa who impulsively decides to exchange identities with an acquaintance he finds dead in a Saharan hotel room. Purloining the corpse's passport and diary, he embarks on a potentially revitalising trip around Europe. Locke also starts a relationship with a beautiful younger woman (Schneider), but the further he goes to escape his previous life, the worse the situation becomes as his mysterious disappearance becomes a matter of great concern not only for his wife and friends back in London, but for the police and some sinister colleagues of the dead man.

Working from a taut, highly imaginative script by Mark Peploe and Peter Wollen, the latter of whom was once a political correspondent in foreign parts, Antonioni creates a haunting, suspenseful and extremely subtle study of psychological and spiritual disenchantment, beginning with visually ravishing scenes of the burnt-out protagonist's progress through the desert (including a sequence in which his jeep becomes stuck in sand, further signposting his stasis), before hinting at a revival of tentative hope in his relationship with the younger woman. The film concludes with Locke sharing the fate of the man whose mask he has taken in what is one of the most memorable and brilliantly audacious codas in cinema. The sequence, a seven-minute take, begins with a shot that passes through the narrow bars of a window to frame Nicholson on his bed, moves into a pretty, picturesque courtyard, then back to look through the bars again. The first time we see Nicholson, he is alive and asleep on his bed. The second time, after it is subtly suggested that one of the men on his tail has slipped into his room, he is dead.

Ravishingly shot by Luciano Tovoli in France, Spain and North Africa, *The Passenger* intimates as much about the contemporary political situation as it does about the state of its protagonist's mind. On a more superficial note, there is also much for car fetishists to enjoy, from Schneider's steely blue and exceedingly stylish convertible to the rows of Fiats and Alfa Romeos lining the streets of Barcelona.

The film was unavailable for many years as, according to the wishes of Nicholson, the former rights-holder, it could only be screened in the presence of Antonioni or his star. However, that changed in 2006 following the acquisition of the film by Sony. Re-released in June 2006 at the National Film Theatre, *The Passenger*, boosted by ecstatic press notices, went on to break the box-office record for a single screen release at the venue. The enduring appeal of Antonioni's remarkable film was emphatically confirmed.

Dir: Michelangelo Antonioni; **Prod**: Carlo Ponti; **Scr**: Mark Peploe, Peter Wollen; **DOP**: Luciano Tovoli; **Edit**: Franco Arcalli; **Score**: Ivan Vandor; **Principal Cast**: Jack Nicholson, Maria Schneider, Jenny Runacre, Ian Hendry, Steven Berkoff.

Planes, Trains and Automobiles
US, 1987 – 93 mins
John Hughes

Promoted as teen-movie guru John Hughes' first adult comedy, no doubt on the strength of a number of profanity-laden sequences, *Planes, Trains and Automobiles* is an enjoyable addition to the mismatched travelling companions road-movie substrata. Ultimately erring towards sentimentality and mawkishness, there is nonetheless an unexpected darkness at the film's core. Hughes quite deftly balances the film's comic and dramatic elements, interspersing the moments of absurdist humour dealing with the horror of interpersonal contact and a world in which even the most mundane objects seem destined to thwart and frustrate with oddly disquieting observations on the impossibility of companionship and what it means to be alone.

En route to Chicago to spend Thanksgiving with his family, irascible businessman Neal Page (Martin) finds that his first-class plane ticket has been demoted, forcing him to share his flight with boorish shower-curtain-ring salesman Del Griffith (Candy). A sudden snowstorm in Chicago forces the plane to land in Wichita, Kansas, and unable to find four-star accommodation, Neal is compelled to accept Del's invitation to flop at his more modest motel. Driven to distraction by Del's annoying personal habits, the ungrateful Neal lets forth with a stream of verbal abuse. Left somewhat shamefaced by Del's obvious offence and hurt, Neal tries to make amends by agreeing to act as a travelling companion back to Chicago. However, tensions soon reappear alongside Del's inane anecdotes as the pair's journey assumes increasingly desperate and ultimately epic levels after encounters involving a train, a tractor and a hired car.

Etching the loneliness of its protagonists in a number of well-written scenes that assert a mutual sense of alienation despite Neal's trappings of money and family, the film ultimately motors towards redemption; in time-honoured fashion the mismatched pair are bosom buddies at the end of their cross-country odyssey, with all quirks and hostilities forgotten. This conciliation is sealed when Del receives an invite to Neal's sumptuous Thanksgiving dinner. But still there lingers the sense that he will undoubtedly have to return to his more modest world, and Neal will similarly revert to reactionary, bullying type.

Though not quite vintage Martin, *Planes, Trains and Automobiles* certainly has more than its fair share of extremely funny moments and is fondly remembered for a scene in which the incompatibles share a bed, only for Neal to confuse Del's buttocks for pillows. Some of the sight gags are similarly crude but nonetheless effective: a seemingly inevitable car crash precipitating the digging of nails into the dashboard followed by a blink-and-you'll-miss-it insert shot to reveal the passenger's reversion to skeleton form. The two leads work well together too, Candy giving a career-best performance as an incorrigible but ultimately endearing travelling companion, the perfect comic foil to Martin's frustrated, maniacal but not too monstrous Everyman.

Dir: John Hughes; **Prod**: John Hughes; **Scr**: John Hughes; **DOP**: Donald Peterman; **Edit**: Paul Hirsch; **Score**: Ira Newborn; **Principal Cast**: Steve Martin, John Candy, Laila Robins.

Poetic Justice
US, 1993 – 109 mins
John Singleton

Set against the backdrop of urban despair and loneliness, John Singleton's follow-up to the landmark *Boyz n the Hood* (1991) is a frustrating but nonetheless uplifting drama about the struggle for love, hope and personal transformation in the face of adversity.

The loss of her lover (played by rapper Q-Tip in a flashback sequence) to gang violence and her alcoholic mother's suicide has made Justice (Jackson) a virtual recluse whose singular form of expression and survival is poetry. A hairstylist at a small salon in South Central Los Angeles, Justice is hired to work at a stylists' event in Oakland, but finds herself left stranded when her car breaks down. Remembering that her friend Iesha (King) is hopping a ride to Oakland with her boyfriend Chicago (Torry), a postal worker heading there with a truck full of mail, Justice tags along only to discover that Chicago's driving partner is none other than Lucky (Shakur), the postman who delivers mail to her shop. Like Justice, Lucky has a creative outlet, spending his weekends at his cousin's eight-track garage studio, recording the rap songs that enable him to creatively voice his inner rage and build hope for his future. The journey is initially a rocky one, with Iesha and Chicago attempting to work out their own fractious relationship, while fate forces Justice to decide if she's ready for a new love – and if Lucky is the man she's waiting for.

Featuring an impressive screen debut for R&B star Janet Jackson alongside a nuanced performance from Tupac Shakur that contrasts with his off-screen persona and previous acting assignments such as Ernest Dickerson's *Juice* (1992), Singleton's merging of the road movie and urban violence genres is a noble if flawed attempt to take black characters and issues out of the macho 'gangsta' ghetto. Expertly capturing the way that anger acts as a barrier to feelings and other less aggressive forms of emotion, Singleton also displays a natural feel for the rhythms, concerns and language of the black American experience, while offering a sobering and progressive comment on the treatment of black women. This is perhaps best illustrated in the comic and extremely explicit barbs Iesha delivers regarding Chicago's sexual inadequacies. Laugh-out-loud funny, they ultimately erupt in violence.

The film is undoubtedly at its best when most direct, Justice angrily reacting to the sexist MTV-style presentation of her peers by lashing out at Lucky with the line 'I am a black woman and I deserve respect'. The film falters in the interior monologues and poetry provided for its central character by celebrated poet Maya Angelou – who also appears in a small cameo. Angelou's maturity and reflection ring false in the mouth of a character barely out of her teens and highlight the fledgling Jackson's acting inexperience. However, the incremental coming together of Justice and Lucky during the road trip is handled with sensitivity and charm and if *Poetic Justice* ultimately teeters under the weight of its responsibility towards the lives of those it depicts, it certainly deserves plaudits for its honourable intentions.

Dir: John Singleton; **Prod**: Steve Nicolaides, John Singleton; **Scr**: John Singleton; **DOP**: Peter Lyons Collister; **Edit**: Bruce Cannon; **Score**: Stanley Clarke; **Principal Cast**: Janet Jackson, Tupac Shakur, Khandi Alexander, Regina King, Joe Torry.

Powwow Highway
UK, 1988 – 91 mins
Jonathan Wacks

Powwow Highway takes two of the standard conventions of the road movie: a mismatched pair with different ideas on how to get to their destination and whose journey is interrupted by a series of serio-comic stopovers and eccentric encounters, and imbues them with a Native American sensibility. Adapted from the novel by David Seals, the premise makes for a genial and entertaining trip that also offers an illuminating meditation on cultural displacement and the psyche of the Native American in late twentieth-century America.

In Santa Fe, New Mexico, a Cheyenne woman is arrested on a trumped-up drugs charge. A few hundred miles north in Lame Deer, Montana, her quick-tempered activist brother, Buddy Red Bow (Martinez), leaves the land hearings he is contesting for his tribe and sets off to bail her out. Lacking transportation, he fortuitously meets old schoolmate Philbert Bono (Farmer) in his self-named 'war pony', a beat-up '64 Buick, and together the pair take to America's limitless highways, initially adopting a route that parallels the Bozeman Trail, the scene of many nineteenth-century battles between white settlers travelling to the gold mines of Virginia City, Montana, and Native Americans eager to protect their northern Wyoming hunting grounds.

As with most buddy movies, the film's foundation is the engaging premise of having two contrasting characters spend time with each other. Philbert clearly doesn't think of the trip to Santa Fe in terms of hours or miles, but in terms of the places he must visit en route to make it into a spiritual journey and not simply the physical relocation of his body. This attitude clearly chafes with the more modern, firebrand Red Bow, who bridles with righteous anger at the indignities heaped upon his people. However, with Philbert – who talks to his car as if it were a pony – in the driving seat, there is no arresting his frequent stops to meditate at sacred sites and visit old friends, and so Red Bow is slowly forced to acknowledge this more philosophical outlook. In doing so, he ultimately reaches a greater clarity of consciousness, realising that simply blaming the white man and what he sees as a system rigged against Native Americans is distracting him from his true mission: to better understand himself and his place in the world. Martinez and Farmer, a former teacher from Ontario perhaps later best known for playing a similar role in Jarmusch's not thematically dissimilar *Dead Man* (1995), create a palpable interplay between two unforgettable characters whose friendship has survived many differences.

Resourcefully shot on location in wintry Montana, director Wacks, the producer of *Repo Man* (1984), and DOP Toyomichi Kurita make the most of available locations – trailer parks, condos, highways, traffic signals and neighbourhood convenience stores – capturing a landscape that is at once iconic and yet depressingly modern.

Dir: Jonathan Wacks; **Prod**: Jan Wieringa; **Scr**: Janet Heaney, Jean Stawarz; **DOP**: Toyomichi Kurita; **Edit**: James Austin Stewart, Hilarie Roope; **Score**: Barry Goldberg; **Principal Cast**: A. Martinez, Gary Farmer, Joanelle Nadine Romero, Geoff Rivas.

Radio On
UK/West Germany, 1979 – 102 mins
Chris Petit

One of the most striking feature debuts in British cinema, Chris Petit's road movie is both a hymn and homage to the dreamed imperatives of the clear highway, while remaining ruefully aware that, in England at least, the road soon runs out and the journey must turn in other directions, not least inward. The film was co-produced by Wim Wenders, whom Petit had seduced into getting involved in his debut feature while working as the editor of the film section at *Time Out* magazine, and if the film does resemble anything it is the vision of road travel and the search for personal identity to be found in Wenders' European road movies of the early 1970s.

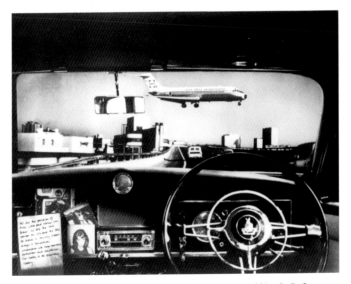

The windscreen as a window to the wider world: Chris Petit's astonishing *Radio On*

Minimalist in plot, *Radio On* follows a young man (Beames) as he travels by car to Bristol to investigate the mysterious death of his brother. As the young man drives, he encounters figures as rootless as himself: an army deserter from Northern Ireland, a German woman looking for her lost child (Kreuzer, on loan from Wenders, who had used her so effectively as a repository for male loneliness in *Kings of the Road*, 1976) and a garage mechanic (Sting in an early and effective cameo). The film offers a quietly compelling and even mythic vision of a late-1970s England stricken by economic decline and stalled between failed hopes of cultural and social change and the imminent upheavals of Thatcherism.

Stunningly photographed in luminous monochrome by Martin Schäfer (another Wenders regular), and driven by a startling new wave soundtrack of *Low*-era Bowie, Kraftwerk, Devo, Robert Fripp and more, Petit echoed punk culture's austere aesthetic, capturing the sense of faltering communication and lurking disenchantment in a country uncertain of its place and future. However, a small but significant note of optimism is struck in the film's suggestion that redemptive change might come, but not necessarily from the expected sources.

Alien and alienating, this haunting, elegiac road movie largely met with suspicion and incomprehension on release. Later celebrated by the writer Iain Sinclair in his book *Lights Out for the Territory*, the rarely screened *Radio On* made a triumphant return to British screens and wider consciousness when it was successfully re-released by the BFI in 2004. Sinclair and Petit later collaborated on *The Cardinal and the Corpse* (1992), *The Falconer* (1997) and *London Orbital* (2002), a loose trilogy for Channel 4 about marginal figures. Accompanying the recent reissue was Petit's twenty-four-minute video-essay *Radio On (remix)* (1998), in which Petit, accompanied by editor Emma Matthews, returned to the original film's locations. While *Radio On* anticipated the significant political transitions of the 1980s, this remix signposts the millennium and catalogues the subsequent shifts in topography and architecture, as well as changes in the medium. An equally intense highway meditation, it collages distressed video with Super-8, archive material with contemporary footage, and original text with Wire's Bruce Gilbert's radical disruption of the original's soundtrack.

Dir: Chris Petit; **Prod**: Keith Griffiths; **Scr**: Chris Petit; **DOP**: Martin Schäfer; **Edit**: Anthony Sloman, Stefna Beames, Stuart de Long; **Score**: Not listed; **Principal Cast**: David Beames, Lisa Kreuzer, Sandy Ratcliff, Sting.

Raising Arizona
US, 1987 – 94 mins
Joel Coen

The follow-up to the Coen Brothers' astonishing *Blood Simple* (1983), *Raising Arizona* replaces the earlier film's labyrinthine plotting and film noir overtones with frantic screwball comedy. Being the Coen Brothers, a whole range of other film references come into play, including Tex Avery cartoons, 1940s B-movies, Sam Raimi horror (an old cohort), baby-boomer comedies and the quest for freedom and escape from conformity associated with the road movie. The Coens were newly married when they embarked upon the film and this, along with the fact that it is set during the heart of the Reagan administration, accounts for the film's satirising of the acquisitive values of the era.

H. I. 'Hi' McDonnough (Cage) is a philosophical but dim career criminal who has been arrested so often that he gets to know 'Ed' (Hunter), the officer who takes his mug shots. Hi takes a shine to Ed and promises to go straight if she marries him. She accepts, and they move to the Arizona desert, where Hi holds down a factory job and blissfully watches the sunsets. Their serenity is shattered, however, when the couple decide they want a child and discover that, as Hi puts it, 'Ed's womb was a rocky place where my seed could find no purchase.' Ed goes into a severe depression until she sees an item in the news: Nathan Arizona (Wilson), owner of a chain of unpainted furniture stores, has become the father of quintuplets, and he and his wife joke that they now have more children than they know what to do with. Hi and Ed decide to kidnap one of the Arizona infants, figuring that they'll have a baby and the Arizonas will have less of a burden. Complications ensue when a pair of Hi's old cellmates turn up in search of sanctuary; and then there's the problem of a hellish, Apocalyptic biker (straight from the *Mad Max* series) hired by Arizona Sr to track down his missing progeny.

A dazzling synthesis of technique, witty dialogue (the Hi voiceover that bookends the film is priceless, as are his various dime-store novel asides) and style, the film's undoubted centrepiece is the moment when Hi decides that he can no longer stand life as an average Joe and, on an errand to buy nappies, impetuously decides to rob the store. Cinematographer Barry Sonnenfeld's low, manic handheld camera tracks Hi as he is pursued down the aisles and through the alleys, gardens and houses of the small town by a pack of dogs, a trigger-happy teenage clerk and Keystone-style cops. The bravura sequence concludes with Ed acting as a getaway driver, Hi scooping the pack of nappies from the tarmac – one of the film's many motifs – as his none-too-pleased wife screeches away.

A film that certainly does things to excess, and is all the better for it, there is also an underlying seriousness in the look at parenting, and more specifically people who want to become parents for all the wrong reasons. The criticism of the government and its clear division of the rich and the poor is more explicit, Ed at one point exclaiming that it isn't easy to 'stand up and fly straight with that son of a bitch Reagan in the White House'.

Dir: Joel Coen; **Prod**: Ethan Coen; **Scr**: Ethan Coen, Joel Coen; **DOP**: Barry Sonnenfeld; **Edit**: Michael R. Miller; **Score**: Carter Burwell; **Principal Cast**: Nicolas Cage, Holly Hunter, John Goodman, Trey Wilson, William Forsythe.

Red Lights
France, 2004 – 100 mins
Cédric Kahn

Confirming his status as one of France's brightest talents, Cédric Kahn
followed up 2001's impressive portrait of Italian multiple killer Roberto
Succo with an equally assured adaptation of a Georges Simenon novel.

Summer in Paris. Antoine (Robert Guédiguian regular Darroussin) and
Hélène (Bouquet) are driving to the south to pick up their children at
summer camp. The roads are packed with holiday traffic and miles of
gridlock is expected. Antoine, annoyed that his wife is running late, tries
to cool himself with beer after beer. By the time they hit the road, he has
laced the beers with whisky but tries to conceal his drunkenness. Traffic
slows and tempers flare as Antoine accuses his wife of not treating him
like a real man. At each forced crawl and stop, they break into
accusations. He takes random turns and continues drinking in small-town
bars. A brief radio announcement reveals that a dangerous killer has
escaped prison and the couple continue quarrelling. Temporarily left
alone in the car and worried by Antoine's inebriated state, Hélène
decides to look for alternative transport. Finding her gone, Antoine
momentarily panics, but soon settles back to enjoy himself like 'a real
man'; it's a long night and every anonymous neon light invites him for
one more drink. He picks up a hitchhiker, who turns out to be the
escaped killer and who has, unbeknown to him, already just encountered
his wife. The events start moving out of Antoine's control and turn into a
night of horror. The film climaxes the next day when he wakes up in the
middle of nowhere and goes looking for his wife . . .

Kahn and co-screenwriter Laurence Ferreira-Barbosa relocate
Simenon's original novel from the US to France, stripping the book down
to the core to concentrate all the action on the two leads. In the
increasingly claustrophobic confines of the car, where the bickering,
bourgeois couple are forced to contend with each other's presence, the
tension slowly builds, reinforced by the dark tones of the music

(*Nocturnes* by Debussy). The human side of the tragedy is central to *Red Lights*: as the night progresses, Antoine's primitive fear colours the film and the ride becomes, rather like Godard's *Weekend* (1967), a nightmare in a world of anonymous roads, cars, consumerism and neon lights. To heighten the sensation that nothing is what it seems and that the apparent familiarity of our lives and our relationships are subject to discomfort and extreme change, Kahn shot all the nighttime car scenes in a studio.

A road movie in which the protagonists seem stuck in stasis, apparently heading nowhere, the film, after highlighting the snail's pace,

Mechanical and emotional breakdown: Jean-Pierre Darroussin searches for the route of the problem in *Red Lights*

frustrations and ennui (an earlier Kahn picture) of modern life, takes a
very disturbing detour. What begins as a detailed dissection of a
deteriorating urban marriage slowly and inexorably transforms into a very
effective and bone-chilling thriller. Kahn's confident flair for narrative
aside, much of the success of this new direction is founded upon the
performances of the two leads. Kahn needed strong actors to play the
couple and preferred well-known stars who had never played together
before. Darroussin's sense of weary resignation and Bouquet's glacial
elegance mesh perfectly.

Dir: Cédric Kahn; Prod: Patrick Godeau; Scr: Cédric Kahn, Laurence Ferreira-Barbosa with
Gilles Marchand; DOP: Patrick Blossier; Edit: Yann Dedet; Score: Claude Debussy, principal
theme 'Nuages', from Nocturnes, conducted by Manuel Rosenthal; Principal Cast: Jean-
Pierre Darroussin, Carole Bouquet, Vincent Deniard, Charline Paul.

The Return
Russia, 2003 – 105 mins
Andrey Zvyagintsev

An astonishing debut feature from Andrey Zvyagintsev, *The Return* is an enigmatic and sombre synthesis of road movie and rites-of-passage drama. Sparse in dialogue and largely devoid of exposition, the absences and allusions to unexplained events also ensure that this is as compelling as the most efficient thriller. Earning its director inevitable comparisons to Tarkovsky, in fact this has little in common, bar a similarly arresting visualisation of landscapes, the film was the most critically fêted of its year.

Andrey Zvyagintsev's *The Return*, a synthesis of road movie and rites-of-passage drama

Carefree teenagers Andrey (Garin) and Vanya (Dobronravov) are given a rude awakening when, returning home after a day of horsing around, they are informed by their mother that their father (Lavronenko), who left home twelve years ago, is upstairs sleeping. The boys are initially wary of this taciturn stranger, but when he asks them to accompany him on a long car trip so that they can re-establish ties, they are forced to grudgingly accept. The trio silently travel through the Russian wilderness, stopping at small, backwater towns for ill-tempered meals, the father having picked up the reins of fatherhood all too easily. Finally arriving at a deserted lake, they take a boat out to a small island to fish. Andrey and Vanya remain unconvinced that the man is their flesh and blood, and frequently compare him to an image in a black-and-white photograph. Slowly, the increasingly enigmatic stranger's motives for being on the island are apparently revealed – the retrieval of a mysterious hidden trunk, the contents of which are unspecified.

The road journey the film reveals is particularly well handled and gruelling for protagonists and spectator alike, with Zvyagintsev incrementally building an atmosphere founded on claustrophobia, brooding silence, paranoia and the impending threat of physical violence. As a result, *The Return* has an incredibly intense emotional and psychological depth. The sense that something awful is about to happen becomes almost unbearable as the trio motor towards an inevitable and ultimately hugely emotive tragedy. The flat Russian countryside and the expansive lakes are rendered with a chilled, meditative beauty by cinematographer Mikhail Krichman, who, working from a largely blue palette, drains his surroundings of all warmth to give the impression of characters unable to escape from their emotional vacuum.

Having been so sparing with background information, the final sequence of the film is startlingly intimate: a series of beautifully shot black-and-white photographs taken by Ivan during the course of the trip. It brings the boys' journey, and their hauling into adulthood, into sudden and sharp relief. Yet with a single, devastating exception, the most important figure here – their father – is as absent as he ever was. Sadly, shortly after filming, one of its young stars, Vladimir Garin, drowned in one of the very lakes where the picture was shot. A film of mythic proportions that examines issues of male authority, glancing back at Russia's past while looking also, tentatively, to its future, *The Return* is a fitting epitaph for his obvious talents.

Dir: Andrey Zvyagintsev; **Prod**: Dmitri Lesnevsky; **Scr**: Alexander Novototsky, Vladimir Moiseenko; **DOP**: Mikhail Krichman; **Edit**: Vladimir Mogilevsky; **Score**: Andrei Dergachyov; **Principal Cast**: Vladimir Garin, Ivan Dobronravov, Konstantin Lavronenko, Natalya Vdovina.

Riding Alone for Thousands of Miles
(Qian li zou dan qi)
Hong Kong/China/Japan, 2005 – 107 mins
Zhang Yimou

More in the intimate, neo-realist vein of *The Road Home* and *Not One Less* (both 1999), as opposed to the spectacular action of *House of Flying Daggers* (2004) and *Hero* (2003), Yimou's *Riding Alone for Thousands of Miles* is a relatively low-key tale about ordinary people in poignant, real-life situations. The film's title refers to a traditional song, 'Romance of the Three Kingdoms', about a general who selflessly went on a long journey to help a friend.

Summoned to Tokyo by his daughter-in-law Rie (Terajima), village fisherman Gou-ichi Takata (Takakura) arrives at a city hospital to find his son Ken-ichi (Nakai) stricken with cancer. Though Gou-ichi attempts to use the visit as a catalyst to heal a decade-long dispute, the stubborn Ken-ichi rejects the attempt at reconciliation. Subsequently handed a videotape by Rie before departing, Gou-ichi returns home unsuccessful in his efforts to build a bridge of peace. Upon watching the videotape, a research project exploring the Chinese folk arts and shot by Ken-ichi in the southern province of Yunnan, Gou-ichi is oddly affected by the on-screen failure of his son in convincing a well-known opera singer, Li Jaimin, to perform the titular song, an operatic piece espousing the values of friendship. Gou-ichi travels to Yunnan to capture the performance that his son could not, only to find that Li cannot sing out of sorrow at losing his own son, who is being cared for in a mountain village far away. Resolving to find the boy and bring him back to his father, Gou-ichi embarks on a personal quest unaware of the miscues and catastrophes that await him.

The veteran Japanese actor Takakura excels in a role especially written for him, conveying with admirable restraint a sense of dignity and longing. Far removed from the taciturn gangsters and violent loners with which he made his name, the mishaps and fiascos his character experiences on the road to China (including inept translators and the discovery that Li Jaimin is serving time for stabbing a man) tread a fine line between sadness and Chekhovian humour, and it is Takakura who deftly establishes this balance, ensuring that the film never tips over into outright farce. Much like the series of hapless disasters that befall the family in *Little Miss Sunshine* (2006) or the would-be wine connoisseurs in *Sideways* (2004), each mounting catastrophe serves to reveal the central protagonist's inner feelings.

Incorporating elements of Japanese music, as well as Chinese opera, Guo Wenjing's poignant score contributes to the film's poignancy and humanist strain; it also serves to highlight Yimou and screenwriter Zou Jingzhi's interest in exploring and ultimately uniting the cultures of China and Japan. A former cinematographer who here displays a keen understanding of the pilgrim's anguish so closely associated with the road-movie genre, Yimou's compositional sense is typically acute and the Yunnan landscapes are spectacular. Equally assured are the opening and closing sequences of Gou-ichi in his seaside home.

Dir: Zhang Yimou; **Prod**: Bill Kong, Xiu Jian, Zhang Weiping; **Scr**: Zou Jingzhi; **DOP**: Zhao Xiaoding; **Edit**: Cheng Long; **Score**: Guo Wenjing; **Principal Cast**: Ken Takakura, Kiichi Nakai, Shinobu Terajima, Qiu Lin.

Road to Morocco
US, 1942 – 83 mins
David Butler

Following *Road to Singapore* (1940) and *Road to Zanzibar* (1941) as the third in a popular series of wisecracking Bob Hope and Bing Crosby comedies that would conclude, after seven features, with 1962's *Road to Hong Kong*, *Road to Morocco* is widely viewed as the best of the bunch. Light-hearted, screwy and frequently nonsensical, *Road to Morocco* certainly represents the point at which the formula for the globe-trotting travelogue series had hit its stride but not yet descended into self-parody. By this time, audiences knew what to expect, and were in on the joke as Bing and Bob sang, in their self-aware opening number that references the previous outings in which they vied for the hand of co-star Lamour, 'Where we're goin', why we're goin', how can we be sure? I'll lay you eight-to-five that we meet Dorothy Lamour!'.

After their freighter accidentally explodes, shipwrecked American stowaways Orville 'Turkey' Jackson (Hope) and his childhood friend Jeff Peters (Crosby) find themselves on the shores of Morocco. Broke and hungry after riding into town on a camel that greeted them by spitting into Jackson's eye (an impromptu moment that Hope reacted to with some surprise and the skill of a seasoned comedian), Jeff decides to sell Orville to slave traders for $200. Troubled after seeing the ghost of his late, revered aunt (Hope in a wig), Jeff relents and decides to rescue Orville, but instead finds him set to marry within a few days the beautiful Princess Shalamar (Lamour). The Princess was supposed to marry the ruthless bandit sheik chieftain Mullay Kasim (Quinn), but the seer warns her that her first husband will die within a week, but the second husband will live a long and happy life. When the seer finds out his calculations were wrong because he mistook fireflies in his dirty telescope for planets, the Princess changes her plans and decides she loves Jeff. Hope hooks up with Mihirmah (Drake), one of the Princess's handmaidens who befriended him, and the foursome try to escape from the wrathful Kasim by taking a boat to New York.

Featuring Bob Hope's well-honed and not entirely sympathetic persona at its most complete – the fast-talking, treacherous conniver who ogles women and yet remains strangely asexual – the film also displays his gift for timing and skill for improvisation. Essentially an extended cabaret act, with scenic locations, run-ins with exotic women and two-dimensional villains (this is not a film that is often emphasised on Quinn's CV), the interplay between Hope and Crosby, who acts as Hope's more pleasant, handsome and sophisticated foil, is undeniable.

Though founded on zany set-pieces, including a camel proclaiming at the film's conclusion that 'This is the screwiest picture I've ever been in,' the Oscar-nominated script by Hartman and Butler does contain a few pearls, not least Lamour's 'A goose is beautiful until it stands next to a peacock.' The music is an improvement on the previous routines found in the earlier *Road* movies series, with Crosby's party-piece crooning of

(From left) Bob Hope, Bing Crosby and Dorothy Lamour wisecracking their way along the *Road to Morocco*

'Moonlight Becomes You' a particular highlight. A road movie in which the quest, as in the rest of the instalments, is ultimately romantic fulfilment, *Road to Morocco* is far from the finest or most representative example of the genre and offers an unenlightened view of the world. However, it is in parts amusing enough and was genial and extremely popular wartime entertainment.

Dir: David Butler; **Prod**: Paul Jones; **Scr**: Frank Butler, Don Hartman; **DOP**: William C. Mellor; **Edit**: Irene Morra; **Score**: Johnny Burke, James Van Heusen; **Principal Cast**: Bing Crosby, Bob Hope, Dorothy Lamour, Dona Drake, Anthony Quinn.

Roadside Prophets
US, 1992 – 96 mins
Abbe Wool

A genuine oddity and one of the few road movies directed by a woman, this debut picture from writer-director-electrician Abbe Wool offers an endearingly offbeat, partly allegorical and partly satirical 1990s update on *Easy Rider* (1969). Equally inspired by Robert M. Pirsig's book *Zen and the Art of Motorcycle Maintenance* and the early 1990s new wave of American independent film-making headed by directors including Hal Hartley, Jim Jarmusch and Richard Linklater, *Roadside Prophets*' US tagline ran 'They weren't born to be wild. It just turned out that way.' It is an apt summation of the film's easygoing, hipster philosophy.

Brooding factory worker Joe Mosely (Doe, front man for Los Angeles punk band X) takes a road trip in order to scatter the ashes of his co-worker Dave Coleman (David Anthony Marshall) who electrocuted himself playing a video game. Riding his vintage Harley Davidson, Joe leaves LA and heads for a small Nevada town to fulfil Dave's final wish. His journey is complicated by a chance meeting with Brooklyn tagalong, Sam (Horowitz, of The Beastie Boys), a wannabe biker whose goofy outlook on life nicely chimes with Joe's studied cool. Joe also has to cope with making daily phone calls to Angie (voice of Sonna Chavez), his co-worker back in LA who is giving him sick days in exchange for the promise of a hot date. While travelling through the arid desert towards their destination, Joe and Sam meet an array of eccentric and bizarre 1960s throwbacks, played by David Carradine, Arlo Guthrie and acid guru Timothy Leary. As with many road movies, it is the journey not the destination that ultimately counts, the Nevada town turning out to be a washed-up gambling backwater called Jackpot.

Assistant director to Alex Cox on *Repo Man* (1984) and scriptwriter on Cox's *Sid and Nancy* (1986), Wool obviously inherited her mentor's fascination for rock-star cameos, counter-culture icons and ironic commentary on those existing on the margins of society. In this regard,

Wool's casting is spot-on, offering a direct route to authenticity, with the likes of Leary – playing a 1960s radical-turned-farmer who spouts roadside philosophies – appearing in cameo roles to validate the film's concern with the disparity between present-day values and those that were rife during the Summer of Love. Now-notable actors such as John Cusack (playing a high-energy criminal who only steals food from restaurants) and Don Cheadle also feature. The pick of the performances, however, is Horowitz, who exudes a nervous and geeky charm that papers over the film's somewhat two-dimensional characters.

There are other flaws, notably Wool's over-strenuous attempts to create moments of existential portent, and an irritating if understandable tendency towards psycho-babble; but the pace of the film rarely flags, the roadside scenery looks wonderful and there is a regular array of quirky walk-ons to keep things interesting. A somewhat simplistic paean to following your heart that offers wry comment on 1990s disaffection, *Roadside Prophets* is an enjoyable and good-natured slice of Americana.

Dir: Abbe Wool; **Prod**: Peter McCarthy, David Swinson; **Scr**: Abbe Wool, David Swinson; **DOP**: Tom Richmond; **Edit**: Nancy Richardson; **Score**: Pray for Rain; **Principal Cast**: John Doe, Adam Horowitz, John Cusack, Arlo Guthrie, David Carradine, Timothy Leary.

The Searchers
US, 1956 – 119 mins
John Ford

Widely considered Ford's masterpiece, *The Searchers* blends the outdoor visual spectacle closely associated with the genre with a complex critique of racism.

Wayne plays Ethan Edwards, a former Confederate soldier who returns to his brother Aaron's frontier home three years after the end of the Civil War. A loner, Ethan harbours a bitter hatred of Indians (though he knows their lore and language well) and trusts no one but himself. Ethan and Martin Pawley (Hunter), Aaron's adopted son, join a makeshift band of Texas Rangers fending off an assault by renegade Comanches, but before they can run off the Indians, several homes are attacked, and Ethan returns to discover his brother and sister-in-law Martha dead, and their two daughters kidnapped. One of the girls is later discovered dead but the other, Debbie (Wood), is still alive, and with obsessive determination, Ethan and Martin spend the next five years in a relentless search for Debbie, and for Scar (Brandon), the fearsome Comanche chief who abducted her. At first reluctant to leave the Indians whose culture she has become a part of, Debbie is at last brought back safely.

Made during the heyday of the psychological Western, with its tormented anti-heroes and ambiguous moral codes, *The Searchers* features Wayne's finest performance, an uncomfortable, troubling depiction of a man driven by hatred and revenge. Preferring to think of Debbie as dead rather than living as Scar's sexual partner, Ethan's vindictiveness is intensified by the fact that prior to slaughtering Martha, with whom Ethan had been secretly in love, Scar had first raped her. Ethan's final scalping of Scar can thus be read as 'asserting his own savagery and his need to root out his quasi-incestuous desire' (Buscombe 2006, p. 179). Wayne's character looks forward to those that would dominate American cinema in the 1970s, *Taxi Driver*'s (1976) Travis Bickle and Clint Eastwood's trigger-happy Harry Callahan (*Dirty Harry*, 1971) being prime examples.

In its rich characterisation and tackling of major themes such as the centrality of home and the dichotomy between civilised and supposedly uncivilised peoples, *The Searchers* is matched by Ford's exemplary staging. One of seven Ford films shot in Monument Valley, Arizona, its Technicolor photography by Winton C. Hoch evocatively captures the arid location's grandeur and punishing, savage beauty. A road movie in that it involves an arduous journey precipitated by a personal quest, the film's denouement is one of the greatest in the history of cinema: a lone Ethan, framed within a doorway, exiting the communal hearth from which he shall, by his own nature, remain forever excluded, wading into the Arizona wilderness.

Dir: John Ford; **Prod**: Merian C. Cooper; **Scr**: Frank S. Nugent; **DOP**: Winton C. Hoch; **Edit**: Jack Murray; **Score**: Max Steiner; **Principal Cast**: John Wayne, Jeffrey Hunter, Vera Miles, Ward Bond, Natalie Wood, Henry Brandon.

SER (*Freedom is Paradise*)
USSR, 1989 – 75 mins
Sergei Bodrov

A former satirical journalist, Sergei Bodrov was one of the leading new Soviet directors to emerge in the wake of the 1986 Fifth Congress of the Film-makers' Association of the USSR, an attempt to 'democratize and decentralize the monolithic Soviet film industry' (Bollag and Posner 1990, p. 55). Beginning from the premise that his countrymen are conditioned to think and behave as prisoners, this exemplary road movie, whose itinerary takes in sites of social and political significance (including Archangel), also typifies the interest in absent fathers that has retained currency in recent Russian works such as *The Return* (2003) and Alexander Sokurov's *Father and Son* (2003).

The film's title refers to the acronym tattooed on the arm of thirteen-year-old Sacha Grigoriev (Kozyrev), SER standing for 'svoboda era rai' ('Freedom is Paradise'). We first encounter Sacha as he breaks out of a reform school in Alma-Ata, the capital of the Soviet Socialist Republic of Kazakhstan. It is revealed that this latest flight of freedom is the first of several jailbreaks in Sacha's short but eventful criminal history. Caught and sent back to the forbidding and oppressive institution, Sacha again manages to escape and, discovering the whereabouts of his father, whom he has never met, sets out on a 7,000-kilometre journey to a prison camp in Russia's extreme north to find him.

We never learn the reason for Kolya Grigoriev's (Alexander Bureyev) incarceration, but after briefly reuniting father and son, Bodrov reveals that Kolya was born in prison, the son of a woman arrested for stealing cucumbers who was then later impregnated by a guard or an inmate. This revelation concerning trans-generational internment and the notion of a class of human beings 'born and raised in prisons, who will acquire their vision of the world there, and who will continue being prisoners as adults with brief intervals of relative freedom' (Bollag and Posner 1990, p. 58) is disturbing and unsettling in the extreme. The denouement, in which Kolya is led back to his cell and Sacha is sent back to his reform school, reinforces the idea that freedom and paradise are either non-existent or unattainable.

Containing traces of autobiography, in that Bodrov, a native of the far east of Russia, was accustomed to taking similarly expansive trips as a child, *SER*'s connection with reality is also apparent in the casting and the director's verité aesthetic. Filming the final sequences in a real prison camp with real guards and inmates (the overriding impression created by this approach, apart from an acute realism, is that the prison is not somewhere one would want to visit), Bodrov cast Kozyrev from 2,000 children he tested for the role. A former reform-school inmate when Bodrov found him, the remarkable young actor was released on parole following the film's shooting after the director intervened on his behalf.

Dir: Sergei Bodrov; **Prod**: Victor Trakhtenberg; **Scr**: Sergei Bodrov; **DOP**: Yuri Skirtladze; **Edit**: Valentina Kulagnina; **Score**: Alexander Raskatov; **Principal Cast**: Volodya Kozyrev, Alexander Bureyev, Svetlana Gaitan, Vitautas Tomkus.

Sherman's March
US, 1985 – 160 mins
Ross McElwee

Beginning his career in his hometown of Charlotte, North Carolina, where he was a studio cameraman for local evening news, housewife-helper shows and 'gospel hour' programmes broadcast by the local television station, Ross McElwee graduated from Massachusetts Institute of Technology, where he received an MS in film-making in a programme headed by documentarian Richard Leacock (*Jane*, 1963). Leacock was one of the pioneers of Direct Cinema, the American response to the cinéma-vérité school of documentary film-makers cultivated by Europeans such as Jean Rouch. The Direct Cinema approach dictated that events were objectively recorded without pre-planned direction or film-maker interference. After working as a freelance cameraman for D. A. Pennebaker, McElwee experimented with a more personal, autobiographical approach to non-fiction film-making.

Acknowledged as a grand epic of its kind, *Sherman's March* introduces an ironic perspective that makes explicit the extent to which the documentarist has knowingly become the subject in his own story. Michael Moore and Nick Broomfield – a self-confessed admirer of the film – are key practitioners of this approach; the proliferation of made-for-television video diaries its ugly conclusion.

An enormously charming and moving personal essay, *Sherman's March* originated when McElwee received a grant to make a documentary tracing American Civil War General William Tecumseh Sherman's devastating march through the American South and the as yet unhealed wounds of the civilian population. The pervading anxieties of the global politics of the 1980s and the impending threat of nuclear war made suitable parallels for Sherman's destructive trail. Abandoned by his girlfriend on the eve of filming, McElwee returned dejectedly to his family home in Charlotte with the intention of aborting the project. Encouraged, however, by his sister's promptings that he use his camera as a conversation piece to meet women, McElwee adopted the unwieldy subtitle *A Meditation on the*

Possibility of Romantic Love in the South during an Era of Nuclear Weapons Proliferation and appropriated Sherman's conquering march for his own road journey in search of an understanding of Southern womanhood and a flickeringly vengeful quest for romantic fulfilment.

Though historical ironies are revealed about the feared general, such as the fact that he marched obsessed with a sense of failure following a series of disastrous business ventures, after the Leacock-narrated introduction Sherman only fleetingly appears as a metaphor for McElwee's own expedition and romantic misadventures. On his travels, McElwee turns his camera on several invariably resilient women, including Mary, a former girlfriend; Pat, an aspiring actress whose dreams centre on meeting Burt Reynolds (a model of the larger-than-life masculinity McElwee feels himself to lack); Claudia, a survivalist; Jackie, a nuclear campaigner; and Charleen, who advises him, 'This isn't art Ross. This is life.' Each responds differently to the attentions of the camera, with McElwee well aware of its intrusive nature. Towards the conclusion, McElwee steps out from behind the camera to be filmed by a third party. The moment, which occurs while addressing a statue at the site of Sherman's final victory, is illustrative of the film's disregard for illusion and its willingness to engage with and discuss its own status as a movie.

Narrated by McElwee in a frequently hilarious and self-mocking voiceover that drew comparison with Woody Allen, the film's intelligence and pioneering interest in structure and representation are slightly disguised and tempered by its comic tone. At the beginning of the film, McElwee appears dressed as the pillaging Sherman but is reduced to addressing his camera in a barely audible whisper so as to not wake his sleeping parents. A personal-quest road movie reminiscent in structure of Jim Jarmusch's *Broken Flowers* (2005), *Sherman's March* spawned *Time Indefinite* (1994), a sequel in which McElwee documents his awkward shift into adulthood, marriage and the death of his father.

Dir: Ross McElwee; **Prod**: Ross McElwee; **Scr**: Ross McElwee; **DOP**: Ross McElwee; **Edit**: Ross McElwee; **Score**: Uncredited; **Principal Cast**: Ross McElwee.

Sideways
US, 2004 – 126 mins
Alexander Payne

An insightful dissection of American social mores from director Alexander
Payne, *Sideways* was among the most critically acclaimed films of its
year. Securing five Academy Award nominations, including Best Picture
and Best Direction, the picture surprisingly triumphed only in the Best
Adapted Screenplay category. A thoughtful and ultimately quietly
profound buddy road movie that deals with tarnished dreams and

College buddies of the increasingly distant variety, Jack (Thomas Haden Church, left) and
Miles (Paul Giamatti) nearing the end of an eventful journey

receding friendship, the film navigates a fertile middle ground between the director's acerbically funny *Election* (1999) and Payne's previous road movie trading in agonised souls, the more overtly bleak *About Schmidt* (2002).

Miles (Giamatti) and Jack (Church) are college buddies of the increasingly distant variety. With his classic all-American looks, Jack's once promising acting career has descended from a central role in a now defunct daytime soap to a radio voiceover 'artiste'. Resigned to the inevitable, Jack accepts a lucrative executive position in a company owned by his girlfriend's father; marriage is the trade-off. An oenophile and failed novelist whose moody introspection and lack of confidence around women make him the antithesis of Jack, Miles organises a pre-wedding trip from Los Angeles to the Californian wine region. His plans to cultivate his pal's palette are quickly sidelined by Jack's desperation for a last fling with the free-spirited Stephanie (Oh), and his attempts to set Miles up with an equally grape-savvy waitress, Maya (Madsen).

Alongside Payne and regular writing partner Jim Taylor's humane and nuanced adaptation of Rex Rickett's novel, the kernel of this picaresque analysis of mid-life crises is the quartet of assured lead performances. A master at portraying tortured self-loathing and frustration (witness his turn as Harvey Pekar in *American Splendor*, 2003), Giamatti excels here. The most self-aware of the anti-heroes Payne has explored with varying degrees of compassion in his four features to date, Giamatti's skill as Miles is to make what in less sure hands could have been an excruciatingly bitter and self-pitying character engaging and, in the closing acceptance of hope as the prospect of a relationship with Maya flickers, ultimately rather heroic. Miles' humanity also seeps through in a scene in which he and Maya, played with warmth and intelligence by Madsen, take turns explaining their love of wine.

Wine is undoubtedly idealised as a byword for culture and conviviality in *Sideways*, but Payne and Taylor also have a keen ear and eye for the snobbery and pretentiousness it generates. This is perhaps most evident in Miles' loathing of Merlot and also in an excruciating, but nonetheless hilarious, wine tasting where Miles' request for a top-up from the seasoned server is met with a disdainful 'Sir, this is not a bar'. Meanwhile, Church, whose CV previous to *Sideways* eerily echoes that of the character he plays, is a revelation, deliciously deadpanning as the fading Casanova whose 'I'm going to get laid before I get married' becomes a personal mantra on this scenic and enjoyable trip through sun-kissed vineyards and along Northern California's rural highways. The film also features one of the most hilarious car crashes in the history of road movies, Miles' prized if ageing Saab convertible colliding with a tree as Jack fights to concoct an alibi to throw his wife-to-be off his musky scent.

Dir: Alexander Payne; **Prod**: Michael London; **Scr**: Alexander Payne, Jim Taylor; **DOP**: Phedon Papamichael; **Edit**: Kevin Tent; **Score**: Rolfe Kent; **Principal Cast**: Paul Giamatti, Thomas Haden Church, Virginia Madsen, Sandra Oh.

Simple Men
UK/US, 1992 – 105 mins
Hal Hartley

The last of Hartley's Long Island pictures – though it was actually filmed in Texas – *Simple Men* gave evidence of the director's desire to explore new thematic, stylistic and geographical terrain while retaining many of the characteristics that had rendered *The Unbelievable Truth* (1989) and *Trust* (1990) so endearing and original. Thus, there is the aphoristic, epigrammatic dialogue; the deadpan performances from repertory actors Robert Burke, Martin Donovan and Elina Löwensohn; crisp, highly stylised compositions courtesy of the ubiquitous Michael Spiller and a determinedly pared-down, minimalist and elliptical approach to narrative and editing.

Simple Men follows Bill McCabe (Burke), an unlucky-in-love, small-time career criminal who is perpetually on the run, and brother Dennis (Sage), an overly serious student, as they embark on a road trip to track down their father. A former baseball shortstop-turned-radical political activist, William McCabe (John Mackay) is readying to make good his escape from the country following his daring prison break-out. Aiding his flight are Kate (Sillas) and Elina (Löwensohn), two women with whom the brothers forge fraught attractions.

A road movie with one flat tyre, *Simple Men* debunks road-movie romance and mythology to reveal that 'There is no such thing as adventure. There's no such thing as romance. There's only trouble and desire.' Other familiar road-movie tropes the film explores through its outsiders on-the-run scenario include the journey towards self-fulfilment, familial dysfunction and the rancour and rumour associated with small-town mentality. All signs point to the need for escape, but it is a route that is frequently frustrated. As with the director's later *Amateur* (1994), the film largely uses the foundations of an established genre to continue Hartley's exploration of the class-versus-culture dichotomy and his emphasis on the stupidity of men, the superior intellect of women and the ways in which men objectify and 'seek to reconcile their various needs in them' (Fuller 1992, p. xi).

Made for $2 million, a sizeable increase from the director's previous, micro-budget features, one of the obvious benefits of the availability of increased funds was increased camera movement. Though still largely defined by its characteristic tableaux-like compositions, the film does make various gestures towards depicting mobility, not least through a number of tracking shots of the brothers en route. The most impressive of these involves their hasty retreat from a small town where they have managed to incur the wrath of a local nun. The escape is made on a motorbike the pair have procured from one of the town's hapless denizens, a wretched, lovelorn loner whose own dreams have long since been dashed. It's instructive that the motorbike constantly breaks down and needs repair, a further metaphor for the impossibility of fulfilling the aspirations that travel and the open road seemingly offer.

Invariably compared to Godard, with whom he shares an interest in referencing popular culture (*Simple Men* contains a sequence in which Madonna's right to exploit her sexuality is discussed), Hartley makes a direct visual reference to *Bande à part* (1964) in a light musical interlude. This beguiling moment, in which the principal characters dance to a Sonic Youth track in a bar, is symptomatic of Hartley's playful irreverence and of the importance he places on the relationship between sound and image. This synergy has historically also played a key role in the development of the road movie, being used as a shorthand for the celebration of freedom, abandonment and mobility from *Easy Rider* (1969) onwards.

Dir: Hal Hartley; **Prod**: Ted Hope, Hal Hartley; **Scr**: Hal Hartley; **DOP**: Michael Spiller; **Edit**: Steve Hamilton; **Score**: Ned Rifle; **Principal Cast**: Robert Burke, William Sage, Karen Sillas, Elina Löwensohn, Martin Donovan.

Soft Top, Hard Shoulder
UK, 1992 – 95 mins
Stefan Schwartz

The likeable feature debut of Stefan Schwartz, *Soft Top, Hard Shoulder* offers an enjoyable take on Frank Capra's *It Happened One Night* (1934) by way of Bill Forsyth. Scripted by lead actor Peter Capaldi, the film adopts a number of the themes and concerns familiar to Forsyth's *That Sinking Feeling* (1980), *Gregory's Girl* (1981) and *Local Hero* (1981), the latter of which featured Capaldi. These include: employment crises, the impossibility of communication between the sexes, self-doubt and the contrasting of natural and rural environments. *Soft Top, Hard Shoulder* also shares Forsyth's laconic, offbeat and unshakeably romantic worldview.

Having failed to make it in London as a comic-book artist, Gavin Bellini (Capaldi) – an Italian-Glaswegian from an ice-cream dynasty – reluctantly yields to his uncle's demands that he return home for his dad's sixtieth birthday party; if he makes it, the uncle (Wilson) may give him a share of the family fortune. But as he heads north in his clapped-out Triumph convertible, Gavin meets countless obstacles. When the car breaks down, a hitcher, Yvonne (Collins), helps to get it going, but Gavin soon tires of her talkative company. Worse, he loses his wallet, and their progress becomes ever slower. Will Gavin reach the party on time? Can he and his feisty passenger put aside their seemingly irreconcilable differences?

Largely included here by virtue of it being one of relatively few British road movies, and one that errs towards happiness rather than gloomy, existential introspection, Schwartz's admittedly modest work does boast some striking cinematography and kinetic travelling shots. These are perhaps most effectively utilised in terms of emphasising the beauty of the Scottish countryside, as opposed to the dreary, constricting environs of London and the myriad frustrations of road travel. Bellini's clapped-out car, with all its quirks and foibles, becomes a character in itself and is the source of many of these frustrations.

Capaldi's script, a London Film Festival Audience Award winner, seems a little overly familiar with road-movie conventions (destination deadline: check; initially hostile but finally compatible travelling companions: check; improbable roadside scrapes and misadventures: check), but the interplay between the two leads is certainly deftly handled and quite beautifully played. Viewers that balk at the film's romantic denouement may be interested to know that Capaldi and Collins would later marry. Karl Golden's *The Honeymooners* (2003) mined a similar terrain, relocating from Scotland to Ireland's Donegal.

Dir: Stefan Schwartz; **Prod**: Richard Holmes; **Scr**: Peter Capaldi; **DOP**: Henry Braham; **Edit**: Derek Trigg; **Score**: Chris Rea; **Principal Cast**: Peter Capaldi, Elaine Collins, Richard Wilson, Frances Barber.

La strada (*The Road*)
Italy, 1954 – 104 mins
Federico Fellini

Considered one of the masterpieces of twentieth-century film-making
(though David Thomson (2002, p. 281) proves a dissenting voice,
labelling it 'desperately portentous') and nestling behind *La dolce vita*
(1960) and *Nights of Cabiria* (1957) as one of the numerous pinnacles of
Italian maestro Federico Fellini's illustrious career, *La strada* is a sad and
poignant remembrance of innocence lost and of the roads that each of
us must choose.

Sold by her impoverished mother to Zampano (Quinn), a brutish
fairground wrestler, waif-like Gelsomina (Masina) lives a life of drudgery
as his assistant. After taking to the road with a travelling circus, a
budding relationship with Il Matto/The Fool (Basehart), a gentle-natured,
tightrope-walking clown, offers a potential refuge from her master's
clutches. Trapped by her own servile nature, Gelsomina wavers, and
Zampano's volcanic temper erupts with tragic consequences.

Characteristically mingling elements of biography with metaphor and
symbolism, *La strada* also combines an easygoing charm with a far
harder-edged realism in the form of domestic violence and the
presentation of Italy's economically deprived and desolate decaying
towns. Though Quinn is a mite histrionic, Masina – Fellini's wife and
sometime muse – is astonishing in the central role, her performance and
the evocative Nino Rota score and Otello Martelli's ravishing photography
combining to make the film a very attractive proposition to the American
Academy voters, who bestowed on it the honour of becoming the
winner of the first official Academy Award for Best Foreign-Language
Film.

Recalling American road movies set in the Depression era for its
focus on Gelsomina's poverty as a catalyst for mobility, the film then
meanders from this theme, becoming more concerned with its central
character's emotional and spiritual alienation and pursuit of creativity. In

A profound influence on the American road movies of the late 1960s and 70s and one of the most striking films with a female protagonist (Giulietta Masina, left, pictured with Anthony Quinn), Federico Fellini's introspective *La strada*

this regard, *Driving Visions* author David Laderman argues that, in conjunction with Bergman's *Wild Strawberries* (1957), the influence of Fellini's film is seismic: 'Bergman and Fellini helped forge the modernist language and landscape that paves the way for the French New Wave, which, in turn, influences the road movie's New American Cinema' (Laderman 2002, p. 248). Though outwardly *La strada* little resembles the first American films of the late 1960s and early 70s, its reliance on a character whose journey narrative is predicated upon introspection and reflection, and whose passage through the landscape becomes 'An allegory of a lost soul seeking the meaning of life' (Laderman, ibid.), undoubtedly loomed large over film-makers such as Hopper, Hellman, Sarafian, Ashby *et al.*

As well as the effective use of travelling shots looking backward from the circus truck in which Gelsomina travels, Fellini also incorporates a series of on-road montage sequences and elaborate moving-camera shots to convey the barren and empty landscape through which the entertainers trek. These flourishes and lyrical camera sequences, which would become a prominent feature of Fellini's work, here brilliantly convey to the spectator of lives lived, very literally, on the road. Finally, the film is notable for being one of the earliest road movies with a female protagonist.

Dir: Federico Fellini; **Prod**: Carlo Ponti, Dino De Laurentis; **Scr**: Federico Fellini, Ennio Flaiano, Tullio Pinelli; **DOP**: Otello Martelli; **Edit**: Leo Cattozzo; **Score**: Nino Rota; **Principal Cast**: Giulietta Masina, Anthony Quinn, Richard Basehart, Aldo Silvani, Marcella Rovena.

The Straight Story
US, 1999 – 111 mins
David Lynch

For a director largely associated with sexual aberration and unrestrained violence, David Lynch seems to offer an uncharacteristically straightforward approach to an engaging true-life tale of an elderly man's journey to reconcile with his brother.

Ailing Alvin Straight (Farnsworth), a stubborn seventy-three-year-old widower who lives with his adult daughter Rose (Spacek), suffers a bad fall and is informed by his doctor that he needs to take better care of himself, but Alvin shows little sign of mending his ways. Rose learns that Alvin's estranged older brother Lyle has had a stroke. Despite Rose's warnings and the incredulity of his fellow townspeople, Alvin is determined to travel from Laurens, Iowa, to Lyle's home in Mt Zion, Wisconsin, and try to patch up their ancient quarrel – using an idiosyncratic means of transport: a motor-driven lawnmower. On his slow chug to Wisconsin, Alvin meets and befriends a variety of people, including coach tourists; a pregnant teenage runaway; a woman whose daily commute to work invariably involves crashing into and killing deer; volunteer fire-fighters; a generous family who allow him to live in their garden while his lawnmower is being repaired by bickering identical-twin mechanics; a World War II veteran with whom Alvin shares anguished memories of combat; and a hospitable priest. At long last, Alvin reaches the ramshackle wooden house where Lyle (Dean Stanton) lives. The two old men sit together on the porch, largely wordless though seemingly deeply moved by their long-deferred reunion.

A project that evolved from Lynch's longtime collaborator Mary Sweeney, who bought the rights to the story of Alvin Straight in 1998, and for the final script retained the names of the real-life characters, the film's title is, of course, a play on words. The surname of the central protagonist, and also a playful reference to the seemingly linear narrative that apparently contrasts with the labyrinthine structure of other Lynch

works, the film is more Lynchian and less clear-cut than initially appears. The director gathers together the majority of his creative team, including costume designer Patricia Morris, composer Angelo Badalamenti, set designer Jack Fisk and cinematographer Freddie Francis (out-ageing Alvin Straight at the time of his journey), and though Lynch stays fairly close to the truth, dramatising the story with relatively few twists and turns and a residual revelation of the past, he somewhat enigmatically declines to reveal the cause of the quarrel. Alvin simply comments, 'Anger, vanity, you mix that with alcohol, you got two brothers that haven't spoken in ten years.'

Taking in the digressions and eccentric character interludes that are common to the road movie, including an early mechanical breakdown, necessitating the purchase of a 1966 John Deere machine in a scene that emphasises the mostly benevolent universe in which the film unfolds, Lynch also playfully incorporates the genre's visual aesthetic. Point-of-view shots from Straight's machine – especially effective and pulse-quickening when the brakes fail on an incline – are juxtaposed with the film's many aerial shots to give a sense of Straight making his slow but steady progress through the picturesque autumn landscapes. As well as flashes of comic brio to suggest the absurdity of Straight's endeavour, including a dramatic pan up into the clouds, which then swiftly descends again to reveal that Straight has only travelled a few yards, Lynch also emphasises the danger, the film's interest in scale being most effective when contrasting Straight's dinky tractor/trailer combo with the monstrous juggernauts that intermittently thunder past him.

Alongside Farnsworth's extraordinary performance (the actor's last, his death coming barely a year after the film's release) and the simmering family feud, it is the sheer scale of the journey that lends the film its tremendous poignancy. This is beautifully underplayed in the final sequence, Lyle simply commenting, 'You came all this way just to see

(*Opposite page*) Alvin Straight (Richard Farnsworth) on his way to visit his brother in David Lynch's *The Straight Story*

me', before the two men become siblings again, taking their places on the porch as Lynch, returning to the film's opening image and recurring motif, cuts to the starry sky of their childhood.

Dir: David Lynch; **Prod**: Alain Sarde, Mary Sweeney, Neal Edelstein; **Scr**: John Roach, Mary Sweeney; **DOP**: Freddie Francis; **Edit**: Mary Sweeney; **Score**: Angelo Badalamenti; **Principal Cast**: Richard Farnsworth, Sissy Spacek, Everett McGill, John Farley, Harry Dean Stanton.

Stranger Than Paradise
US/West Germany, 1984 – 89 mins
Jim Jarmusch

One of American independent cinema's defining moments, *Stranger Than Paradise* was responsible for pushing many new films and directors into production and for auguring what John Pierson perceives as a halcyon period (1984–94) in intelligent, esoteric but accessible low-budget movies. Jarmusch's second film after 1982's disappointing *Permanent Vacation* also coined a laconic, minimalist visual style and general sensibility in part informed by the works of Bresson, Ozu and Rivette but also borrowing from avant-garde and punk-rock aesthetics. Adding a European perspective to the existentialist American road movies of the 1970s, the film revisits road-movie staples such as travel and mobility as wish fulfilment and escape, and ennui inducing on-road aimlessness. Though it 'possesses little of the driving fetishism of most road movies, its detached, blasé, nonchalant interest in driving is characteristic of the emergent postmodern road movie, where driving is treated as a kind of joke' (Laderman 2002, p. 145).

Originating as a thirty-minute short shot on leftover stock donated by Wim Wenders following *The State of Things* (1982), the film was screened on portable projectors at clubs throughout New York to attract completion finance. The expanded feature explores the effects of an unwanted visit from a Hungarian cousin (Balint) on detached, taciturn New Yorker Willie (Lurie) and his gambling buddy Eddie (Edson). Offering a perceptive look at exile, affectionately mocked solitude and the possibilities of communication beyond cultural differences, Jarmusch also studies the effects of geography on human emotions, tracking the trio as they travel by car from New York, to snowy Cleveland (a journey for which the catalyst is a small-time crime) and then on to an out-of-season Florida. Shots of driving per se are minimised, though the language of the genre is adhered to in a series of frontal shots in which the characters are shown through their car windscreen. However, as the film opens with shots of Eva watching a plane land, 'the theme of travel and migration is built into its fundamental framework' (Laderman 2002, p. 146).

Made for just $110,000, *Stranger Than Paradise* was set apart by Tom DiCillo's elegant black-and-white photography and its part poignant, part deadpan minimalism that serves to magnify the import of every gesture and wry comment. Divided into three chapters – 'The New World', 'One year later' and 'Paradise' – the film displays a discrete approach to style and grammar, with no dissolves, cuts or wipes in the long, uninterrupted stationary scenes with which the film proceeds. A film in which little is resolved – it concludes with Willie flying to Hungary, mistakenly believing that Eva has returned there – the film's philosophy, and that of the road movies that followed it, can be summed up by Eddie's words on arriving in Cleveland: 'when you come to some place new, everything looks the same'.

With *Stranger Than Paradise*, Jarmusch became the first American to win the Camera d'Or for best first feature at Cannes. The film also exerted a seismic influence on the way American independent films were made, distributed and marketed, with the poster audaciously proclaiming 'a new American film by Jim Jarmusch'. Moreover, it began Jarmusch's interest in the road movie, subsequently revised, with characteristic understatement, in subsequent works such as *Mystery Train* (1989), *Night on Earth* (1991), *Dead Man* (1995) and more explicitly in *Broken Flowers* (2005).

Dir: Jim Jarmusch; **Prod**: Sara Driver; **Scr**: Jim Jarmusch; **DOP**: Tom DiCillo; **Edit**: Jim Jarmusch, Melody London; **Score**: John Lurie; **Principal Cast**: John Lurie, Richard Edson, Eszter Balint, Cecillia Stark.

The Sugarland Express
US, 1974 – 110 mins
Steven Spielberg

Loosely based on a 1969 incident involving Bobby and Ila Faye Dent's flight from the Texas State Police following their attempts to keep their family together by any means necessary, Steven Spielberg's first theatrical feature and second road movie following the made-for-television *Duel* (1972) provides a 'benchmark example of the highway chase, that most ubiquitous of road movie sub-strata' (Williams 1982, p. 101).

Opening in iconic road-movie fashion with a shot of multiple interstate signs accompanying a drifter picking through the carcass of an abandoned automobile, *The Sugarland Express* finds recently released jailbird Lou Jean Poplin (Hawn) visiting her obedient convict husband Clovis (Atherton) at a Texan pre-release correctional facility. Determined not to lose their son Langsten to the authorities, Lou Jean coerces a reluctant Clovis into breaking out to participate in a hair-brained scheme to travel to Sugarland, Texas, to kidnap Langsten from his foster parents. Plans go awry from the outset, and with their freshly acquired hostage, Officer Slide (Sacks), in tow, the fugitives head across the vast open plains to their destination, pursued by a flotilla of patrol cars, TV cameras and general sightseers. Even though Slide gradually sympathises with the nervy, adolescent Poplin's plight, the Law, presided over by the gruff Capt Tanner (Johnson), is hell-bent on capturing its outlaw quarry.

Beautifully shot by Vilmos Zsigmond and possessing a majestic sense of scope, space and mood, the film shares innumerable similarities with Malick's *Badlands* (1973). Perhaps most notable is a mutual interest in the increasingly dominant role of the media in the shaping of American life, notions of heroism, the loss of innocence and the capturing of an American society extensively enthralled by commercialisation. *The Sugarland Express* ostensibly seems a more conservative and conventional piece, anticipating the director's subsequent career in its emphasis on the family unit and respect for the law, the sympathetic portrayal of cops foreshadowing 1991's *Thelma & Louise*.

The cloying sentimentality that would later become insufferable in Spielberg's work is here largely kept at bay despite the Poplins' wide-eyed wonderment. The killing of Clovis by a police marksman delivers a particular sucker punch for any audience seduced into believing that the righteousness of the protagonists' cause renders them invincible, the film also making clear that the Poplins are 'wrongheaded in their quest to reclaim parental responsibility' (Gilbey 2003, p. 63). We must also pay heed to Spielberg's own claim during publicity for the film that Hawn is the real villain of the piece. Denounced in a radio bulletin by her father as 'no good', from the start Lou Jean is a screw-up whose selfishness and skewed perceptions of paternity get her husband killed. A brilliant deconstruction of Hawn's vivacious and endearing star persona, *The Sugarland Express*, with its de rigueur unhappy 1970s ending, finds Spielberg doing uncharacteristically well in the cynicism stakes.

Extremely assured on a technical level, Spielberg's background on made-for-TV fare serves him well as he expertly navigates the logistical demands of the multi-vehicle-pursuit aspect of the narrative. Working from an extremely detailed, Cannes prize-winning script from Barwood and Robbins originally entitled *Carte Blanche*, Spielberg meticulously pre-planned every shot, even having a graphic artist sketch the film in its entirety so that he could obtain a bird's-eye view of it as it progressed from one police car to fifty. Equally accomplished is Spielberg's incorporation of a sequence from a *Road Runner* cartoon to provide a chilling moment of illumination as it dawns on the captivated Clovis that

(*Opposite page*) Road-movie iconography: Goldie Hawn as Lou Jean Poplin in Steven Spielberg's *The Sugarland Express*

in reality any pain suffered is real. Suddenly, his journey's end becomes all too clear to him.

Dir: Steven Spielberg; **Prod**: David Brown, Richard D. Zanuck; **Scr**: Hal Barwood, Matthew Robbins from a story by Steven Spielberg; **DOP**: Vilmos Zsigmond; **Edit**: Edward M. Abroms, Verna Fields; **Score**: John Williams; **Principal Cast**: Goldie Hawn, William Atherton, Ben Johnson, Michael Sacks.

Sullivan's Travels
US, 1941 – 91 mins
Preston Sturges

An irresistible tale of a Hollywood hotshot bent on making an arthouse epic, Sturges' *Sullivan's Travels* is the most ambitious of the director's 1940s classics and one of the finest films about the movies ever made. Blending uproarious comedy and grim tragedy to almost Shakespearean effect, it is also a prime example of a road movie in which journeying and mobility are used to express a rebellious response to the social crisis of the American Depression.

In one of his best roles, McCrea plays John L. Sullivan, Hollywood's top director of lightweight hits. Fed up with directing profitable comedies like *Ants in Your Plants of 1939*, Sullivan is consumed with the desire to make a serious social statement with the breadline picture *Oh, Brother,*

Momentarily forgetting their woes, convicts experience the joy of a Disney cartoon in Preston Sturges' *Sullivan's Travels*, a road movie in which journeying and mobility is used to express a rebellious response to the social crisis of the American Depression

Where Art Thou?. Unable to function in the rarefied atmosphere of Hollywood, Sullivan decides to hit the road disguised as a tramp and touch base with the 'real' people of America. But Sullivan's horrified studio transforms his odyssey into a publicity stunt, providing the would-be nomad with a luxury van, complete with butler and valet. Advised by his servants that the poor resent having the rich intrude upon them, Sullivan escapes his entourage and continues his travels incognito, where he meets The Girl (Lake), a down-on-her-luck actress. Returning to Hollywood riddled with bleeding-heart fervour, Sullivan heads to the rail yards to hand out ten thousand dollars to the needy. Fate intervenes, and Sullivan is cold-cocked by a tramp, who steals his clothes and ID. When the tramp is run over by a speeding train, the world at large is convinced that the great John L. Sullivan is dead. Meanwhile, the dazed Sullivan, dressed like a bum with no identification on his person, is arrested and put to work on a brutal Southern chain gang, where he realises that the world values laughter more than social realism.

Made while Sturges was at the height of his commercial and satirical powers, the choice of a misguided film director as the main character has led many to assume that the film has an autobiographical slant, with Sturges making a case for Hollywood escapism while criticising the liberal solemnities of 'issue' pictures. One of the film's standout sequences, a Thomas Hardyesque moment in which a bunch of hardened convicts momentarily forget their misery by enjoying a Disney cartoon, is often cited as evidence in this regard. But the film, a bravura mix of tone and genres taking in melodrama, musical, slapstick, farce, chain-gang drama, travelogue and even film noir (the DOP John F. Seitz would go on to shoot *Double Indemnity*, 1944, and *Sunset Boulevard*, 1950), also seems to suggest that comedy and serious drama – and in its latter sequences including *Sullivan's Travels* is quite astonishingly brutal – can co-exist quite happily after all.

Like Billy Wilder, Sturges was not averse to biting the hand that fed him, and the pithy script, especially enjoyable in the earlier, more dialogue-driven sequences that feature some classic exchanges between

Sullivan and his Hollywood producers (Warwick and Hall), rarely misses its target, delightedly poking fun at the absurd and shallow frothiness of Hollywood hedonism and the posturing of guilt-ridden artistes. A film whose relevance and power has rarely dimmed, it was lent added currency by the Coen Brothers' engaging nod to Sturges' vision with their own Deep South Depression-era semi-musical road comedy, *O' Brother, Where Art Thou?* (2000).

Dir: Preston Sturges; **Prod**: Paul Jones; **Scr**: Preston Sturges; **DOP**: John F. Seitz; **Edit**: Stuart Gilmore; **Score**: Leo Shuken, Charles Bradshaw; **Principal Cast**: Joel McCrea, Veronica Lake, Robert Warwick, Porter Hall, William Demarest, Franklin Pangborn.

The Sure Thing
US, 1985 – 94 mins
Rob Reiner

A witty, 1980s teen variation on *It Happened One Night* (1934), the affectionately regarded *The Sure Thing* was an early success for Capra-loving director Rob Reiner. The film also set Cusack, who was the same age as the eighteen-year-old character he portrays, on the road to an estimable career in which he has excelled at playing doubting, somewhat sour-faced cynics who nonetheless win over and engage audience sympathies.

Walter 'Gib' Gibson (Cusack) is a self-obsessed college freshman at an East Coast school who finds himself floundering in a sea of confusion and despair during his first semester. Unsurprisingly, he jumps at the chance to join his buddy Lance (Edwards) in Los Angeles for a Christmas break, especially after Lance vows to set Gibson up with a 'sure thing' (Nicolette Sheridan), a voluptuous, bikini-clad blonde described as being 'just released from parochial school and in her experimental phase'. But getting to California involves having to take a road trip with priggish co-ed Allison (Zuniga), who is venturing to LA to join her wealthy fiancé. The two despise each other on sight, and memorably have to begin their 3,000-mile journey with show-tune-loving preppies played by Tim Robbins and Lisa Jane Persky. However, as the kilometres rack up, Gib and Allison begin to realise that sometimes love can spring from unexpected sources.

Retrospectively viewed as a dry run for *When Harry Met Sally* (1989), *The Sure Thing* gets good mileage from the incompatible travelling companions format, its initial in-car claustrophobia and jarring of personalities made all the more palpable by having to endure listening to 'The Age of Aquarius' at high volume. Sartre claimed that hell is other people; he could just as correctly have asserted that it is other people's records. As the film progresses, the show tunes give way to a soundtrack of familiar 1980s hits such as Wang Chung's 'Dancehall Days' and Peter

Wolf's 'Lights Out'. Dreadful at the time, their awfulness has since been dulled by the cosy patina of nostalgia. There is a wistfulness, too, regarding the initial year of college life, when education takes a firm back seat to pursuing romantic fulfilment and coming up with smart one-liners.

Sharply written by Steven L. Bloom and Jonathan Roberts, the film has a ready supply of snappy banter, the writers arming Cusack with a series of withering put-downs. 'Have you ever considered a sexual encounter so intense it could conceivably change your political views?' is just one quotable line. Cusack approaches customary perfection in the lead role, wearing a trademark wry smile as he charmingly clowns through such incidents as plunging fully clothed into a swimming pool to get Zuniga's attention, or pretending to be an insane hitchhiker to scare off a horny truck driver. One of the few films of its kind that is actually as good as you remember, it's a light-hearted journey but enjoyable all the same.

Dir: Rob Reiner; **Prod**: Roger Birnbaum; **Scr**: Steven L. Bloom, Jonathan Roberts; **DOP**: Robert Elswit; **Edit**: Robert Leighton; **Score**: Tom Scott; **Principal Cast**: John Cusack, Daphne Zuniga, Boyd Gaines, Anthony Edwards, Tim Robbins, Lisa Jane Persky.

Thelma & Louise
US, 1991 – 129 mins
Ridley Scott

Originally viewed as offering a radical revision of the traditionally male road movie in its feminist skew and progressive sexual politics, the undeniably influential *Thelma & Louise* is a more complex proposition. 'Ostensibly presenting women without men' (Dick 1997, p. 22) and painting a picture of a repressive and patronising patriarchal society in which men offer homilies such as 'Talk nice to her when she calls, women love that shit', the film ultimately punishes its female protagonists' quest for freedom and equality, offering simplistic, kneejerk reactions to the ideologies it seeks to address.

Leaving her tyrannical husband Daryl (McDonald) a pre-made meal, Thelma (Davis) sets off with her friend Louise (Sarandon) for a forbidden weekend getaway. Louise also has problems in her domestic life, her boyfriend Jimmy (Madsen) displaying a maddening fear of commitment. Though the road trip starts out on a high, the pair's first stop sees them drinking and dancing at a rowdy bar. When Thelma is almost raped, Louise shoots the assailant dead. The carefree mood instantly evaporates and Louise, who makes veiled references to an incident in her own past, persuades Thelma that they need to go on the run and head for the sanctuary of Mexico. Growing into their newfound fugitive roles, the pair become bolder, robbing a convenience store, shooting up a leering driver's truck and locking a cop in his car boot after lecturing him about the need to respect women. Thelma finally 'learns what all the fuss is about' after a wild sexual encounter with a young criminal (Pitt). Pursued by a police officer (Keitel) sympathetic towards their plight, the pair motor towards the Grand Canyon and a fateful decision about their lives.

Blisteringly directed by Scott and performed with gusto and conviction by its two female leads (a young Pitt also catches the eye in a formative role), *Thelma & Louise* is in many ways superior genre fare. Making fine use of landscape in the voyage across the American heartland, Scott also displays an astute eye for the nuts and bolts of the genre. This ranges from the visual iconography, including the endlessly stretching dusty highways and the long, low tracking shots of Louise's aqua 1966 Thunderbird convertible (combining both, a publicity still featured the car travelling along an empty road flanked by rows of telephone poles), to the buddies-on-the-run/fugitive narrative structure. Scott also 'instigates the crosscutting format typical of many road movies', juxtaposing the 'stable, grounded and oppressive society they are leaving behind with their mobility away from it – with the effect of enhancing the thrill of such mobility' (Laderman 2002, p. 186).

Garnering debutant screenwriter Khouri a Best Original Screenplay Academy Award, the film's sexual politics and notions of freedom are compromised and in the final analysis confused. Rarely rising above stereotypical characterisation (the sensitive cop, the Neanderthal husband), most troubling is the insistence on punishing Thelma and Louise's each and every attempt at liberation. After the women let their hair down in a bar, one of them is almost raped, and when Thelma finally experiences sexual gratification at the hands of Pitt's young buck, she is immediately robbed. Dick highlights the film's puritanical streak: 'whenever Thelma has fun with men, something terrible happens' (Dick 1997, p. 22).

The ambivalent and self-consciously provocative denouement has been a subject of endless debate. The two women decide to 'Keep on going', driving off the edge of the Grand Canyon in slow motion to elude capture from the pursuing hordes of cops, boyfriends, husbands and lovers. An affirmation of female solidarity and self-empowerment (though it is also worth noting that the power Thelma and Louise accumulate has much to do with their mastering of handguns)? Or a powerful re-enforcement of what happens to women who refuse to know their place?

Dir: Ridley Scott; **Prod**: Ridley Scott, Mimi Polk; **Scr**: Callie Khouri; **DOP**: Adrian Biddle; **Edit**: Thom Noble; **Score**: Hans Zimmer; **Principal Cast**: Susan Sarandon, Geena Davis, Harvey Keitel, Brad Pitt, Michael Madsen, Christopher McDonald.

(*Next page*) Cars and girls: Thelma (Geena Davis, left) and Louise (Susan Sarandon) in Ridley Scott's Callie Khouri-scripted *Thelma & Louise*, a road movie with a feminist skew

Thieves Like Us
US, 1973 – 123 mins
Robert Altman

Adapted from the same 1937 Edward Anderson novel as Nicholas Ray's *They Live by Night* (1949), Robert Altman's *Thieves Like Us* emerged during a remarkably productive five-year period for the idiosyncratic director. Beginning with *M*A*S*H* (1970) and ending with *Nashville* (1975), Altman worked in a number of genres, producing in a short time span a body of work that arguably remains unequalled in modern American cinema. A melancholic account of doomed outlaws in love that found itself on cinema screens during the same twelve months as Malick's *Badlands* (1973) and Spielberg's *The Sugarland Express* (1974), the film resides alongside *Nashville* and the similarly revisionist and lovelorn *McCabe and Mrs Miller* (1970) at the pinnacle of Altman's career.

Depression-era criminals T-Dub (Remsen), Chicamaw (Schuck) and Bowie (Carradine) band together to rob banks after escaping from a prison farm. Hiding out with Dee Mobley (Skerritt) and Keechie (Duvall), and then with T-Dub's in-law Mattie (Fletcher), between bank jobs, the three crooks are a loyal group, but increasingly sensational news accounts of their bloodless robberies force them to split up before their next crime. After a car accident, Chicamaw leaves the injured Bowie in Keechie's care and love blossoms between the two naïfs, compelling Bowie to find a way to balance his bond to Keechie with his loyalty to his friends. On the run and with the law closing in, the pair conspire to flee to Mexico but soon discover that their need to survive is ultimately compromised by the finite honour among thieves.

Sharing a number of obvious similarities with *Bonnie and Clyde* (1967), not least its period setting and interest in a romantic union between two misfits that is doomed to failure, *Thieves Like Us* eschews myth-making and stylised shoot-outs and car chases to show the unglamorous life that was an outlaw's lot. Working with the esteemed

French cinematographer Jean Boffety, the camera takes an observational stance, highlighting place and emotion through the beautiful rendering of the verdant greens and browns of the delta and the more earthy tones of the ramshackle, rain-drenched, dirt-poor Southern towns (reminiscent Walker Evans' photographs). The typically innovative sound design brings the era fabulously to life, snatches of 1930s radio shows, news reports and political speeches brilliantly functioning in lieu of a score. Playful at times, the use of sound and the frequently clownish antics of T-Dub also hint at the more gentle and wistful air that underpins the film's fatalistic exterior.

Drawing from what would become a loyal and long-standing repertory of stock players, Altman, facilitated by co-writers Calder Willingham and Joan Tewkesbury (who cameos), coaxes particularly endearing and affecting performances from Carradine and Duvall as the Coca-Cola-loving young innocents from the wrong side of the tracks. Duvall, particularly, stands out in the film's final scene. Pregnant and alone after Bowie has been betrayed and gunned down, Keechie boards a train unsure of its destination. Asked if she might be heading to Fort Worth, she replies, quite simply, 'I guess so'.

Not for the first or the last time, Altman found that his films were out of kilter with American audiences, *Thieves Like Us* making the most minimal of impressions on the box office. A haunting and unsentimental work that extends its characters compassion but rarely pity, it is another milestone moment in a remarkable career.

Dir: Robert Altman; **Prod**: Jerry Bick; **Scr**: Calder Willingham, Joan Tewkesbury, Robert Altman; **DOP**: Jean Boffety; **Edit**: Lou Lombardo; **Score**: N/A; **Principal Cast**: Keith Carradine, Shelley Duvall, John Schuck, Bert Remsen, Louise Fletcher, Tom Skerritt.

Thunder Road
US, 1958 – 92 mins
Arthur Ripley

Directed by a personally selected Arthur Ripley, whose preceding feature film, twelve years earlier, had been the eerie Cornell Woolrich-based thriller *The Chase*, and taken from a story provided by its executive producer and star Robert Mitchum, *Thunder Road* is the definitive moonshine bootlegging drama. Featuring a quintessential performance, it is also, as Mitchum biographer points out, the film closest to the star's heart:

> From the sympathetic subject matter to the alienated, outside-the-law hero who feels without a home even in his mother's kitchen, the glimpses of a close yet dysfunctional family, the film's religious belief in rugged individualism, the obsession with the Deep South, the fetish for high-speed cars, liquor, lonely open roads and an all-night life, the pessimistic, fatalistic perspective that harkened back to his ten years in the noir trenches – here was Mitchum's ultimate cinematic statement, his personal vision of life transposed into lurid, downbeat, entertainment. (Server 2001, p. 331)

A magnetic Mitchum plays Lucas Doolin, who has returned from duty in Korea to rural North Carolina where his father Vernon (Bardette) has continued their family business of illegally making and distributing alcohol. Transporting the booze to various states (mostly Memphis) in 'tankers' (cars that have been modified so that the gas tank can carry booze), Doolin is pursued by the authorities but uses his driving skills and canny know-how to outwit them. Doolin's younger brother, Robin (Mitchum's son James), is a mechanic who fixes the car but grudgingly

(*Opposite page*) Robert Mitchum and son James (right) in *Thunder Road*, one of Mitchum's most personal works and a paean to the American South

promises their mother (Francis Koon) that he'll otherwise never participate in the family business. Even though Lucas' success has led to a higher concentration of cops and Treasury Agents in the area, the real threat to his continued exploits comes from Carl Kogan (Aubuchon), a gangster determined to buy up or put out of business all the other bootleggers in the region.

Working in tandem with second-unit directors James Casey and Jack Lannan, and second unit photographer Karl Malkames, Ripley whips the action along at breakneck speed, peppering the film with a number of expertly executed chase sequences on Tennessee's dusty back roads. James Bond fans may well admire Doolin's specially modified 1950 Ford Coupe, with its quick-release whiskey tank in the trunk and primitive but effective switch-operated oil-spurting jets that derail pursuing lawmen.

A B-movie that became a sizeable success upon release, *Thunder Road* understandably acquired a special resonance in Mitchum's native South. The film in fact continued to generate annual five- and six-figure ticket sales from drive-ins on the border and in Southern states for twenty-five years after its original release, a factor that caused United Artists and its successor organisations to purposefully delay its release on home video until the end of the 1980s. As further evidence of the heart and soul Mitchum put into the film, the erstwhile crooner even recorded two songs for the picture, 'The Ballad of Thunder Road' and 'Whiporwil', but sadly neither made the final cut (though they did dent the pop charts). The inspiration for Bruce Springsteen's song of the same name, *Thunder Road*'s cult status is enhanced by the fact that Mitchum originally wanted Elvis Presley to play his brother. However, Colonel Parker's outrageous wage demands and prevarications chaffed with Mitchum's more straight-talking approach to business, and indeed to life.

Dir: Arthur Ripley; **Prod**: Robert Mitchum; **Scr**: James Atlee Phillips, Walter Wise; **DOP**: Alan Stensvold, David Ettenson; **Edit**: Harry Marker; **Score**: Jack Marshall; **Principal Cast**: Robert Mitchum, Gene Barry, Jacques Aubuchon, Keely Smith, Trevor Bardette.

Thunderbolt and Lightfoot
US, 1974 – 115 mins
Michael Cimino

Michael Cimino's first film as a director after penning *Silent Running* (1972) and the subsequent year's *Magnum Force* (in conjunction with John Milius), *Thunderbolt and Lightfoot* came to Cimino at the behest of star Clint Eastwood and was made under the aegis of his Malpaso production company. A road/buddy-movie fusion, the film also offers an offbeat and eccentric character study revolving around a quartet of misfits and their life of crime.

Opening, quite brilliantly, with retired thief John Doherty (Eastwood), nicknamed Thunderbolt because of his skill at cracking safes, having his cover as a preacher blown and pursued across wheat fields by a murderous ex-colleague, the film then pitches him alongside fast-living young drifter, Lightfoot (Bridges), who happens to be passing in his stolen sports car. Declining Lightfoot's offer of a partnership founded on a life of good times and crime, Thunderbolt is made to swiftly reverse his decision when the sadistic Red Leary (Kennedy) and the cretinous Goody (Lewis), two more vengeful associates, make their intentions clear. Thunderbolt and Lightfoot's plans to recover some stolen money from its resting place in an old schoolhouse go awry when it transpires that the building has made way for a more modern structure. Despite Red's intense loathing of his new, younger nemesis, the four thieves join forces, renting a house and working legitimate jobs while they plan a lucrative heist. With stakes so high, it's not too long before the code of honour among thieves begins to ebb, the rising to the fore of old scores threatening Lightfoot and Thunderbolt's burgeoning relationship.

A slight step-aside from his tough-guy Western persona and a gentle introduction to the comedy that would flourish with varying degrees of success in later Eastwood pictures, *Thunderbolt and Lightfoot* sees the iconic star giving one of the most relaxed and natural performances of his 1970s period. Playfully parodying the gangster couple on the lam of crime pictures such as *Bonnie and Clyde* (1967), the film features some delightful interplay between Eastwood and Bridges, who, as the wisecracking, cocksure young upstart whose mouth gets him into women's beds as much as it does into trouble, earned his second Best Supporting Actor Academy Award nomination. The relationship between the older, wiser man and his younger charge is a beguiling combination of the paternal and the sexual, the gay subtext perhaps most overt in the bristling jealousy the easy-on-the-eye Lightfoot inspires in Red. The largely ineffectual and weak Goody is a poor surrogate for Eastwood's potent safecracker, and the more time the quartet spend together, the higher the sexual tension rises.

A film in which car culture runs deep, Lightfoot's lifelong wish is to purchase a brand new Cadillac. The dream is realised at the conclusion, Thunderbolt at the wheel as Lightfoot slowly succumbs to a vicious beating dispensed by Red, leaving his companion alone once more on the open road. Cimino also presents a series of entertaining encounters with left-of-centre road-movie types. These include a couple of floozies (it was the 1970s), a credit-card heavy couple who appear to transport the contents of their wardrobe in the back of their car and, most notably, a deranged hick (it was the 1970s, and, of course, said hick is played by the estimable Bill McKinney [*Deliverance*, 1972]) who keeps rabbits in the trunk of his souped-up Dodge for the purposes of shooting.

Referencing *Vanishing Point* (1971) with its use of stunt choreographer (Gary Loftin) and closing title music ('Where Do We Go from Here?'), the film earned Cimino the keys to the Hollywood kingdom, leading to *The Deer Hunter* (1978) and the unjustly maligned *Heaven's Gate* (1980).

Dir: Michael Cimino; **Prod**: Robert Daley; **Scr**: Michael Cimino; **DOP**: Frank Stanley; **Edit**: Ferris Webster; **Score**: Dee Barton; **Principal Cast**: Clint Eastwood, Jeff Bridges, George Kennedy, Geoffrey Lewis, Catherine Bach, Gary Busey, Jack Dodson.

Two-Lane Blacktop
US, 1971 – 101 mins
Monte Hellman

A protégé of Roger Corman, Hellman's early pictures configure to the low-budget, genre knock-offs with which Corman made his name. However, though made at Corman's behest and shot back-to-back for a combined $150,000, Hellman's starkly original Westerns *Ride in the Whirlwind* (1965) and *The Shooting* (1966) display a less commercial and more cryptic, European sensibility. *Two-Lane Blacktop* advanced Hellman's wilfully esoteric approach and withdrawn visual style, replacing the Western genre template with that of the road movie to consider man's abject futility and mythical search for identity in a pessimistic, existentialist landscape of the kind more commonly found in the films of Antonioni and the literature of Sartre, Camus and Beckett.

Greenlit by Universal alongside Hopper's *The Last Movie* (1971) and Peter Fonda's *The Hired Hand* (1971), the $850,000 project was seen as an opportunity to capitalise on the chord that *Easy Rider* (1969) had struck with America's youth market. The omens were initially good: *Esquire* was so impressed by the Wurlitzer/Corry screenplay that it made the film its April 1971 cover, printed the script in its entirety and proclaimed the film, which they had yet to see, 'the movie of the year'. Though accorded a few positive endorsements by critics who admired director-editor Hellman's capturing of the contemporary mood of alienation without resorting to the visual clichés of drugs, sex and violence, *Two-Lane Blacktop* was largely marginalised by reviewers and public left cold by its wilfully inert, apathetic characters.

Opaque, with little investment in character or plot consequentiality, the film centres on two young car enthusiasts, The Driver (singer James Taylor) and The Mechanic (Beach Boy Wilson), who trek across the American Southwest in their finely tuned, primer-grey '55 Chevy occasionally competing in drag races to maintain the car's upkeep. Barely speaking, except when a discussion of the car necessitates (dialogue is pared down to the minimum and revolves around aphorisms such as 'you can never go fast enough'), the duo experience friction after allowing a girl (Bird) to enter their circle. At a gas station the trio encounter GTO (Oates), a middle-aged braggart who travels the highways in his Pontiac picking up hitchhikers and listening to loud music; in one of the more lucid moments he divulges that his job and family have 'fallen apart'. A challenge is suggested, a race over the two-lane blacktops of Oklahoma to Washington DC in which the victor will claim the loser's car. Wearing the 'thin guise of a racing film, this relatively superficial narrative context quickly evaporates, revealing an exploration of the meaning (lessness) of road travel' (Laderman 2002, p. 94) as gradually the race fizzles out and the nomadic participants lose first the girl – the only character who seems interested in exercising any control over her own destiny – to the attentions of a biker, and then interest altogether. GTO continues his aimless odyssey, while The Driver and The Mechanic take on one final symbolic challenge.

As the pair face down another drag driver, the revving of engines is replaced by industrial white noise as The Driver stares without emotion through his front windscreen. Shot from the back seat of the car from over The Driver's shoulder (Jack Deerson's photography is minimalist but effective throughout), the film slows as he starts to drive, before the celluloid flips out of the projector and ignites. Illustrating Hellman's disregard for convention, this remarkable image would act as a metaphor for the director's subsequent career as, unable to assimilate into the system, he returned to the fringes with the relentlessly bleak *Cockfighter* (1974). This notorious burning and fragmentation of the film frame has also come to be seen as condensing the spirit of the 1970s road movie to a single moment that effectively, if abstractly, communicates the pointlessness of travel in an America in which everyone is lost, endlessly searching, but unable to find themselves or each other. Subsequently attaining mythic status, *Two-Lane Blacktop* is now commonly considered a quintessential road movie, 1970s or otherwise, standing alongside *Five Easy Pieces* (1970) and *Vanishing Point* (1971) in its articulation of nihilistic drift.

Dir: Monte Hellman; **Prod**: Michael Laughlin; **Scr**: Rudolph Wurlitzer, Will Corry; **DOP**: Jack Deerson; **Edit**: Monte Hellman; **Score**: Billy James; **Principal Cast**: James Taylor, Warren Oates, Laurie Bird, Dennis Wilson.

Vagabonde (Sans toit ni loi)
France, 1985 – 106 mins
Agnès Varda

A subtly disturbing portrait of alienation and lost direction, *Vagabonde* opens with the death of its main character, the perpetual drifter Mona Bergeron (Bonnaire), and proceeds to piece together the events of her life until that fatal moment. Found frozen to death in a ditch, Mona is revealed as an inscrutable young woman from a good home with employable skills who chooses, quite simply, to drop out of society.

Varda tells Mona's story in a series of flashbacks and semi-documentary-style anecdotal interviews with the people who have known or crossed paths with her during the last few weeks of her life, including a trucker who Mona insulted by criticising his vehicle. Along the way, several missed opportunities for help and stability are revealed: a kind Turkish migrant worker who works in a vineyard, a house-sitter who envies her freedom and simple passion, and a kindly research professor who learns of Mona's dream to own a piece of land and become self-sufficient; this ambition is seemingly interchangeable with toiling as a caretaker in a large house. Given the opportunity to experience both, Mona simply walks away, seemingly resigned to accepting defeat at the hands of life's daily struggle.

Featuring a formidable and entirely unsentimental performance by Sandrine Bonnaire as the unlikeable and rather callous central enigma, Varda's audacious approach to character allows Mona to act as a mirror for the foibles, failings and prejudices of those around her, many of whom are played by non-professional actors. Though the director seems to suggest that modern culture has left people like Mona emotionally void, and that the notion of coasting through life as a free spirit is therefore farcical, the film's objectivity and refusal to offer straightforward answers render *Vagabonde* a tantalisingly ambiguous work. However one wishes to interpret the film, it undoubtedly offers a fascinating and complex glimpse into the human soul.

Matching Varda's audacious deconstruction of the storytelling process and her formally free take on reality is the film's spare poetic visual beauty. Betraying Varda's beginnings as a photographer and her instinctive awareness of detail, the film is elegantly framed and the mid-winter landscapes rendered cold, bleak and yet eerily beautiful. The winner of the prestigious Venice Golden Lion, *Vagabonde*'s employment of differing perspectives and the artistic use of the unpredicted (many of the 'interviews' have an improvised feel and begin mid-conversation) for artistic effect would forcefully recur in Varda's exceptional 2000 documentary *The Gleaners and I*. A look at those who survive on what other members of society discard, it is another road movie of sorts that would certainly, space allowing, have merited an entry of its own in this volume.

Dir: Agnès Varda; **Prod**: Oury Milshtein; **Scr**: Agnès Varda; **DOP**: Patrick Blossier; **Edit**: Agnès Varda; **Score**: Joanna Bruzdowicz; **Principal Cast**: Sandrine Bonnaire, Macha Méril, Yolande Moreau, Stéphane Freiss.

Les Valseuses (*Going Places*)
France, 1974 – 118 mins
Bertrand Blier

An enormous hit in its native France, *Les Valseuses* furthered the consideration of director Bertrand Blier as the French Buñuel. A bourgeois-baiting, anarchistic satire that is violent, sexually explicit and open to charges of misogyny, the film radically polarised critical opinion in France, attracting accusations of fascism while at the same time being celebrated as an escapist and radical referencing of popular culture.

Two petty criminals, Jean-Claude (Depardieu) and Pierrot (Dewaere), lead an anarchic lifestyle, drifting through the idyllic French countryside, stealing, fighting and always trying to stay one step ahead of the law. Sex is perhaps the activity to which they dedicate most of their attention, the film beginning with the pair molesting and robbing a middle-aged woman before being chased away by an angry mob. From there, the duo bounce from one *ménage à trois* to another, their conquests including a bored young hairdresser, Marie-Ange (Miou-Miou), who they ultimately kidnap. Adopting a freewheeling structure to deliberately mirror the protagonists' free-spirited, chaotic lifestyle and racy on-road adventures, the film takes a sharp turn into romantic outlaw territory when a death transforms Jean-Claude and Pierrot into genuine fugitives from the law. One of the pair's final conquests brings a degree of reflection, a middle-aged mystery woman, Jeanne (Moreau), who is fresh out of jail and apparently desperate to fuck. The encounter takes an unexpectedly tragic turn, leaving both men shaken and searching for the next chapter in their hedonistic odyssey.

Les Valseuses (French slang for testicles) arguably marked the moment when Depardieu became an international star and certainly forged his reputation for playing brutish if undeniably charismatic outcasts. Later revelations about the actor's own youth, in tandem with similar turns in fare such as *Buffet Froid* (1979, again directed by Blier, with whom Depardieu would work on numerous occasions), to many eyes blurred the distinction between the man and his movies. Whatever reservations one may have about the film and its attitude towards women, many of whom are shown as perfectly happy to be screwed, slapped around and subservient, one of its more engaging ingredients is the easygoing chemistry and interplay between Depardieu and Dewaere. Always animated, whether brawling, bantering or espousing their personal philosophies, the obvious bond between the two miscreants brings an undeniable homoeroticism to their frequent threesomes.

Apologists for the film view it not only as a radical critique of French society and its bourgeois conservatism, but take the aggression of the male characters as offering a reflection of masculinity in crisis, a crisis precipitated by rising unemployment and a subsequent sense of emasculation. This is perhaps overt in one not especially subtle moment in the film when a bullet narrowly misses one of the characters' testicles.

Dir: Bertrand Blier; **Prod**: Paul Claudon; **Scr**: Bertrand Blier, Philippe Dumarçay; **DOP**: Bruno Nyutten; **Edit**: Kénout Peltier; **Score**: Stéphane Grappelli; **Principal Cast**: Gérard Depardieu, Patrick Dewaere, Miou-Miou, Jeanne Moreau, Jacques Chailleux.

Vanishing Point
US, 1971 – 107 mins
Richard Sarafian

A vintage road movie that is considered to be one of the masterpieces of the genre, *Vanishing Point* is a symbolically charged work that bridges the gap between *Two-Lane Blacktop* (1971) and *Badlands* (1973), two other venerated American films of the 1970s. Combing the genre's quest and outlaw tendencies, Sarafian's film also reaches back to *Easy Rider* (1969) in its use of soundtrack music (a touch heavy-handed) and its suggestion of spirituality as an antidote to a prejudiced, uptight and hypocritical America.

In a role originally intended for George C. Scott, Newman plays Stanley Kowalski, an ex-marine and ex-racing car driver, who arrives in Denver with a car he's ferried from San Francisco. Kowalski informs his receiving agent that he wants to make the fifteen-hour drive back to San Francisco immediately and is given a supercharged Dodge for the trip. Stopping off to visit his drug dealer, Kowalski stocks up on amphetamines and strikes a seemingly impossible wager: that he won't make it back to San Francisco by three the following afternoon. If he does, the drugs are his for free. Screeching off, Kowalski is apprehended by the police but refuses to stop and a high-speed chase ensues. Incidents abound en route, including an attempted abduction by two honeymooning homosexuals (a somewhat crass reference to the counter-culture), a fierce spat with a Jaguar driver, a visit to a religious sect and the avoidance of a police roadblock with the aid of a Hell's Angel and his girlfriend. Kowalski's quest is commented on throughout by blind black DJ Super Soul (Little), who deifies the speedster on his local radio show as 'The last American to whom speed means freedom of the soul'.

One of the relatively few films of the genre in which a black character plays a positive role (and though the DJ is not actually in the car, he is very much presented as the driver's buddy or partner), Super Soul's turning of Kowalski into a minor but undoubtedly rebellious national hero leads to his vicious beating and the broadcasting of false information that will lead Kowalski into a police trap. We see this trap being erected at the film's beginning, evoking a sense of fatalism while also marking *Vanishing Point* out as radical in terms of its approach to temporal continuity. This technique of beginning with the end recalls the fatalistic and foregone conclusion of *Detour* (1945) and more generally corresponds to the complex backward narrative structure of film noir.

Sarafian injects plenty of road-movie iconography, including cars speeding through small towns, deserted highways and desert vistas, but distinguishes *Vanishing Point* from other road movies of the period through the use of flashbacks and references to Kowalski's past. In the European-influenced, modernist tradition, there are allusions to demons, including a failed relationship, but Kowalski's addiction to speed is never fully explained. The film is also significant in its presentation of perspective, crosscutting through a series of montages between Kowalski's frenzied drive and Super Soul's 'bird's-eye' view.

Operating as an allegory concerning the inevitable journey towards death (the film's vanishing point?) and capturing the disillusionment of the post-Woodstock generation, *Vanishing Point* also functions on a more primitive level as a cracking chase movie. Stunt director Cary Loftin executes a number of faultless set-pieces and ensures that the on-road action never lets up and the rendering of the actual mechanics of driving is infectious and equally dynamic. The film acquired further cultural currency when Primal Scream named their 1997 album after it.

Dir: Richard Sarafian; **Prod**: Norman Spencer; **Scr**: Guillermo Cain; **DOP**: John A. Alonzo; **Edit**: Stefan Arnsten; **Score**: Jimmy Brown; **Principal Cast**: Barry Newman, Cleavon Little, Dean Jagger, Victoria Medlin.

(*Next page*) Stanley Kowalski (Barry Newman) attempts to elude the cops and win his wager in *Vanishing Point*, widely considered one of the masterpieces of the genre

Vendredi soir
France, 2002 – 89 mins
Claire Denis

A lyrical and characteristically visual portrayal of a one-night stand from Claire Denis, one of contemporary French cinema's most consistently satisfying directors, *Vendredi soir*, an adaptation of the novel by Emmanuèle Bernheim, is a Gallic road movie that begins from a premise shared by Godard's *Weekend* (1967) and Cédric Kahn's *Red Lights* (2004). Unlike her male counterparts, however, Denis uses the metaphor of blocked roads and unmoving cars not as a symbol for the decline of western civilisation and the stagnation of contemporary society, but as a springboard to an altogether more optimistic and sensual journey of self-discovery.

Friday night, Paris. Laure (Lemercier) has finished packing and shuts the door of her apartment behind her. Early next morning, the removal men arrive to transport her belongings to her boyfriend's home, the pair having decided to cohabitate. Tonight, however, she is going out to dinner with good friends, but getting into her car remembers that traffic in the city has degenerated into chaos because of a public transport strike. It doesn't budge. But Laure feels good in her car, the only place she can call her own right now. It's nice and warm and she has music. Around her, people hoot their horns and get worked up. Everyone that is, except for one man, Jean (Lindon). He is standing in the street, in the glow of an illuminated sign, calm and self-assured. Motivated by a radio announcement that motorists should help stranded pedestrians, Laure invites Jean into her car. Before long, he transports her down a number of side streets and away from all the confusion. Attraction between the two strangers mounts.

Though the plot of *Vendredi soir* may be fairly routine erotica – albeit from a distinctly female perspective – and the theme of illicit attraction familiar to followers of the director's work, Denis' languid and surreal romance (in one Jane Campionesque sequence anchovies atop a pizza slice wriggle to life) reverberates with a sense of seduction and a level of emotional truth that few contemporary film-makers can match. Denis resists insinuating that her two star-crossed lovers are brought together by fate or metaphysics; in fact, rarely does she suggest that they have anything in common other than the physical. Desire here is not a disruptive factor as in other Denis films such as *Beau travail* (1998), but a liberating means to a moment of sexual self-expression.

With dialogue stripped to the bare minimum, the physical is a concept to which Denis is devoted here, skilfully emphasising the space, or lack of it, between two people in a car, at a restaurant table and finally in bed. Conventionally titillating sex scenes are avoided, with regular cinematographer Agnès Godard's luminous photography taking centre stage to lend the attraction between Laure and the emphatically non-predatorial Jean a palpable frisson as the camera focuses on hands, shifting positions and the details of foreplay. The shimmering, rain-sodden streets of nighttime, wintry Paris rarely looked more beautiful and inviting; ditto the womb-like comfort of Laure's car interior. A beguiling, Dickon Hinchliffe (The Tindersticks)-scored hymn to the vicissitudes of day-to-day personal interaction that offers one of the few commendations of traffic, this is cinema to make you swoon.

Dir: Claire Denis; **Prod**: Bruno Pesery; **Scr**: Emmanuèle Bernheim; **DOP**: Agnès Godard; **Edit**: Nelly Quettier; **Score**: Dickon Hinchliffe; **Principal Cast**: Valérie Lemercier, Vincent Lindon, Grégoire Colin, Hélène Fillières, Hélène de Saint-Père.

El viaje (*The Voyage*)
Argentina/France, 1991 – 150 mins
Fernando E. Solanas

One of the most influential figures in Argentinian cinema and a key proponent of the radical, leftist school of film-making that developed during the 1960s and 70s, Solanas' most enduring work is perhaps the four-hour documentary *The Hour of the Furnaces* (1966). The film marked a seminal moment in what has become known as Third Cinema, a style of film-making that eschewed the values and techniques of both Hollywood and European productions in favour of making films with a revolutionary bent. Turning to fiction films when Peron was swept to power in 1973, Solanas fled to Paris three years later when Peron was usurped in a military coup and did not return until 1983. Considered among the finest of the director's post-documentary work, and retaining a commitment to political discourse and social comment, *El viaje* concerns a young Argentine boy whose urge to see his long-absent father sends him on an epic bicycle trip throughout South America.

Martin Nunca (Quiroz) is a student at a remote college in Tierra del Fuego. His father Nicolás (Berman) is a former comic-strip-artist-turned-anthropologist, last reported as working in Brazil. Leaving behind his mother and stepfather, and the local girl who resists his pleas not to abort their baby, Martin travels northwards, encountering scenes of exploitation and destruction and abject subjugation to America. There are also a number of incidents involving colourful characters en route, including a blind truck driver who lets fate decide his direction and a mysterious girl in a red dress who accepts a ride on his crossbars. Learning about environmental and cultural destruction, particularly in reference to indigenous cultures and peoples, Martin suffers the loss of his bicycle and extreme exhaustion – being cared for by a peasant family in Peru – before continuing to Teotihuacan, Mexico, where he hears that his father has a studio. Finding the studio deserted, it dawns on Martin that the journey has been experience enough and he relinquishes his search.

Structured in three parts – 'The End of the World', 'To Buenos Aires' and 'Across Amerindia' – *El viaje* replaces the militancy of Solanas' early works with a wry and quizzical exasperation at the ineffective and inept bureaucracy that seems to grip not only Argentina but, as the visits to Nicaragua and Salvador suggest, Latin America as a whole. Solanas, whose outspoken criticisms for Carlos Menem's administration led to an attempt on his life, confining him to a wheelchair for *El viaje*'s post-production, also points out the steady collapse of public services and the pervading mood of discontentment and frustration. Some of the satire is of the Nanni Moretti variety, including a buffoonish president of a Buenos Aires outskirt liable to flooding who dons flippers. But Solanas' intentions here are barbed, using the swamp lands of the 'Venice of the South' as a metaphor for his drowning country. Lucrecia Martel returned to the allusion ten years later for her remarkable *La ciénaga*.

The surname of the protagonist and his absent father translates to 'Never' and it can be no coincidence that the name of Martin is also that of José de san Martin, the founding father of Argentinian independence, a crumbling statue of whom appears in the film. Visually eye-catching and impressively expansive in terms of the geography and subjects it covers, *El viaje* perhaps most importantly offers 'a travelogue through a country's identity crisis' (Strick 1993, p. 55).

Dir: Fernando E. Solanas; **Prod**: Fernando E. Solanas; **Scr**: Fernando E. Solanas; **DOP**: Felix Monti; **Edit**: Alberto Borello, Jacqueline Meppiel, Jacques Gaillard; **Score**: Jacques Morelembaum; **Principal Cast**: Walter Quiroz, Soledad Alfaro, Ricardo Bartis, Cristina Becerra, Marc Berman.

Voyage to Italy (*Viaggio in Italia*)
Italy, 1953 – 100 mins
Roberto Rossellini

Voyage to Italy is a deceptively simple, though utterly captivating and brilliantly written study of a once happy marriage finally dashed by boredom, blame, deception and denial. Perhaps the high point of the director's collaboration with his wife Ingrid Bergman, the film's examination of isolation and communication breakdown was to prove portentous, hastening the collapse of the pair's own marriage following the film's less than enthusiastic reception when it was released. Perhaps too advanced for the audiences of the time in its meandering travelogue of a plot and languorous pace, the film's fortunes were subsequently substantially revived and it is now regarded as one of the finest human dramas of Roberto Rossellini's post-neo-realist period. Aided by superb performances from the two leads, it is certainly one of the most honest portrayals of a marriage ever committed to film.

The opening scene is a masterwork of cinematic shorthand. We meet Alexander (Sanders) and Katherine (Bergman) Joyce, a privileged, wealthy English couple: she wears furs, he drives a Bentley. They're travelling to the south of Italy to sell a villa that Katherine has inherited from a wayward uncle. Alexander is caustic and cynical, baffled into hostility by the customs of a country he doesn't understand. 'It's incredible the way some people drive,' he says after a Fiat whizzes past. 'What noisy people. I've never seen noise and boredom go so well together.' Katherine is more easy and accepting of life 'abroad' ('It should amuse you,' she rebuffs her grumbling husband), but is introspective and emotional. She realises that this road trip is the first time that she and her husband have been alone in eight years of marriage. 'We are like strangers,' she says. She also begins to understand that she bores him. The scene is set for a marital crisis and a profound exploration of alienation, desire, communication and expression.

One of the most remarkable aspects of the film is the fact that it leaves so much unresolved. By its conclusion, the villa still waits to be sold and the Joyces' differences are equally in limbo. And yet Rossellini deftly shows us so much more, introducing a number of seemingly minor details and revelations – amid the torrid arguments and fleeting misadventures – that gradually accumulate to provide a fascinating and rather complex insight into Katherine and Alexander's individual characters, and their union as a whole. There is mild alarm when each realises that the other is a charming flirt, and further surprise at the introduction of hitherto unnoticed quirks and peccadilloes.

Rossellini also reveals much about the mental state of his characters by setting the tale against the backdrop of the striking and strikingly photographed Neapolitan countryside, and against the backdrop of Italian history. In one of the film's many moments of overt symbolism, Katherine wanders among the ruins of Pompeii and the cinders of Vesuvius, the very physical manifestation of the natural world a marked contrast to her repressed turmoil. A man of repressed emotion, Alexander meanwhile sinks into a sullen silence in an Italian café, taking respite from the noisy, effervescent Italian streets that are so alien to his sense of Englishness and repressed, stiff-upper-lip mentality. Alexander's inability to speak Italian further alienates him from his wife and his surroundings, resulting in one humorous moment when he frustratingly labels a whore a 'Shameless brazen hussy' after failing to converse with her in his mother tongue.

Dir: Roberto Rossellini; **Prod**: Roberto Rossellini, Adolfo Fossataro, Alfredo Guarini; **Scr**: Roberto Rossellini, Vitaliano Brancati; **DOP**: Enzo Serafin; **Edit**: Jolanda Benvenuti; **Score**: Renzo Rossellini; **Principal Cast**: Ingrid Bergman, George Sanders, Paul Muller, Leslie Daniels, Natalia Ray.

The Wages of Fear (Le Salaire de la peur)
France, 1953 – 144 mins
Henri-Georges Clouzot

One of the finest writer-directors of the war and post-war years, Henri-Georges Clouzot was also one of the most neglected until recent retrospectives at the Edinburgh International Film Festival and the National Film Theatre did much to restore his reputation. Frequently dubbed the French Hitchcock, Clouzot is a master of suspense with a distinctive, sour worldview founded on what Geoff Andrew in his NFT introduction referred to as 'a wholly unsentimental awareness of humanity's capacity for cruelty, greed, envy and violence'. This unerring pessimism is in plentiful supply in *The Wages of Fear*, a suspenseful adaptation of Georges Arnaud's novel.

In the village of Las Piedras in an unnamed Central American country, the Southern Oil Company rules the roost. When an inferno breaks out at an oil well three hundred miles away, the company sends out a call for long-distance truck drivers to transport highly volatile nitro-glycerine to the site. Despite hazardous terrain, the $2,000 offered per shipment proves enough to attract a quartet of ruthless mercenaries. Through expository dialogue, tense interactions and flashbacks, we become intimately acquainted with the four drivers who sign up for this death-defying mission: a Corsican (Montand), an Italian (Lulli), a German (van Eyck) and a Frenchman (Vanel).

The first half methodically introduces the characters and their disparate motivations; the scenes of the grimy quartet hanging out in feverish bars seemingly inviting comparison to the close-knit male camaraderie beloved of Howard Hawks in films such as *Only Angels Have Wings* (1939). However, the film's second half, the fatalistic and utterly nerve-shredding drive itself, becomes a more corrosive presentation of masculinity, revealing the desperate, loathsome and chauvinistic reprobates as entirely lacking in redeeming features. One of Clouzot's first images, a Peckinpahesque close-up of insects being tortured by children, is a perfect metaphor for the men's morality, and for the general cruelty of life.

Once on the road with the hardened expatriates, who, unlike Hawks' heroes, are unified only in their desperation, Clouzot makes the journey one to remember through a series of brilliantly orchestrated set-pieces and a since-imitated schematic involving the need to maintain a constant speed to prevent the cargo from discharging in transit. One of Clouzot's other great touches is that when disaster does strike, such as one of the trucks exploding, the event is never shown. It is hard to imagine a more chilling illustration of the sheer arbitrariness of life and death.

The winner of the Grand Prix at Cannes and one of Clouzot's greatest commercial successes, *The Wages of Fear* originated after Clouzot married Véra Gibson-Amado (who appears in the film as a barmaid who catches Montand's eye) in 1950. The pair honeymooned in Gibson-Amado's native Brazil, giving the director a fascination for the region that is present in every frame. William Friedkin remade the film in

A genuine white-knuckle ride: Clouzot's relentlessly pessimistic action-road movie hybrid, *The Wages of Fear*

1977 as *Sorcerer*. Few would argue that he came anywhere near to matching the original.

Dir: Henri-Georges Clouzot; **Prod**: Raymond Borderie, Henri-Georges Clouzot; **Scr**: Henri-Georges Clouzot, Jérôme Géronimi; **DOP**: Armand Thirard; **Edit**: Madeleine Gug, Etienette Muse, Henri Rust; **Score**: Georges Auric; **Principal Cast**: Yves Montand, Charles Vanel, Peter van Eyck, Folco Lulli, Véra Clouzot.

Weekend
France, 1967 – 90 mins
Jean-Luc Godard

A brutal satire that serves as a ferocious attack on consumerism, capitalism and imperialism, *Weekend* was Godard's most ambitious and unconventional film before he positioned himself even further left-of-centre with the Dziga Vertov group. A revolutionary work about the prospect of a bourgeois apocalypse, the film also serves as an attack on cinema aesthetics.

Opening with a psychiatric-session monologue by the delicate Corinne (Darc), clad only in panties and perched first on a desk, then on a refrigerator as she hesitantly describes a sexual encounter involving an egg and an orifice, *Weekend* then moves to the road as Corinne and her husband Roland (Yanne) embark on a trip from their upmarket Parisian home to the French countryside to claim an inheritance by nefarious means. Almost immediately, the bickering, bourgeois pair become entangled in a cataclysmic traffic jam – captured in a staggeringly audacious ten-minute tracking shot revealing a long line of stalled automobiles on a French country highway lined with poplars. Making little progress on a road that becomes increasingly littered with burnt-out cars and bored, murderous motorists, the couple then find themselves mixed up with a band of forest-dwelling Maoists who rape, loot, murder and cannibalise.

Godard's famously dystopian work is a consistently relentless and ferocious attack on the bourgeois values of his own country, as represented by the superficial and ruthlessly self-centred central couple. 'My Hermès handbag!' Corinne wails as she crawls from her flame-engulfed car, later going on to strip corpses of their designer clothing. Her shallow consumerist mentality is matched by the avarice of her husband, who rifles through the pockets of the dead bodies and whose greed takes him to even more violent and extreme lengths when his mother-in-law won't agree to a share of the millions that have been left as an inheritance. The couple's selfish indifference to the plight of others extends to a mutual despising of each other: Roland sits by unconcerned while his wife is raped at the roadside; while Corinne, newly radicalised, tells graphic stories of sexual encounters with other men and cannibalistically feasts on her husband's bones by the film's end.

Unfolding as a series of provocative digressions, frequently linked by title cards bearing such slogans as 'Faux . . . tography' and 'Anal . . . yse', the film shatters all cinematic conventions. Characters directly address the camera, as Godard aims for, and achieves, a cathartic chaos. At one

Jean-Luc Godard mischievously surveys the on-road carnage he creates in the satirical *Weekend*

point during the film, Roland complains to the audience about how ludicrous the film is; at another, an African garbage collector with no obvious connection to the narrative applies Marxist-Leninist principles to highlight social and economic problems and denounce imperialism to an off-camera interviewer. In a further assault on the senses, the music wells up at inappropriate times only to stop suddenly; and the camera spins and moves without any respect for traditional cinema space.

A black, bitter and frequently very funny depiction of society as road rage, *Weekend*, which ends with the title card 'End of Film, End of Cinema', was uncannily in touch with its times, as demonstrated by the subsequent events in Paris in 1968. Considered the apotheosis of Godard's work, it is complex, absurd and frequently difficult. In an interview on Artificial Eye's recent DVD reissue, cinematographer Raoul Coutard cites the film as being capable of both testing the patience of the viewer to the limits while also demonstrating flashes of inspiration and inventiveness far beyond anything achieved by the director's contemporaries.

Dir: Jean-Luc Godard; **Prod**: N/A; **Scr**: Jean-Luc Godard; **DOP**: Raoul Coutard; **Edit**: Agnès Guillemot; **Score**: Antoine Duhamel, Wolfgang Amadeus Mozart; **Principal Cast**: Mireille Darc, Jean Yanne, Jean-Pierre Kalfon, Jean-Pierre Léaud.

Where is My Friend's House? (*Khaneh-je doost kojast?*)
Iran, 1987 – 85 mins
Abbas Kiarostami

Of the current film-makers working in Iran today, Kiarostami is considered the most direct heir to the cinema of Shahid Saless. Simple narratives, poetic meditations on life's daily struggles, the use of non-professional actors and the blurring of the lines between fiction and documentary are characteristic of Kiarostami's work. Although he has been active in film production since 1970, it was *Where is My Friend's House?* that initially brought him international recognition, gaining the director his first European honour, the Bronze Leopard at the Locarno Film Festival.

The first and most straightforward of a series of films now known as the Koker Trilogy that was completed by *And Life Goes On* (1992) and *Through the Olive Trees* (1994), the trilogy is set around the Koker villages in northwestern Iran. An enthralling blend of low-key realism, gentle comedy and self-reflexivity, in *Where is My Friend's House?*, Kiarostami focuses upon Ahmed's (Babek Ahmed Poor) realisation that he has accidentally taken home a classmate's exercise book. Knowing that the failure of his classmate Reza (Ahmed Ahmed Poor) to complete his homework will have dire consequences, Ahmed sets out on foot to the neighbouring village to seek out his friend and return the book. Ahmed's quest is beset by problems, the most grave of which is that despite the various clues he picks up along the way (for example, we learn that the house has a blue door), he does not know his school colleague's actual address.

Showing a great sympathy for young Ahmed as he comes into contact with various older and mostly unhelpful authoritarians, Kiarostami's fable-like tale – comparable to Vittorio De Sica's *Bicycle Thieves* (1948) – also offers a poetic evocation of the landscape through which Ahmed moves. Produced for the Institute for the Intellectual

Development of Children and Young Adults, *Where is My Friend's House?* is symptomatic of much contemporary Iranian cinema in that it treats its child characters with intelligence and respect and refuses to burden the narrative and ideological challenges they face with cheap sentiment. Working exclusively with local non-professional actors, Kiarostami draws a number of remarkable performances from his cast, not least the engaging Babek Ahmed Poor in the central role.

Existing in what may be considered a particular road-movie subgenre, in which the journey is largely undertaken on foot (Wim Wenders' *Paris, Texas*, 1984, being perhaps the most obvious example), *Where is My Friend's House?* contains not a single extraneous frame or emotion. The film's wonderful pay-off – which I'll not reveal here – may fleetingly revive in the most ardent pessimist belief in the essential generosity of the human spirit.

Dir: Abbas Kiarostami; **Prod**: Ali Reza Zarrin; **Scr**: Abbas Kiarostami; **DOP**: Farhad Saba; **Edit**: Naamet Allah Alizadah; **Score**: Amine Allah Hessine; **Principal Cast**: Babek Ahmed Poor, Ahmed Ahmed Poor, Kheda Barech Defai, Iran Outari.

Wild Strawberries (*Smultronstället*)
Sweden, 1957 – 94 mins
Ingmar Bergman

An influential work not least for its transformation of the road trip into an allegorical contemplation of the passage of life and its emphasis on the significance of the journey over the final destination, *Wild Strawberries* remains among Bergman's most humane, compassionate and accessible works and is unarguably a landmark moment in post-war cinema.

Legendary Scandinavian director and silent-film actor Victor Sjöström plays Isak Borg, a 78-year-old medical professor who reassesses his life while journeying to his former university in Lund to receive an honorary degree. Borg travels with his unhappy daughter-in-law Marianne (Thulin), who although pregnant is planning to leave her husband. En route she and Isak meet a ceaselessly bickering married couple and a trio of hitchhikers, one of whom, Sara (Andersson), reminds the old man of his long-lost childhood love and stirs up hazy flashbacks and half-remembered memories. There is also a stop-off at Isak's childhood summer home, a detour to the house of his embittered mother (Wifstrand) and an encounter with his cold and resentful son. All the while, Isak experiences a number of dreams, premonitions and nightmares that serve to remind him of his many disappointments and abject sense of disillusionment.

The winner of the Golden Bear at the 1958 Berlin Film Festival, the script for *Wild Strawberries* was completed by Bergman while convalescing in hospital following treatment for gastric ulcers. Rich in symbolism and elegiacally sliding between past and present, and between dream and reality, the film turns the physical journey of its central protagonist into a spiritual and emotional voyage back to his very origins. A devastatingly perceptive study in isolationism that effectively provides a glimpse into the external and internal world of its central character, the film arguably set the tone for the numerous psychological studies – European and American – that followed in its wake.

Though referencing more traditional American road movies through the incorporation of visual shorthand such as driving montage sequences, chance encounters and speeding close-ups of tarmac, all masterfully shot by cinematographer Gunnar Fischer, Bergman's film is nonetheless distinguished from the American road movie's frontier spirit. Interspersing the pastoral idyll with interpersonal communication breakdowns and moments of acute expressionistic distress, the director ultimately derives his exploration of ethical and philosophical issues more from 'the likes of Descartes, Kant, Kierkegaard and Nietzsche' (Laderman 2002, p. 254).

The film's Swedish title is another key to understanding Bergman's vision. Translating as 'strawberry field patch', the Swedish *smultronstället* also refers not only to the location where strawberries can be picked but also to a personal place or a time in the past that is particularly cherished and that one may frequently revisit in one's mind.

Dir: Ingmar Bergman; **Prod**: Allan Ekelund; **Scr**: Ingmar Bergman; **DOP**: Gunnar Fischer; **Edit**: Oscar Rosander; **Score**: Erik Nordgren; **Principal Cast**: Victor Sjöström, Bibi Andersson, Ingrid Thulin, Gunnar Björnstrand, Naima Wifstrand, Max von Sydow.

The Wizard of Oz
US, 1939 – 101 mins
Victor Fleming

Following versions in 1910 and 1933 by Otis Turner and Ted Eshbaugh respectively, this third feature-length adaptation of L. Frank Baum's 1900 children's fantasy adventure is the definitive article. A lavish MGM production that lost over a million dollars on release, and whose 1955 re-release also failed to turn a profit, *The Wizard of Oz* is now estimated to be the most seen film ever made due to its perennial Christmas appearances on television. One of the first films ever to be sold to TV for prime-time broadcast, a new and perhaps very different audience was introduced to it following David Lynch's multiple allusions in 1990's hyper-violent *Wild at Heart*.

In a star-making turn, Judy Garland plays Dorothy Gale, an orphaned young girl unhappy with her drab black-and-white existence on her aunt and uncle's dusty Kansas farm. Dorothy yearns to travel 'over the rainbow' to a different world, and she gets her wish when a tornado whisks her and her little dog, Toto, to the Technicolor land of Oz. Having offended the Wicked Witch of the West (Margaret Hamilton), Dorothy is protected from the old crone's wrath by the ruby slippers that she wears. At the suggestion of Glinda, the Good Witch of the North (Burke), Dorothy heads down the Yellow Brick Road to the Emerald City, where dwells the all-powerful Wizard of Oz, who might be able to help the girl return home. En route, she befriends a Scarecrow (Bolger), a Tin Man (Haley) and a Cowardly Lion (Lahr). The Scarecrow would like to have some brains, the Tin Man craves a heart and the Lion wants to attain courage; hoping that the Wizard will help them too, they join Dorothy on her odyssey to the Emerald City.

The transfer to the screen was far from easy. Fired after only two weeks and all his footage scrapped, original director Richard Thorpe was replaced by George Cukor, who himself lasted just one week. Victor Fleming was then bought onboard, with an uncredited King Vidor filming the Kansas sequences, including Garland's performance of 'Over the Rainbow'. It is impossible to think of *The Wizard of Oz* without recalling the song and its performance by a then sixteen-year-old Judy Garland (wearing a tightly binding corset to make her appear Dorothy's twelve), but it almost didn't make the final cut, studio executives considering it too dour and gloomy for children. Garland was second choice for the part, getting the nod only after Shirley Temple dropped out, and Bolger was to have played the Tin Man but talked co-star Buddy Ebsen into switching roles. When Ebsen proved allergic to the chemicals used in his silver makeup, Haley took over. Gale Sondergaard was originally to have played the Wicked Witch of the West in a glamorous fashion, until the decision was made to opt for belligerent ugliness, and the Wizard was written for W. C. Fields, who reportedly turned it down because MGM refused to meet his wage demands. To all this is added a stunt going wrong and leaving Margaret Hamilton with second-degree burns and reports of drunken, lecherous behaviour among the actors playing the Munchkins.

Despite failing to find commercial success on release, *The Wizard of Oz* was recognised for its impressive production values. Cedric Gibbons' art direction was widely admired, and Rosson's sparkling cinematography helped convince audiences and the industry of the creative potential of the Technicolor process. The film duly earned several Academy Award nominations in technical categories, though won for Stothart's score and Arlen and Harburg's 'Over the Rainbow'. One of the few films in this selection in which the journey is taken on foot without the use of a vehicle or mode of transport of some kind, *The Wizard of Oz* also stands out as a road movie that despite emphasising some of the benefits of travel (meeting new companions, self-discovery and the appreciation of loved ones), rigorously emphasises that there really is no place like home.

Dir: Victor Fleming; **Prod**: Mervyn Leroy; **Scr**: Noel Langley, Florence Ryerson, Edgar Allan Woolf; **DOP**: Harold Rosson; **Edit**: Blanche Sewell; **Score**: Herbert Stothart, songs by E. Y. Harburg, Harold Arlen; **Principal Cast**: Judy Garland, Ray Bolger, Bert Lahr, Jack Haley, Frank Morgan, Billie Burke.

Wolf Creek
Australia, 2005 – 99 mins
Greg McLean

Opening with the claim that 'The following is based on actual events', writer-director Greg McLean's *Wolf Creek* has a chilling veracity. Though not based on any specific incident, McLean readily evokes the spectres of Ivan Milat, the Backpacker Killer, and Bradley Murdoch in a grimly realistic and disconcertingly credible tale that taps into fears concerning the unknown and travel in the vast expanse of Australia's desolate back-country.

Highlighting the horror that comes later and a technique that whips away feelings of equilibrium, McLean begins the film with naturalistic sequences showing three backpackers – English girls Liz (Magrath) and Kristy (Morassi), and Australian alpha-male Ben (Phillips) – flirting and whooping it up in Broome, Western Australia. The trio purchase an ailing car, to head off to Wolf Creek, a meteor crater, before continuing on a three-week road trip. Beautiful montages of the natural habitat and the endlessly stretching roads accompany the protagonists' journey inland, but as they near Wolf Creek, a menacing note arises as the skies turn grey and the soundtrack incrementally incorporates strange and unnerving ambient noises. In a portentous moment reminiscent of Peter Weir's *Picnic at Hanging Rock* (1975), the protagonists' watches stop before their car refuses to start. Cold and afraid, salvation seemingly arrives in the form of Mick (Jarratt), a grizzled, Crocodile Dundee type who offers to tow them to his camp for refreshment and repairs. Though in the middle of nowhere, relations around the campfire at Mick's base are genial until he takes offence at an innocuous remark and the inexperienced backpackers find themselves plunged into their worse nightmares and trapped in a grisly fight for survival.

Citing the Dogme-95 manifesto as inspiration, McLean shoots on high-definition digital video using handheld cameras, limited lighting and sound, and largely unknown actors (though Jarratt, creating one of cinema's most terrifying bogeymen, is well known in Australia as a soap star, an inspired piece of counter-casting) to create a highly credible and horribly realistic journey into primal terror. To the tradition of Australian outback movies, as exemplified by *The Cars That Ate Paris* (1974) and George Miller's *Mad Max* trilogy, McLean moulds the determinedly relentless and frills-free horror of 1970s American classics such as *The Last House on the Left* (1972) and *The Texas Chansaw Massacre* (1974). Employing another effective method of ensuring that the spectator is unable to take anything for granted, McLean also borrows from these latter pictures the narrative device of escape and recapture, ensuring that the empathy we feel for the protagonists, who suffer rape, torture and dismemberment as a prelude to death, is all too realistic.

In the press notes, McLean described the film as 'Exploring the dull, mundane nature of violence', countering claims that it was exploitative and gratuitous with the comment that while taking an admittedly voyeuristic journey into pure evil, 'I believe it's the artist's job in some form to "not look away"'. *Wolf Creek* certainly offers an interesting meditation on the real-life crimes it refers to, while also contemplating with some distinction the question of how and why we relate to on-screen horror. Unlikely to do much for Australia's travel industry, the film has since spawned Ray Lawrence's similar, if more sober, *Jindabyne* (2006).

Dir: Greg McLean; **Prod**: Greg McLean, David Lightfoot; **Scr**: Greg McLean; **DOP**: Will Gibson; **Edit**: Jason Ballantine; **Score**: François Tetaz; **Principal Cast**: John Jarratt, Cassandra Magrath, Kestie Morassi, Nathan Phillips.

Y tu mamá también
Mexico, 2001 – 106 mins
Alfonso Cuarón

Emerging alongside compatriot Alejandro González Iñárritu's *Amores perros* (2000), *Y tu mamá también* alerted the eyes of the world to the riches to be found in Mexican cinema. While the former marked a remarkably confident and audacious debut, the latter, a merging of the road movie with a frank coming-of-age drama, signalled the work of an experienced film-maker returning home for a personal project after a Hollywood sojourn. Having dragged Mexican cinema from its 1980s doldrums with *Solo con tu pareja* (1991), Alfonso Cuarón had answered American overtures, making two successful and well-received pictures there: *A Little Princess* (1995) and *Great Expectations* (1997).

Luisa (Maribel Verdú, far left), Tenoch (Diego Luna) and Julio (Gael García Bernal) prepare to get to know each other intimately while also discovering something about their Mexican homeland in Alfonso Cuarón's phenomenally popular *Y tu mamá también*

It is difficult not to discuss *Amores perros* and *Y tu mamá también* in tandem when considering the manner in which they exploded onto the international scene. Both feature the poster-boy looks and electrifying screen presence of Gael García Bernal. Each is confident, stylishly shot and structurally complex. Moreover, these films are thematically provocative in their treatment of prescient social issues, and thrillingly forthright in their willingness to address the ills afflicting contemporary Mexican society. This is no doubt also a contributing factor to their phenomenal domestic success. Each was the highest-grossing picture of its year in Mexico, challenging the dominance of American imports and enticing young Mexican audiences back to see local product in which their hopes, aspirations and sensibilities are authentically replicated on screen.

With their respective girlfriends away in Europe, Julio (García Bernal) and his upper-class friend Tenoch (Luna) are looking forward to a hedonistic summer of drink, drugs and sex. During a wedding, they meet Luisa (Verdú), the twenty-eight-year-old wife of Tenoch's scholarly cousin, and try to convince her to go on a road trip to Heaven's Mouth, a golden beach paradise. To their surprise, Luisa agrees but tension simmers after she has sex with them both in an attempt to teach the boys a thing or two about love and life. Soon enough the excitable Julio and Tenoch are prepared to destroy their friendship to vie for Luisa's undivided affections.

Confidently helmed by Cuarón, and sumptuously shot by his regular cinematographer Emmanuel Lubezki, prominent among the film's many pleasures is the poignant interplay between real-life childhood friends and former Mexican soap-star colleagues García Bernal and Luna. Utilising a number of autobiographical elements, right down to the naming of the car in the film, Betsabé, after one they actually owned, Alfonso and brother Carlos also use the geographical journey from the sprawling city to a mythical paradise and the emotional journey from adolescence to adulthood as an allegory for Mexico itself:

The premise Carlos and I had from the get-go was about these two kids looking for their identity as adults; this woman seeking her identity as a liberated woman and an observation of a country that was in our opinion a teenage country seeking its identity as an adult country. (Interview with the author conducted for, but not used, in *The Faber Book of Mexican Cinema*, 2006).

The journey that the trio take indeed reveals a lot both about themselves and about the social climate in Mexico at the time of the film's making. There is a reference to a migrant worker killed in an accident because of a poorly located pedestrian crossing; on reaching the fabled Heaven's Mouth, which proves not to be the answer to their aspirations, the film also shows a fisherman who has lost his livelihood to the more economically lucrative tourism industry. These elements were seemingly lost on Mexican critics, who unjustly dismissed the admittedly raunchy *Y tu mamá también* as a south-of-the-border Beavis and Butthead. Thankfully, others were more receptive to its political subtleties and bittersweet charms.

Dir: Alfonso Cuarón; **Prod**: Jorge Vergara, Alfonso Cuarón; **Scr**: Carlos Cuarón, Alfonso Cuarón; **DOP**: Emmanuel Lubezki; **Edit**: Alfonso Cuarón, Alex Rodríguez; **Score**: Liza Richardson, Annette Fradera; **Principal Cast**: Gael García Bernal, Diego Luna, Maribel Verdú, María Aura.

Bibliography

Aftab, Kaleem (2005), *Spike Lee: That's My Story and I'm Sticking to It* (London: Faber & Faber).

Andrew, Geoff (1998), *Stranger Than Paradise: Maverick Film-makers in Recent American Cinema* (London: Prion Books).

Atkinson, Michael (1994), 'Crossing the Frontiers', *Sight and Sound*, vol. 4 no. 1, January.

Bedell, Geraldine (2004), 'A Winterbottom's Tale', interview with Michael Winterbottom, *The Observer*, Sunday 1 February.

Bollag, Brenda, and Posner, Roland (1990), review of *Freedom is Paradise*, *Film Quarterly*, vol. 44 no. 1, Autumn.

Boorman, John (2003), *Adventures of a Suburban Boy* (London: Faber & Faber).

Buscombe, Edward (2006), *100 Westerns* (London: BFI).

Chion, Michel (2006), *David Lynch*, 2nd edition (London: BFI).

Cohan, Steven, and Hark, Ina Rae (eds) (1997), *The Road Movie Book* (London: Routledge).

Dargis, Manohla (1991), 'Roads to Freedom', *Sight and Sound*, vol. 1 no. 3, July.

Darke, Chris (2000), 'TV Afterlife', *Film Comment*, July/August.

Dick, Leslie (1997), '*Sight and Sound* A–Z of Cinema', *Sight and Sound*, vol. 7 no. 11, November.

Fuller, Graham (1992), 'Finding the Essential', Hal Hartley interview that precedes the scripts for *Simple Men* and *Trust* (London: Faber & Faber).

Geist, Kathe (1988), *The Cinema of Wim Wenders: From Paris, France to Paris, Texas* (Ann Arbor, MI: UMI Research Press).

Gilbey, Ryan (2003), *It Don't Worry Me: Nashville, Star Wars, Jaws and Beyond* (London: Faber & Faber).

Hillier, Jim (ed.) (2001), *American Independent Cinema: A Sight and Sound Reader* (London: BFI).

Jaafar, Ali (2005), 'Le Grand Voyage' review, Sight & Sound, vol. 15 no. 11, November.

James, Caryn (1990), 'Today's Yellow Brick Road leads straight to hell', The New York Times, 19 August.

Kolker, Robert Philip (1993), A Cinema of Loneliness (New York: Cambridge University Press).

Kolker, Robert Philip (1993), 'On the Road: Exile and Innocence: Major Themes and Images in Wenders' Films', in The Films of Wim Wenders: Cinema as Vision and Desire (Cambridge: Cambridge University Press).

Laderman, David (2002), Driving Visions (Austin: University of Texas Press).

Lang, Robert (2002), 'My Own Private Idaho and the New Queer Road Movies', in Masculine Interests: Homoerotics in Hollywood Films (New York: Columbia University Press).

Maher, Kevin (2005), 'To haj and haj not on the road to Mecca', The Times, 13 October.

Malcolm, Derek (2000), 'Michelangelo Antonioni: Passenger', extract from Derek Malcolm's Century of Films, Guardian, Thursday 1 June.

North, Sam (2006), 'The Road Movie: An Introduction', <www.hackwriters.com>.

Pierson, John (1996), Spike Mike Slackers & Dykes: A Guided Tour across a Decade of Independent American Cinema (London: Faber & Faber).

Pym, John (ed.) (2005), The Time Out Film Guide, 14th edition (London: Time Out Guides Ltd).

Ranaldo, Lee (2005), Road Movies (New York: Soft Skull Press).

Roddick, Nick (2005), 'Taking Care of Is-ness', Sight & Sound, vol. 15 no. 11, November.

Sandu, Sukhdev (2003), 'Brilliantly Exasperating', online Cannes daily report for the Daily Telegraph, filed 22 May, <www.telegraph.co.uk/arts/main.jhtml?xml=/arts/2003/05/22/bfbunn22.xml>.

Sargeant, Jack, and Watson, Stephanie (eds) (2000), Lost Highways: An Illustrated History of Road Movies (London: Creation Books).

Server, Lee (2001), Robert Mitchum: Baby, I Don't Care (London: Faber & Faber).

Strick, Philip (1993), 'El Viaje' review, Sight and Sound, vol. 3 no. 9, September.

Thomson, David (2002), *The New Biographical Dictionary of Film* (London: Little, Brown).

Weingroff, Richard F. (1996), 'Road Movies', Federal Highway Administration, Office of the Associate Administrator for Program Development <www.tfhrc.gov/pubrds/summer96/p96su42.htm>, vol. 60 no. 1, Summer 1996.

Williams, Mark (1982), *Road Movies: The Complete Guide to Cinema on Wheels* (New York: Proteus Books).

Wood, Jason (2006), *The Faber Book of Mexican Cinema* (London: Faber & Faber).

Wurlitzer, Rudolph, and Corry, Will (1971), 'Two-Lane Blacktop', full script reproduced in *Esquire*, April.

Index

Page numbers in *italics* denote illustrations

List of Illustrations

While considerable effort has been made to correctly identify the copyright holders, this has not been possible in all cases. We apologise for any apparent negligence and any omissions or corrections brought to our attention will be remedied in future editions.

The Adventures of Priscilla, Queen of the Desert, Latent Image Productions/Specific Films; *Badlands*, Pressman Williams Enterprises; *Bombón el perro*, © Guacamole Films/© OK Films; *Broken Flowers*, © Dead Flowers, Inc.; *The Brown Bunny*, Vincent Gallo Productions; *Butterfly Kiss*, Dan Films; *Cold Fever*, Icelandic Film Corporation/Film Fonds Hamburg/Icicle Films/Sunrise A.G./Pandora Filmproduktion/Zentropa Entertainments ApS/Alta Films; *Dear Diary*, © Banfilm/© Sept Cinéma/© Canal+/© Sacher Film; *Easy Rider*, Pando Company/Raybert Productions; *Familia rodante*, © Matanza Cine/© Paradis Films/© Pandora Filmprodukton; *Gallivant*, Tall Stories; *Get on the Bus*, 40 Acres and a Mule Filmworks/Columbia Pictures Corporation; *The Grapes of Wrath*, Twentieth Century-Fox Film Corporation; *Kikujiro*, © Bandai Visual/© Tokyo FM/© Nippon Herald Films/© Office Kitano; *Kings of the Road*, Wim Wenders Filmproduktion/Filmverlag der Autoren; *Last Orders*, © Scala (Last Orders) Limited/© MBP; *Leningrad Cowboys Go America*, Villealfa Filmproductions Oy/Svenska Filminstitutet/Finnkino/Megamania/Esselte; *(Mad Max 2) The Road Warrior*, Kennedy Miller Productions; *Messidor*, Citel Film/SSR Télévision Suisse/Action Films/Société Nouvelle des Etablissements Gaumont; *Midnight Run*, Universal Pictures/City Light Films; *The Motorcycle Diaries*, © FilmFour; *Natural Born Killers*, © Warner Bros. Productions/© Monarchy Enterprises B.V.; *The Passenger*, Compagnia Cinematografica Champion; *Radio On*, © National Film Trustee Company; *Red Lights*, © Aliceléo/© France 3 Cinéma/© Gimages Films; *The Return*, Ren Film; *Road to Morocco*, Paramount Pictures; *Sideways*, © Twentieth Century Fox Film Corporation/© TCF Hungary Film Rights Exploitation Ltd; *La Strada*, Ponti-De Laurentiis; *The Straight Story*, © Straight Story Inc.; *The Sugarland Express*, Universal Pictures; *Sullivan's Travels*, Paramount Pictures; *Thelma & Louise*, Pathé Entertainment Inc./Percy Main; *Thunder Road*, © D.R.M. Productions; *Vanishing Point*, Cupid Productions; *The Wages of Fear*, Compagnie Industrielle et Commerciale Cinématographique/Filmsonor/Véra Films/Fono Roma; *Weekend*, Comacico/Lira Films/Cinecidi; *Y tu mamá también*, © Producciones Anhelo.